Praise for

BORN TO THE WILD

An *Association of Book Publishers of British Columbia* Bestseller

"Veteran warden Rob Kaye has become a bestselling author with *Born to the Wild.* One wonders how a...park warden can be included in BC Bestsellers List since August. But as soon as one opens Kaye's book it becomes apparent...he tells it like it is."

—*BC Bookworld*

"This book is pure gold. Kaye's adventures are exciting, fascinating and even frightening....very engaging and quite captivating. Not only does he do a masterful job of describing his natural surroundings, but he tells the stories of his and his friends' and predecessors' backcountry adventures in an easy, entertaining and nearly flawless manner....This is one of those few books that I highly recommend you add to your own library."

—*International Game Warden*

"After reading this book, I was so jealous of Rob's many years of adventures and encounters in such a gorgeous part of the world!...Rob brings that amazing period of Rocky Mountain history to life, and in exquisite detail—the adventure, the danger, and the beauty of the...wilderness."

—*Nature Alberta*

"A gifted writer, Kaye describes backcountry wildlife encounters, tales of adversity and accounts of survival....If you have ever known or longed for the wilderness, you must read this beautifully illustrated *Born to the Wild.*"

—*BC Nature*

"Thanks for this book, Rob! Your tales of childhood adventures made me laugh, your encounters with wildlife were magical, and your love of nature and of Jasper National Park is obvious. I will recommend your book to anyone who wants to understand the life of a warden, the history of the park, and the need for continued conservation."

—*Canadian Parks and Wilderness Society (CPAWS)*

"The book is very readable, a real page-turner if you like the outdoors and are concerned about the future of wildlife and the environment in general....Kaye's stories are engrossing, if not terrifying at times – the backcountry is still quite wild, though some species populations are greatly diminished. Importantly, the book is a plea for greater protection of our mountain spaces and species....Please, read this book and pass it on...."

—*The Canadian Society of Environmental Biologists*

"The romantic image of a national park warden, sitting high astride a steed while exploring the untamed backcountry for months on end with the purpose of studying and protecting our natural environment has all but disappeared from modern times....The author paints vivid pictures of the majestic beauty of the deep wilds that humans scarcely experience."

—*Bow Valley Crag & Canyon*

BORN TO THE WILD

Journals of a National Park Warden
In the Canadian Rockies

Rob Kaye

Published by GREY WOLF BOOKS
www. robkaye.ca

Library and Archives Canada Cataloguing in Publication

Kaye, Rob, author
Born to the wild : journals of a national park warden in the Canadian Rockies / Rob Kaye.

ISBN 978-0-9940518-0-6 (pbk.)

1. Kaye, Rob, 1954-.
2. National parks and reserves--Rocky Mountains, Canadian (B.C. and Alta.).
3. Park wardens--Canada--Biography.
I. Title.

SB481.6.K39A3 2015 333.78'3092 C2015-902338-6

Front and back cover photographs: Rob Kaye Collection.
Cover design by Iryna Spica
Typeset in *Plantin* at SpicaBookDesign

Printed in Canada

10 9 8 7 6 5 4 3

Contents

Maps

INTRODUCTION

This Moment is My Life

Tired from nine days of following the movements of hunters in the basins and along the ridges straddling the park boundary in the Moosehorn Valley and adjacent Wolf Pass area, I hit the hay not long after dark. Sometime around midnight I awoke feeling fully refreshed. I had slept soundly. Moonlight was filtering through the windows, casting a soft light on the interior log walls of the old warden cabin. The window nearest the bed was partially open, with a light cool breeze wafting through. It was dead quiet. A silence one only experiences far from human activity, a peacefulness that city dwellers may never know. "This is my element," I thought, "the only place I feel truly connected—in the wilderness." It was the last night of my shift in the Moosehorn and the horses and I would be heading out to Devona on the banks of the Snake Indian River in the morning. I didn't want to leave. I rolled over and closed my eyes.

I was wide awake again at 4:00 a.m. The moon had sunk behind the towering peaks, but a light still glowed through the windows. It was an eerie defused light, a different spectrum, and it was pulsating. I looked out. Half the sky was lit up with incredibly vivid green arcs of light, dancing and flickering against the backdrop of mountains on each side of the valley—the aurora borealis at its best. I dressed, walked out into the meadow, and watched the show. The majestic mountain panorama encircled the valley and the galaxies extended endlessly above. I felt small, but not alone. I stood and gazed in awe and wonder: the vast expanse of the aurora surrounded by bright stars along its glowing flanks; the silhouettes of ancient peaks against the gigantic movie screen in the sky; a reflection of the iridescent green aurora in the sparkling clear waters of a cool mountain creek; and the musky autumn scent of mother Earth at my feet. Life couldn't be better than this. I felt...*this moment is my life*.

I thought of a poem that had been carved into a wood plank by Park Warden Monrad Kjorlien at Adolphus warden cabin many years before. Inspired by the scenery near the headwaters of the Athabasca River, RCMP Officer Sydney R. Montague had written the poem in the early 1900s.

THIS MOMENT IS MY LIFE

Here on the dust of countless ages past,
I stand, this moment is my life.
All the past is but a memory,
therefore the future is only hope.
Amid the towering peaks so cold, serene and high,
Life is eternal.
The roaring rivers at my feet,
the sun, the moon, the stars, the sky,
I am a part of all this universe,
I am tomorrow's dust.
Here on the dust of countless ages past, I stand,
This moment is my life.

As I stood spellbound by the brilliant display around me, I heard the familiar "ting" of a horse bell. Indeed, I was not alone. My companions were close by, perhaps a couple hundred metres upstream from the cabin. The sound of the bell told me that they were awake and had commenced their morning feeding. Enraptured by the lightshow, I didn't feel like going back inside the cabin and I certainly wasn't going back to bed. I wanted to make the best of my last day in the Moosehorn Valley. Picking up a halter, I went for my last jingle, the glow from the stars and aurora lighting the path enough so that I could find my way. I found Lucky and Harvey grazing in their favourite meadow. I sat near them for half an hour as they continued to feed. I drifted to thoughts of thankfulness for my cherished companions in the wilderness, for their countless hours carrying my weight and guiding me along ancient trails. Lucky and Harvey took a break from their feeding, sauntered over to where I sat, and stood over me. "Yes, buddies, it's time," I said. I slipped the halter over Lucky and led him back to the cabin, with Harvey following behind. They both nickered in anticipation of their treats and Lucky impatiently pawed the ground as I filled their canvas bags with oats from the 45-gallon bin. By the time they had finished their morning treat, the aurora was fading and I went inside.

Not wanting the bright hissing light of the gas lantern in the cabin to interfere with the now softening glow of the aurora outside, I lit a few candles and then placed some kindling in the wood stove. With the strike of a match, I soon felt the warmth of the fire. Before long I had pancakes on the griddle, my last ration of bacon sizzling in a pan, and hot tea in my mug. The horses were dozing soundly at the hitching rail, their stomachs satisfied. I ate my breakfast slowly and reflected on the last nine days. I didn't care to hurry—we'd be out to the trailhead at Devona, and from there, back to the busy world soon enough.

I wanted to prolong *this moment that was my life.*

CHAPTER ONE

Bears In Our Backyard

My first memories of black bears go back as far as...well, my first memories.

I lived with my parents and my older brother Gary behind the Astoria Hotel and its adjoining restaurant in Jasper, Alberta. Jasper is a small town located near the banks of the Athabasca River in the largest park in the Canadian Rockies—Jasper National Park. Our unfenced yard was at the end of a street called Pyramid Lake Road. The road came off the Pyramid Bench, a plateau above the northern and western perimeters of the townsite. During the summer, black bears sauntered down from the plateau every night, cut through our yard, and feasted on the garbage in the back alley and behind the restaurant.

Garbage management in the mid-1950s was very different from what it is today. Townsite residents discarded their garbage in old 45-gallon drums in the back alleys, and restaurants disposed of their waste in the same way. The top lid of the drums was cut off, exposing the food waste to the open air, and garbage pickup was once a week. This gave the bears plenty of time to sift through the most desirable edibles (almost anything) before a new batch of waste conveniently appeared for them in the alleyways.

My parents' evening ritual was to make sure that my brother and I were inside the house before the bears made their way through our yard. I have many recollections, from the time I was a toddler, of standing inside the house by our dining room window and waiting for the bears to show up for their nightly rounds. At about the age of six, I occasionally eluded the watchful eyes of my parents and snuck outside to watch the bears from a safe vantage point in our yard as they made their rounds. I quickly learned how to read each bear's body language for cues that signalled uneasiness—and responded by staying far enough away to accommodate their comfort zone. I understood when very young that wandering too close to an animal would provoke a fight-or-flight response. I never encountered any problems with the bears—I think I was lucky.

One evening our family went out to a movie at the Chaba Theatre, leaving the yard to the bears. When we came home, we saw that one of the living room windows, left partially open to air the house, was broken off its frame. Shards of glass lay on the floor, a coffee table had been knocked over and other furniture moved about, but otherwise the house seemed in order. Then we heard a knock at the door—it was Papa George (George Andrew), the owner of the Astoria Hotel. He had heard a crashing sound coming from the side of our house while he was at the back of his restaurant and had come to investigate. Seeing the smashed window, he looked inside and was shocked to see a black bear pacing around the house. To provide an exit for the bear, Papa George opened the back door; then he ran around to the front door, stepped into the house, and hollered at the bear. The bear immediately ran for the back door and out of the house.

One of my brother's favourite bear stories involved his first (and I think last) attempt at entrepreneurship. He had been watching some of the neighbourhood kids making a few pennies selling Kool-Aid at their roadside stands and figured he could do better. Early one evening he found a cardboard box, crossed the alley over to the back of the Astoria Restaurant, and went through the garbage before the bears could get at it. He found some spoiled potatoes, tomatoes, and other assorted vegetables and fruit. He then took the box back to our screened-in front porch to store for the night and went to bed with plans to open up his street market stall business in the morning.

Following its nose, a bear came into the yard that night, tore through the porch screen, and headed straight for the cardboard box. Mom chased the bear off the porch before it could eat all of Gary's produce. Gary received a good scolding—enough to keep him from thinking up another misadventure for a few days.

Not long after his failed business venture, Gary came up with a plan to trap the bears coming through the yard. I was not privy to this plan. He recruited two of our next-door neighbours, the Hudson brothers, Harold and Ron, to dig a huge pit in our yard. They were a little older than Gary and therefore had the strength to dig the pit. The three of them then covered the big hole with poles and cardboard on which they layered some dirt. (Our yard was not landscaped and didn't have a conventional lawn).

Next, they needed to test the trap. So Gary and the Hudsons asked me to come out of the house to play with them, and some well-planned teasing on their part resulted in my giving chase. As we rounded one corner of the yard, they took an extra-long stride to leap over the pit. Sure enough, I fell into the hole. Dad heard my cries for help and rushed out of the house to investigate. After a good laugh at my expense, he put the kibosh on Gary's bear trapping plans. Good thing, as I don't think Gary had really considered what he would do with a trapped bear once it was caught.

About a year after that incident, we moved to a newer house at the west end of town. Nightly summertime black bear visits were a way of life there as well. There were no restaurant food waste drums near our new house, but resident 45-gallon garbage containers remained fixtures in the back alley. We had one of the best bear viewing yards on the block. A fork in a pine tree about eight metres off the ground on one side of our garage was an ideal sleeping place for whatever bear claimed it. Butting up against the garage, the tree gave direct access to the garage roof. Many a bear found refuge there, away from neighbourhood dogs and young boys with increasing testosterone levels demonstrating their bravery (or stupidity) in bear treeing techniques. Of course, we were trying to impress the young girls on the block, oblivious to the fact that they likely thought of us as a bunch of idiots.

Standing up to the bears was a part of our initiation into early manhood, fully accepted by our peers but condemned by our parents. (If only my parents had known that it was a huge part of my learning curve, necessary for my future career as a park warden.) I could not show fear around wild animals, but at the same time I had to learn how to respect them and not breach the thresholds of harassment or my own safety. I learned how to bluff to fend off potential physical encounters with animals larger and stronger than myself.

We had almost daily encounters with bears in those days. Jasperites simply considered it a normal part of life to see them wandering around town looking for garbage, trying their best to avoid humans and dogs. The closest I got to a bear back then was the length of a broom. I was at home alone when I heard our dog barking outside with much more energy and urgency than normal. I opened the back door to the deck and stared in disbelief at what I saw before me. Part way under the deck, our small mixed-breed dog was spinning around in circles, snarling and barking like mad under the legs of a big adult black bear. The bear, huffing and puffing, was rotating its body in circles in the opposite direction as it tried to get a swat at the dog while at the same time vainly attempting to find a dignified way out of the mess in which it had somehow found itself. Our dog was furiously defending its territory. I grabbed a broom and swung it at the bear, hitting it across the back. Before I could wind up for another hit, the bear hightailed it out of the yard with the dog in hot pursuit. Our dog soon returned, none the worse for wear—incredibly without so much as a scratch.

Many of my friends had similar stories. John Kofin had a much closer black bear encounter when he was three years old. Like many Jasper homes in the late 1950s, his parents' yard wasn't fenced. John was out with his mother, Gertrude, in the backyard. She was busy in the garden taking care of her flowers when she briefly lost track of her young toddler. It wasn't long before John noticed a black bear feeding in an overturned garbage container in the back alley behind the flower garden. He just had to investigate. John's mom heard her son yell, "Get out of my backyard. Get out!" She turned to see John just as he was smacking the bear on the rump. Fortunately, the bear's head and upper body were still deep inside the garbage can and Gertrude was able to pull John away from the bear before it had even noticed what was happening. Gertrude then let out a shout. The bear pulled its head out of the garbage container and fled down the alley in a shower of gravel and dust.

John still vividly recalls another encounter when he was about eight years old. He was out in the next-door neighbours' backyard with his sister Chris and the Thomson daughters, Maxine and Debbie. Once again a black bear had its head deep into an overturned 45-gallon garbage container, enjoying the smorgasbord of leftovers.

John came up with the idea of throwing rocks at the container, hoping the noise would cause the bear to make a hasty retreat. The four of them scrambled up to the top of a gravel pile next to the bear and proceeded to pelt the container with rocks. Alarmed by the rattling of rocks echoing inside the drum, the bear immediately thrust its head out. It spun around, glanced at the kids, and bolted down the alley. The bear however, was back a short time later to resume its feeding. The kids responded by throwing rocks at the garbage container again. Once more the bear retreated, only to come back a short time later to stick its head back inside the container.

Amused and very pleased with their antics, John and the girls pelted the bear and container with rocks for a third time. The bear pulled out, spun around, and charged them. They all turned and ran for the house but Debbie fell while scampering off the gravel pile. John says he will never forget looking back and seeing Debbie prone and frozen in fright, crying out for help as the bear pulled up short just behind her. The bear hung its head close to the ground, slowly waved it from side to side, and gave a loud huff—a warning that the fun was over. It then retreated back to the garbage container. The rest of the group helped Debbie to her feet and left the bear alone. They learned a new respect for bears that day.

I mention these stories to demonstrate the incredible tolerance black bears have for humans. In those days, encounters like these were played out and witnessed daily by Jasper residents. I have often pondered why bears typically avoid even the slightest physical confrontation with us, in spite of the harassment they may face or however abrupt a surprise encounter might be. For the most part, black bears avoid people. If we respect them, encounters rarely result in a bluff charge or an all-out attack by the bear.

There seems to be a law of nature that if we ignore the bear, it will ignore us under all but a very few isolated circumstances.

I recall my parents relating the story of a young girl killed by a black bear in the park. In August 1958, Barbara Coates was picking berries with her five-year-old sister behind their rented Sunwapta Bungalows cottage, 55 kilometres south of Jasper townsite. A black bear, conditioned to obtaining food handouts from park visitors, came out of the woods and charged the two girls. Barbara's sister made it back to the cottage door but the bear caught Barbara on the cabin steps, dragged her into the woods, and mauled her before her mother and other vacationers chased the bear away. Barbara died en route to hospital. This unfortunate encounter is the only reported incident of a fatal black bear attack and the only serious black bear mauling to occur in Jasper National Park.

Before Barbara's mauling, several vacationers and a few Jasper residents had been clawed or bitten by black bears. All of these incidents involved food-conditioned bears that associated handouts or unattended food with people. Most human injury was a result of feeding bears from inside cars along park roadways or approaching bears on foot and enticing them with food. On a few occasions, campers were clawed or bitten through their tents at night by bears attracted by the odour of food kept inside. Fortunately, none of these incidents resulted in serious injury.

Bear related issues in the 1950s were not just a result of their increasing reliance on human food from resident garbage containers, campground garbage, and direct feeding. Large, unfenced, open pit garbage dumps had been used throughout Jasper National Park from the early 1900s through to the early 1970s. The largest unfenced, open pit site, located two kilometres above town on the Pyramid Bench, handled residential garbage as well as waste from the many picnic areas and campgrounds located around the park.

Jasper Park Lodge used another large dumpsite, located a half kilometre east of this famous resort. Although both the Pyramid Bench and Jasper Park Lodge dumps had incinerator facilities, much of the garbage was left unburned. Most of the outlying commercial resorts in the park also used open pit garbage dumps. During the summer, bears wandered freely throughout these resort areas and their associated dumpsites seeking handouts from park visitors and the garbage they left behind.

◆ ◆ ◆

In the early 1960s, about the time I started school, my parents began taking Gary and me to the Pyramid Bench and Jasper Park Lodge dumps in the evening to watch grizzlies feed on the garbage, then a common practice for both tourists and Jasper residents. Grizzlies are generally much more timid than black bears around humans and human occupied areas and were rarely observed close to town. I cannot recall a single incident of a grizzly actually being spotted in town.

We'd arrive at the dumps in the early evening when the black bears were feeding, and we'd sit and wait in our cars until dusk. Watching black bears was no big deal for us as we interacted with them in town every summer day. The first time my parents took us to the Jasper Park Lodge dumpsite is still fresh in my mind as Gary and I had not yet seen a grizzly bear. As my dad parked our old '49 Dodge overlooking the disgusting heaps of garbage, he told my brother and me that we must remain quiet and not open the car door. He said that just before dusk, the dozen or so black bears would leave and we might see some grizzlies. I watched with intense anticipation. Not long before dusk, the black bears began slowly dispersing into the forest, all leaving via a well-trodden trail.

After several minutes all the bears had vacated the dump except for one, left behind with its head deep in garbage. The bear eventually lifted its head and saw that it was alone. It spun around comically, scattering garbage in several directions, and with all four legs spinning out wildly from underneath its body, bolted into the forest.

The dump and surrounding forest became ghostly quiet. Then, on the opposite side of the dump from where the black bears had left, a large brown-coloured bear emerged from the trees and into the open area. As it lumbered towards us, I could see the silver tipped hairs on its shoulder hump glistening in the evening light. I could feel the vibrations in the air; this was a bear that demanded respect and attention—it was a huge dominant boar. I stared in fascination. I remember clutching the top of the front car seat and shaking, not from fear, but with awe. Then several more grizzlies, all somewhat smaller than the first, emerged from the shadows of the forest. I was wonderstruck by their presence. Although I was very young, I sensed a future with these magnificent animals.

◆ ◆ ◆

By the mid-1960s, I was old enough to ride my bike for some distance outside of town. This gave my friends and me the opportunity to explore the park farther than a couple of hours' walk from home. We continued to learn the ways of nature, observing bears, elk, moose, deer, coyotes, and many smaller mammals and birds in their natural habitat.

At this same time, I was looking for ways to supplement my meagre one-dollar-a-week allowance. Dad suggested I use my bike to collect beer bottles. Dad worked as a locomotive engineer for the Canadian National Railway (CNR). Many of the younger men he worked with partied during weekends at picnic sites not far out of town. He was usually privy to the locations of these sites, some of which were local bush hangouts. As several of these were within sight of the railway, Dad often spotted the parties from the train when coming back into town from work in the evening. Dad would tell me about these parties, where a lot of beer was consumed, and early the next morning I'd bike out alone and collect the empty bottles. If I couldn't take all the bottles back home in my bike carrier, I stashed them in the bush and Dad would drive out later and help me collect them.

One day I had a brainwave—I could corner the market in beer bottle collecting! And where might I find the most beer bottles with the least amount of effort? The Pyramid Bench garbage dumpsite of course! I had been around the dumps long enough to know that they were a goldmine for bottles; back then, few people recycled their empties. I also knew that on weekends the park waste collection staff had their days off.

As the weekend approached, I geared up for my business venture. I cleaned and oiled my bike, made sure the carrier was securely attached, and asked Mom to make me a sandwich. My parents always allowed my brother and me free rein to explore and were never overly worried. We only had to inform them where we were going, and if not alone, with whom. (For the record, I told Mom I was merely taking a ride up Pyramid Lake Road.)

The first time I rode my bike past the gated dumpsite entrance and into the open pit, I knew what to expect. I had to compete with the many black bears—at times as many as 15—feeding there. Well, not really compete, as they were seeking food and I was seeking fortune. I found that if I moved around slowly collecting the discarded bottles, the bears ignored me. I was careful to keep my distance, always staying far enough away to avoid confrontation. Occasionally, when a bear came too close to my comfort zone, I would slap my hands, shout "Hey!" in a loud voice, and make a motion towards it. This simple method of deterrence worked for most bears, most of the time. When a bear refused to back away, I gave it a wider berth.

After two or three weeks of this, I was bringing in quite a haul. It was a lot of work getting all the bottles back to our garage myself, as I didn't care to let my dad know where I was getting them. Then one day I arrived at the dumpsite feeling cocky. Not paying much attention to the black bears, I began collecting bottles. After a while, I lifted my head up and found myself surrounded by bears, including a couple of sows with cubs. I became a bit nervous, and then, I panicked, just a little. Instead of letting the circle of bears open enough to give me an escape route, I tried to walk out, and in the process I inadvertently got too close to one of the bears. I had stepped from the invisible perimeter of its comfort zone into its fight-or-flight zone. The bear chose fight.

It charged 10 metres forward, came to an abrupt stop right in front of me, and gave out a loud huff (this is what is called a "bluff charge"—an extremely frightening encounter). It wanted to avoid contact but clearly gave me the message to back off or else. With my heart pounding, I backed away slowly. Thankfully, the bear went back to its business of scrounging for food waste.

I waited several minutes until a few other bears had moved further away from me, giving me an opening to walk back to my bike. I realized that I had been foolish about this venture and that it was time to stop. I was fortunate not to have had a more direct confrontation. I thought about the recent mauling of a young man by a sow grizzly in the Maligne Lake dumpsite area, and I realized that I was pushing the boundaries. I knew that the much more dangerous grizzlies did not enter the dumpsite until the late evening—but why take the chance?

Sometime later I asked my dad for a ride to the collection depot with my bottles. He was proud of me when he saw my large stash of bottles all neatly placed in closed cases in the garage. When we arrived at the bottle depot, the collector, a friend of Dad's I might add, sensed something was amiss. He checked my cases to be sure there were twelve bottles in each and that none were broken. He pulled out a few bottles and inspected them. It was obvious that some of the bottles were too dirty for reuse and quite clearly smelled somewhat of a...well, a garbage dump. The price for a case of empty bottles dropped right then and there from 25 cents to 15 cents. My business venture collapsed, and of course, I had some explaining to do when we got home.

CHAPTER TWO

Running Wild

With my bottle collecting business washed up, I left the garbage dump to the bears and got back to exploring nature with my friends. This, I knew, was where I really belonged. I had recently made friends with Earl Bruce, who lived down the alley from me. The day we met, we were hanging out with a few mutual friends in the alley and looking for mischief. At first meeting, Earl and I were somewhat cool with one another, a bit like a couple of dogs sniffing each other out. Perhaps we knew that we had similar interests and that one day we might compete to lead the "pack" of friends we had. Earl claims that he gave me a good hard punch in the nose just to make it clear that he was someone to be reckoned with, although I don't recall that at all.

Around the time we turned 12, Earl and I became interested in horses. We wanted to learn how to ride and started hanging out at a couple of the local horse stables. We got to know the stable hands and guides at Clint's Pony Barn and occasionally they let us help out around the corral and barn. We were learning a fair bit about horses and the equipment required to care for and ride them. On one particular day the guides were saddling up the horses to take a group of about 10 dudes out for a trail ride on the Pyramid Bench. A couple of horses had not yet been out that day and the head guide asked if we wanted to come along. Was he kidding?

We were put at the back of the trail ride and had to ride our horses at a slow walk, eating the dust kicked up by the horses in front of us. I wondered why we had reins as each horse pretty well stuck its nose on the rear of the horse in front and followed. After a while, Earl and I sized up the situation and agreed we'd had enough of that. At one point, the guide was far enough ahead to be out of sight around a bend, and this gave us the opportunity for a little fun. We reined our horses back for several minutes while the rest of the party rode on; our goal was to practice trotting. Those that know horses will understand that this situation posed a problem. Horses are by nature herd animals, and they generally dislike being away from their group. They'll resist the bit when you try to hold them back from their buddies, and if they lose sight of the lead horses, they'll gallop to catch up.

Earl and I held our horses back long enough to get some distance from the group, and when we could no longer restrain them, we gave the horses free rein. Our horses immediately broke into a gallop, and we bounced all over our saddles with our arms and legs flailing—not quite what we had envisioned. As we came bounding up to the rest of the party, the other horses spooked and created a stampede. Earl and I didn't know whether to laugh our heads off or head for the hills. The guide didn't see the humour in our antics. However, once the mess of horses and riders was straightened out and we got back to the barn, I think he saw a little of himself in us. We had perhaps bitten off a little more than we could chew, but we thrived on an element of risk.

Earl's older brother, Don, was earning money during the summer working as a horse wrangler and trail guide at another stable at Jasper Park Lodge. Now that we had some experience under our belts, we had an opportunity to plan our next move in the equine world. We got to know some of the cowboys at the stable and gained their trust. They occasionally permitted us to ride a few of the horses. This allowed us to practice trotting and galloping as long as we gave the horses long walking breaks to keep them from lathering up. We were learning to ride and we loved every minute of it.

◆ ◆ ◆

The Jasper Rodeo and parade were very popular events for Jasperites and tourists alike. The parade, always held in town, kicked off the annual rodeo. I particularly admired the local park wardens, horse outfitters, Royal Canadian Mounted Police (RCMP), and members of the Stoney Nakoda First Nations Band as they paraded by on their horses.

I stood on the side of the street in silence and wonderment as I watched the neatly groomed horses stride by with their steel shoes clacking on the hard paved road surface. The wardens rode high in the saddle, radiating confidence in their roles as guardians of the wild. They wore their green dress uniforms and trademark Stetson hats with the brass park warden badge displayed on the headband. Usually at least two members of the group led a pack horse behind their riding horses. Many of the wardens that I admired—and tried my best to imitate in my pint-sized cowboy boots—rode in the annual parade. Park Wardens Mac Elder, Alfie Burstrom, Norm Woody, and Bob Barker often participated. Bob always stood out in the group, waving enthusiastically. He is a jovial character and draws attention with his loud voice and spirited laugh. As one of the younger wardens, Bob related well to the kids in town and rarely turned down an opportunity to chat with us. Senior Horseman Denny Welsh also took part in the parade. He was responsible for the care and training of the horses used by park wardens for their backcountry patrols. Years later, my dreams of becoming a warden realized, I worked alongside Denny and these wardens.

The horse outfitters, along with their guides and wranglers who led camping trips into the backcountry areas of the park and into the neighbouring Willmore Wilderness Park north of Jasper, dressed in their everyday western attire for the parade. They resembled cowboys in a Hollywood western—but even better—they were real cowboys, and because Jasper was a small town, we knew most of them. I saw these horse outfitters, like the wardens, as representatives of the wilderness they worked and lived in. Some of the outfitters were the direct descendants of the pioneers who first cleared the backcountry trails through Jasper and Willmore Wilderness long before they became parks. This was a feat they never would have accomplished without their horses or without the skills and knowledge of Aboriginal guides familiar with the areas they ventured into. A few of these outfitters were Métis with roots stretching back to the fur trade era.

Members of the local RCMP detachment also participated in the parade. They wore their iconic, brilliant red serge jackets, black trousers with yellow vertical strips down the sides, and high-topped, immaculately polished brown boots. Like the wardens, they sported their trademark Stetson hat. They marched with military precision, heads focused straight ahead and arms swinging in perfect unison as they kept in stride with the flow of the parade and the tempo of a local Jasper band playing behind them. Every second or third year there'd be a few RCMP members with riding experience, some of whom had ridden in the famous RCMP Musical Ride. They rode tall, black horses from the Warden Service stock.

I was particularly awestruck by the beaded leather clothing worn by members of the Stoney Nakoda First Nations Band from the Kootenay Plains who participated in the rodeo for many years. Some of them rode bareback, their horses decorated with feathers, paint, and leather strapping.

In 1926, a group of local outfitters, park wardens, and other horse enthusiasts from the surrounding area established the Jasper Rodeo. The rodeo presented an opportunity for horse owners to get together and evaluate suitable breeding stock for mountainous terrain and for camaraderie and competition. It was held at Henry House Flats, northeast of town, before it was moved in 1929 to Marmot Meadows just south of present-day Whistlers Campground.

Unlike modern-day rodeos where safety measures protect spectators from the animals, we were allowed to get close to the action, and we often sat on top of the arena's wood rail fence. Sometimes the cowboys allowed us onto the catwalk immediately above the bucking chutes where we could look down on the riders as they got ready for the gates to open. Now that was exciting! We could also walk around to the other side of the arena and sit on a hill above the fence—never a bad seat in the house.

Naturally, we couldn't sit for too long. Earl and I, along with a few other friends, often climbed the fence to get into the staging area behind the bucking chutes. What a thrill—all the cowboys hung out back there, either preparing for their turn or hobbling around wounded after their rides. We wore our western outfits, complete with boots, and looked like we belonged, walking around as if we owned the place. We scuffed up our clothes and boots with dirt for added affect, so we looked the part. I think the cowboys thought that we were back there to see our dads—except our dads weren't cowboys.

On one occasion, a group of us was hanging out in the staging area with the cowboys, looking for a little excitement. The smell of leather riding gear, horse sweat, and cowhide heightened our own sense of competition. The Brahma bull corral was situated slightly back from us, connected by a gated alley to the staging area, and we dared each other to run across the corral and through the Brahma bull herd.

Let me explain a little about these bulls. Before the rider mounts, a flank strap is buckled around the bull's flank, which makes the Brahma bull kick out straighter and higher when trying to buck off its rider. When rodeo horses buck, they arch their backs, throw their heads down, and jump stiff legged in their attempt to toss the rider. The much more ferocious Brahma bulls jump and throw out their back legs much like a horse, but they also twist and turn in tight arcs at the same time. The cowboy must stay atop the bucking bull for eight seconds—a very risky endeavour that has been called "the most dangerous eight seconds in sport." If a bull succeeds in dumping its rider, it may whirl around and turn on the hapless cowboy, and that's when the real danger begins. The nearly one-tonne bull will often try to spear the rider with his horns or pummel him with his sharp hooves. This is where the rodeo clown comes in. It's the clown's job to lure the bull away from the fallen rider. And if he can't, well, that accounts for all the cowboys hobbling around.

Back to our challenge to run through the Brahma bull herd. With the bulls mainly crowded towards one end of the corral, we dared each other to run across. When it was my turn, I made a quick dash for the opposite fence, slipped, and almost fell in a steamy pile of dung, but we all made it across without provoking much of a reaction from the bulls. Naturally, we then had to turn up the challenge a notch. In response to a flurry of double and triple dares, we made successive mad dashes across the pen, inching ever closer to the bulls with each round of idiocy.

About the time the bulls were becoming agitated, a rodeo official discovered us. I explained that we were in training to be cowboys—after all, that's what we all wanted to be. Didn't everyone want to be a cowboy? Not to mention how impressed the girls on our street would be with our bravado. Or so we liked to think. Of course, the real cowboys weren't impressed with our foolishness and we were unceremoniously ushered from the area and taken to our parents.

We received the usual reprimand but it was worth it and we looked forward to our next misadventure. We later learned that the Brahma bull is generally a docile breed until it feels the weight of the cowboy on its back in the bucking chutes—or perhaps, until it becomes agitated with a few foolish kids trying to be cowboys. We were proud of ourselves nonetheless; we felt we had "run with the bulls."

The rodeo attracted cowboys from all over Alberta and British Columbia, and some came from as far away as Saskatchewan and Montana. Many of the local outfitters and wardens organized and/or participated in the roping and riding events, as did a few locals who were still in, or just out of, high school. Injuries were common, and the town had only one ambulance to cart away the unfortunate. On each day of the rodeo, the ambulance was either en route to Jasper with one broken body or returning to the rodeo grounds in anticipation of another. Many times, after a rider had fallen hard or been kicked by his mount and needed medical attention, the event announcer would request the service of someone in attendance with a station wagon. I think every Jasper family with a station wagon carted an injured cowboy or two to the hospital.

One memorable day, when we were back home after the rodeo had finished, Dad told us that there would be something very special happening at the rodeo grounds that evening, something very few people ever got the opportunity to witness. Despite our pleas, he wouldn't divulge any details; but at what was usually our bedtime, we piled into the car and drove back to the rodeo grounds.

The dust of the daily rodeo events had long settled and twilight was fading into darkness. A bonfire had been lit at one end of the grounds and it was now a circle of small flames and glowing embers. We gathered with other Jasper residents and many of the cowboys and sat quietly in a large circle around the fire. I waited with mounting excitement.

Soon, at the outer fringes of light cast by the glowing fire, ghostly figures slowly stepped forward. They were members of the Stoney Nakoda Band carrying hide drums. They sat down amongst us and readied their drums to play. From out of the same shadows, dancers in striking Aboriginal regalia merged into the inner circle. The deep base sounds of chanting and drumming soon filled the air, accompanied by the rhythmic dancers silhouetted against a backdrop of fire and night. I was mesmerized. The ceremonial singing and dancing was a celebration of the First Nations' connection to tradition, spirituality, and Mother Earth. That night's ceremony remains forever etched in my mind.

To our great disappointment, the outdoor rodeo was phased out in 1969. In 1976, it was replaced by the new indoor Jasper Heritage Rodeo at the Jasper Activity Centre. During the summer following the last outdoor rodeo event, I met a family from Utah vacationing in the park. I befriended the two sons, both close to my age, and took them to the old rodeo grounds to show them around.

We were walking around the back corrals when we noticed movement beneath a black tarp covering part of a storage shed. We could not see the animal behind the tarp, but it appeared to be the size of a small cat. The two brothers picked up a board and shouted "Rat!" I yelled that it couldn't be a rat because Alberta was rat free. They paid no attention to me and smashed the moving form behind the tarp until it was dead. I was shocked and furious that they would do this and I was curious to see what wild animal they had just killed.

I pulled out my jackknife and slit open the tarp. A huge, repulsive rat dropped to the ground. This was not the wild and somewhat cute-looking bushy-tailed wood rat found at higher elevations in the Rockies. This was a Norway rat that must have come in on a horse trailer the summer before and somehow survived the winter. If I recall correctly, the storage shed had some oats in it, providing the rat with at least one food source. We searched the area for signs of other rats but found nothing. Thanks to my American friends' well-aimed swings with a piece of lumber, Alberta could again be declared rat free.

◆ ◆ ◆

My brother Gary and his buddies spent a lot of their time roaming around an area just west of town, and a few of my friends thought we would do the same. We began learning how to climb on a rock outcropping called Little Mountain, situated right alongside the railway about a kilometre outside of town. As best we could with our flat-soled running shoes and without ropes or other climbing equipment, we honed our climbing skills on the steep faces of the rocks immediately above the railway tracks.

Another area we liked to wander around in was between town and Little Mountain—an area now partially taken over by new housing development. We called the area "Hobo Sandpit." A number of unemployed men looking for work or adventure were still hitching rides on the rails in the early and mid-1960s—a throwback from the Dirty '30s, I suppose. These men frequently camped or simply rested at Hobo Sandpit while waiting for the next train to take them wherever it might be going.

We often took our longbows and pellet guns with us when roaming the woods. One of our favourite spots to set up targets and practice our shooting skills was Hobo Sandpit. As longbows are considered firearms, just as rifles are, this is something that would never be allowed in a national park today. However, we were fortunate that the park wardens generally looked the other way and rarely went after us for possessing firearms. If the wardens trusted that we weren't shooting at wildlife, they usually left us alone. And if some youngster was not following the rules—well, we lived in a small town and word travelled fast.

We ran into many hobos as they came off the trains and we never had any trouble with them. They often went to the first house they saw as they jumped off the trains pulling into the west end of town near Hobo Sandpit, and they would ask for food from the lady who lived there. She was the mother of a friend of ours and was always kind to the hobos. She gave them food, encouragement in their travels or job search, and her blessings.

We used to watch those hobos as they jumped on and off the trains as they pulled into and out of town. Gary and his friends, being a little older than me, mastered the feat of jumping onto a boxcar as a train was pulling into town. Note that I said *into* town. They'd run alongside the tracks as a train was pulling into town from the west, then reach out and grab for the steel ladder on either end of a boxcar. They'd "ride the rails" towards town just as the hobos did and safely jump off before they reached the rail yards. Cool. I followed my brother out to Hobo Sandpit one day to watch him and his friends engage in this dangerous activity. I was impressed, albeit a little frightened by the whole idea, but vowed I would do the same someday soon.

Now, it so happened that I had a new friend who lived across the alley from us, Ricky Baxter. Ricky was a little younger than me and had just moved to Jasper. Naturally, I decided to do something to impress him. So off we went to Hobo Sandpit, I with my bow slung over my shoulder and my arrow quiver on my back. We waited until a train came *out of* town, heading west on its way past Little Mountain. It somehow escaped me that trains pulling *out of* town would be accelerating as they moved westward, and not decelerating as they would be when moving eastward *into* town. It was much safer to jump the inbound train (like my brother always did) as it was slowing down, which meant you could disembark at a lower and safer speed. My brother understood this, but he was always better at the theory of mechanics than I was.

The train was pulling 80-odd boxcars as it moved out of town and picking up momentum. As it was approaching us, I explained everything I knew to Ricky about hopping trains. I knew almost nothing about this dangerous activity (and was about to demonstrate that), apart from having watched my brother, his friends, and the hobos jumping on and off trains. I had also watched westerns at the Chaba Theatre in town many times, observing carefully the train robbers' technique of jumping from galloping horses onto moving trains. I *did* know that it was wise to hide in the trees until the engine passed by so I wouldn't be noticed, especially if the engineer on the train happened to be my dad. The trick was to run out of the trees and simply (or so I thought) hop onto the passing train.

After the big engine thundered by, I threw my bow and quiver to Ricky for added effect, and peeled off towards the nearest boxcar. It was at this time that I noticed the train was quickly gaining speed. My heart was thumping out of my chest and the palms of my hands were sweating as I leaped up to grab the second from the bottom rung of the ladder on the side of the boxcar. I missed. In a fraction of a second, my momentum carried me downwards as I grabbed for the bottom rung. Amazingly my hands caught the rung and held. But now the momentum inwards carried my legs under the outside floor of the boxcar towards the rolling wheels. To this day, I don't know how I was able to hold on, swing out, and then let go at the right moment. I landed hard, and rolled and tumbled along the gravel bed beside the track—just like in the movies but much less gracefully. I was bruised and scraped but got away without major injury. I was very lucky, to say the least. But I was shaking like a leaf in a stiff wind, and Ricky was not impressed. My clothes were ripped to tatters and not without a few blood stains. I had some explaining to do when I got home—another misadventure and another reprimand.

After all this, I realized that working for the railway, like my father and both of my grandfathers, was not going to be the career for me. My activities, once more, turned back to nature.

CHAPTER THREE

Wilderness At Our Doorstep

I started fishing with my dad and grandfather when I was still a young boy. My grandfather, Herb Karran, was the locomotive shop foreman with the CNR in Jasper, but on weekends during the fishing season, he hired himself out as a fishing guide for tourists interested in trying out their luck at the many good fishing lakes in the park.

We fished for various species of trout: mostly rainbow, eastern brook, cutthroat, and dolly varden. My dad and grandfather often drove my brother and me, or one of my friends and me, to the many lakes in the park that were too far away to reach on foot or by bicycle. We had a small three-metre wooden fishing boat that we transported on the car top carrier to the lakes situated close to the roads.

We usually ventured out in the very early morning when the chances of catching fish were greater. If successful, we brought our catch home before lunchtime, cleaned the fish, and then let Mom take over. Mom battered the freshly caught trout with flour and spices and pan-fried them, sometimes with leftover potatoes. This was a delicacy for everyone in the family, including our Siamese cat, who would pace the kitchen floor until she got her share. Our dog, though, could never understand what all the fuss was about.

On warm summer evenings, I frequently cycled with my friends Ben Hodgkiss and Richard Ireland up to Patricia and Pyramid lakes on the Pyramid Bench, or to Annette or Trefoil lakes on the other side of the Athabasca River across the valley from town. We carried our rods to fish for trout from the lakeshores. If my friends weren't around, I'd head off alone on foot or with my bike to the various lakes scattered around the valley. I'd find quiet locations along the shoreline away from other people and observe the natural world around me while I fished. I was captivated by the comings and goings of the many duck species, Canada geese, grebes, and loons. I marvelled at the enchanting calls of the loons, watched the small hand-sized belted kingfishers dive for minnows from tree branches overhanging the lakes, and was always on the lookout for osprey flying overhead. All three bird species depend on fish for their survival. Angling, as with all my outdoor activities, instilled in me the love of nature, and I knew, even as a youngster, that this would lead to a career working with wildlife.

◆ ◆ ◆

To gain an understanding of how angling became an acceptable practice in the mountains, we have to go back to the late 1880s when the Rocky Mountains began to attract the first tourists. Banff, Canada's first national park, established in 1885, emphasized visitor recreation and appreciation of the area's scenic wonders. The establishment of Jasper National Park (1907) and other Rocky Mountain parks followed. Hunting, trapping, and fishing remained, to one extent or another, common pursuits for a few decades afterwards.

The National Parks Act abolished hunting in the national parks in 1930. The Act prohibited the disturbing, hunting, or destruction of wildlife unless under special permit. Park wardens retained the authority, however, to destroy an animal that was injured or presented a risk to the public. In most parks, sport fishing (really another form of hunting) continues to be permitted. For a nominal fee anyone can get a permit.

Anglers must purchase permits when fishing in national parks, and a brochure with a condensed version of fishing regulations is included with all permits. These regulations state which species can be caught, the number of fish anglers are allowed to have in their possession each day, the lakes and waterways where fishing is allowed, the permissible baits, and the time of year fishing is allowed (with separate time periods for different lakes and species).

Many mountain lakes were naturally barren of fish before the establishment of the Rocky Mountain national parks. In the early part of the 1900s, wardens stocked park lakes and streams with both native and non-native fish. As a child, I can recall many of the older wardens explaining how, on cool spring or autumn days, they would fill specially lined boxes with cold water and fingerling fish and then load the boxes onto pack horses. They would then ride out to the designated lakes or streams in their districts and release the fingerlings. Some of the early pioneers and backcountry horse outfitters did the same.

Past fisheries management programs in Jasper National Park were mandated to provide optimal fishing. To achieve this goal, the federal government constructed a fish hatchery in 1942, situated just off the Maligne Lake Road and alongside the Maligne River, seven kilometres north of the townsite. For almost three decades, cultured fish were introduced en masse to virtually all of the park's accessible lakes and streams. Some of these waters contained native fish, but introduced stocks were regarded as superior sport fish or innocuous supplements to native fish stocks. Park managers assumed, or at least hoped, that these fish would thrive in the wide variety of habitats found in the park.

Such bounty, however, did not last long. The lack of biological productivity and the often silt-laden waters of many mountain lakes could not support large numbers of fish. As well, many of the lakes did not contain suitable spawning environments.

The cost of operating the fish hatchery became an issue and hatchery operations were phased out in the late 1960s. The old fish hatchery buildings were subsequently used as the Park Warden Office from 1975 until the mid-1990s, when the Warden Office was re-located to the government compound on the outskirts of Jasper.

There were other issues with fish stocking. Many of the exotic species brought into the park did not survive. On the other hand, some of the introduced fish species did alarmingly well in their new surroundings, and many native fish populations, suffering from competition for food and the limited spawning sites, declined. Bull trout, for example, was once the most widespread native trout in the mountain parks, but this species has disappeared from much of its former range. To protect the remaining populations of bull trout, all mountain national parks have instituted a zero catch and possession limit for this species. Mountain park waters are no longer stocked with non-native fish, and some species of native fish are being re-introduced into selected waters to re-establish their populations.

Fishing in the Rocky Mountain national parks no longer provides anglers with the plentiful food resource it once did. We were very fortunate to have grown up in Jasper when we did and to have had so many lakes and streams at our disposal to fish from.

◆ ◆ ◆

Each year, as summer progressed into autumn and autumn to winter, we looked forward to cold weather activities. When we entered elementary school, our parents gave my brother and me the choice of either taking up hockey at the local arena or learning to ski at Whistlers Ski Hill; they couldn't afford the equipment for both. We chose skiing. Ski lessons were offered during school hours to all students starting from grade four and continuing up to grade twelve. A dedicated group of ski instructors gave lessons to as many as 130 kids each week. I had to wait three years before I could take lessons through school.

My skis were hand-me-downs made from wood and fitted with non-release bear trap bindings. My poles were long sticks of bamboo with leather-wrapped handles and wide baskets. I learned to ski on the bunny hill that had straight fall lines from top to bottom and ran just short of 200 metres with a slope of approximately 25 degrees. I couldn't turn well with those ancient boards, so my way of getting to the bottom was to tuck and swoosh. The level run-out at the bottom of the hill was very short, and by the time I got there I was usually going very fast. To break my descent (remember, I couldn't turn), I would invariably end up crashing at full speed into the willows beyond the run-out area. Dad always came over and picked me up, and then he searched for my poles, either half-buried in the snow or hung up in the branches of the willows. Sometimes, a group of adults, gathered at the bottom of the hill to watch their kids, would slog through the snow and willows to join in the search for my mitts and toque. This was after they had enjoyed a good belly laugh watching my unique stopping technique. Then Mom would put me on the rope tow, and up I'd go to the top of the hill to repeat the whole process.

After a few weeks of this, my dad figured that perhaps if I had my ski edges sharpened and my bases hot-waxed by head ski patrolman Tom McCready, I might learn how to push into my turns better, slow down, and end my dangerous dash, crash, and burn style of skiing. I recall with great clarity walking into the basement of the ski lodge with Dad and ambling over to Tom's ski shop. As Tom busied himself repairing some skis, Dad engaged him in conversation and then asked him if he would hot-wax my skis for me. Tom had witnessed my skiing ability (or lack of) on the hill. He looked over at Dad with obvious amusement on his face and pointed out that a fresh coating of wax would place a smooth layer between the wood at the bottom of the skis and the snow, allowing for a much faster ski surface. Dad realized his mistake, and I wasn't too young to know what that meant. Dad stated that perhaps this wasn't a good idea after all, but I would have none of that and I made a huge fuss; I wanted my skis waxed. Dad relented and Tom waxed my boards. Big mistake.

Off we went to the bunny hill again. As soon as I put my skis on, I noticed the difference the wax created; I could barely stand without the skis taking off from underneath my feet. My eagerness in getting to the top of the lift and onto the hill caused my mother much anxiety as she placed me on the rope tow. After she sent me off, I turned around and saw Dad lining up a group of men at the end of the run-out in anticipation of stopping a speeding bullet. I reached the ski lift tower at the top of the hill, let go of the rope before it carried on around the bull wheel, and glided into position. Were my parents not aware that I had no intention of making turns on the newly waxed skis because I loved speed? This was all just too cool.

I looked for a clear line between the other skiers on the hill, pushed off with my oversized poles and ancient hot-waxed boards, and tucked. The rapid acceleration was more than I could ever have imagined. The rush of wind made my eyes tear, causing me to stray somewhat off course. As I raised my head slightly out of my tuck position, I could see the line of men that Dad had arranged at the end of the run-out area. They were moving back and forth across the slope as a group, trying to anticipate my fall line, hoping that they could stop me at the bottom of the slope rather than in the willows I preferred to crash into. As the world rushed by me in a blur, I remember thinking what a ridiculous idea this was—and that we'd all get hurt.

I never made it to the bottom of the hill. As I was reaching the run-out area, an elderly man cut across the hill between me and the safety net of adults lined up below. I slammed into him at breakneck speed before he knew what hit him. Once the snow had settled, the group of men came over and untangled us. One of the ski patrollers on the hill raced over and checked us for injuries. Although he announced that I had survived the crash, I felt sore all over and I was slow in getting up because the wind had been knocked out of me. The elderly man was very shaken but seemed okay. As he was slowly helped onto his feet, my dad, with a grim look on his face, walked up to him carrying one of the man's bamboo poles busted in half. The man then proceeded to verbally tear into Dad for not being in control of his crazy son. I remember listening to a long exchange of words, some that I'd never heard before.

About a half hour later, I once again ambled up to Tom McCready's ski shop with Dad. I think Tom was expecting our return because he looked up at Dad with a twinkle in his eye and a mischievous grin. Dad, without engaging in any unnecessary conversation, bought a new set of adult bamboo poles for the elderly man and had Tom sign me up for ski lessons.

By the late 1960s, my brother and my friends and I had become fairly proficient skiers and had graduated to the expansive and newly established ski hill, Marmot Basin, situated farther south of town. Although I continued to downhill ski as I entered high school, I also became more interested in cross-country skiing and snowshoeing. These pursuits took me away from the bustle of the ski hill into undisturbed wilderness. It was here that I could observe and learn the ways of wildlife during the cold months of the year, as they lived their lives in various habitats in the mountains.

◆ ◆ ◆

As I moved into my teen years, I became increasingly interested in the lives of wildlife species, their interactions with one another, and how they reacted to humans. Bear sightings continued to be a daily occurrence during the summer months and an accepted part of everyday life. It was also common to see elk and deer close to home as well as coyotes wandering around the perimeters of the townsite. Unlike wolves, coyotes often skulk into inhabited areas searching for small, wild prey and the occasional domestic animal. I had yet to experience my first wolf sighting. Wolves, being far less tolerant of human activity than their canine cousins, will usually go to great lengths to avoid humans. Seeing a wolf anywhere near town was a rare experience.

So I turned my interest towards an animal that I could watch in silence and in a completely natural setting. During the autumn of my first year in high school I searched out a location along the Miette River, about five kilometres west of town, where a family of beavers had established its territory. I sat quietly out of their view on a low ridge just above the river and watched them for several weeks before the water began to freeze over. They busied themselves cutting branches off the large mature aspen trees they felled along the riverbank and stockpiled them in the water around their lodge for their winter food supply. Once the river froze over, they accessed the stockpile from an underwater entrance in their lodge. It is an amazing experience to watch these industrious rodents at work.

It was during this particular autumn that Jasper residents, for the first time in anyone's memory, reported seeing a wolf moving about the townsite at night. My dad caught a quick glimpse of the wolf in an alley when he was walking home from work late one night. When the wolf saw Dad, it vanished into the darkness. This was a lone wolf that didn't appear to belong to a pack. It may have been sick, injured, or old and unable to keep up with its former pack, a young wolf looking to break into a new pack, or just alone for some other reason.

After observing the beavers one evening and returning from Miette River in near darkness, I was about to step out of the forest and into the lights of an alley that ended at the west end of town when I suddenly spotted the large canine loping down the alley. It was headed straight towards me from approximately 50 metres away. There was no mistaking this to be the wolf that many Jasper residents had seen.

I immediately crouched down in the dark and waited behind a bush, hoping that the wolf would pass close by. The wind direction must have been right as the wolf failed to sense me when it crossed a road bisecting the alley and headed into the trees where I was waiting. I couldn't believe my eyes as the wolf approached to within 10 metres before it noticed me. Totally startled by my presence, it sidestepped, completed a quick 90-degree turn, ran along the bush line next to the road, and then faded back into the trees away from me. Although it would have been a more memorable experience to have this happen in a natural setting, it was exhilarating to have come so close to this beautiful animal.

◆ ◆ ◆

After sighting my first wolf, I gave much thought to the intensive wolf control programs that had been implemented in the national parks and in many other wild areas in North America for over a century.

John Palliser, an Irish-born geographer and explorer, first recorded the persecution of wolves in 1860 in what was to become Jasper National Park. Fur traders in the Athabasca River Valley killed wolves with strychnine. Later, park regulations and policies that encouraged the killing of wolves, bears, and other large predatory species in the mountain national parks between 1890 and 1930, drastically reduced wolf populations in Jasper National Park. Wolf population numbers, along with the population of other predators, recovered to some degree in the years between 1930 and the late 1940s when their persecution was somewhat reprieved.

By the late 1940s, park management again considered wolves undesirable park residents, and wardens were encouraged to shoot, snare, or poison as many as they could. Baits laced with strychnine or bait-triggered cyanide capsules nailed to trees was an effective way to eliminate wolves. Unfortunately, these poisons resulted in the deaths of any fur-bearing animals that took the bait. Strychnine has far-reaching and unintended consequences along the subsequent food chain, killing many mammals and birds that feed on poisoned carcasses.

Wolves and other predatory wildlife again faced large-scale slaughter in 1952 when rabid foxes brought rabies into Alberta from the Northwest Territories. Fearing the disease would spread to other predatory species, and ultimately to humans from bites or scratches by infected animals, the federal and provincial governments initiated an intensive predator control program. Tens of thousands of black and grizzly bears, foxes, coyotes, wolves, cougar, lynx, and wolverine were trapped, shot, and poisoned throughout Alberta (including the mountain national parks) over a two-year period.

Wolves and other predators weren't the only animals to face steep population declines with the arrival of Europeans. Widespread hunting in the late 1800s drastically reduced elk numbers to the point where local populations became extirpated. By the early 1900s, elk were reported to be absent from the Jasper area. As a result, park officials initiated an elk reintroduction program in the 1920s. Approximately 100 elk were brought into the park by rail from Yellowstone National Park in Wyoming.

Elk numbers grew, and by the early 1940s, park managers became increasingly concerned about their high numbers in the Athabasca River Valley and the subsequent deterioration of ungulate winter range. An annual winter elk cull began in 1942 and continued into the late 1950s. Periodic culls also took place several times in the 1960s when park wardens killed over 2200 elk. The elk carcasses were stripped of their hides, quartered, and shipped by railway to several First Nations reserves in Alberta. The antlers were sent to a cutlery factory to be made into elk-horn knife handles.

Ironically, the elk slaughter program was underway at the same time that intensive predator control programs nearly eliminated wolves from the park and across much of North America. Elk make up the largest portion of the wolves' diet within the Athabasca River Valley during the winter months. By 1954 (the end of the rabies scare), periodic predator control programs had been implemented in Jasper National Park for over 90 years. The especially intensive control programs in the decade up to 1954 had a major impact on natural predator/prey interactions; and the drastic reduction in the wolf population had played a large part in the increase of elk numbers. Subsequently, an overabundance of elk resulted in the decline of available graze on their winter range.

The park wardens and other park employees working in the field during these years of intensive predator control programs and elk slaughters were, to varying degrees, aware of this irony. At the same time, they treated it as a condition of their continued employment. They did the best job they could, given the knowledge they had at the time. In retrospect, there was a clear contradiction in the national parks' wildlife management policies. One day a park warden might be shooting elk and poisoning wolves and other wildlife, while the next day he could be on patrol ensuring that all park visitors were abiding by the many regulations in place to protect and preserve the park's flora and fauna.

Something else seemed out of balance with the ecosystem in the 1960s. Ecologists and wildland fire experts were beginning to acknowledge that forest fire suppression throughout North America for most of the 20th century was having a detrimental impact on the environment. National park fire crews were still vigorously fighting all fires in the park system, whether caused by lightning or by human carelessness. However, parks policies governing wildfire suppression were slowly changing in response to ecological studies that recognized fire as a natural process. This process, which had been around since the appearance of forests 400 million years ago, is necessary to promote new growth and increase biological diversity.

As I sat watching the beavers on the bank of the Miette River that autumn over the course of a few weeks, I gave much thought to the natural processes going on around me. I understood by this time how the predator control programs and elk slaughters had affected the natural equilibrium of predator/prey dynamics. I could see that fire suppression had led to the creation of many large tracts of equal-age, over-mature pine and spruce forests in Jasper. And it was evident that the biodiversity of plants and animals within these forests was very low compared to the mixed forests or the small stands of aspen forests in the park. Through fire suppression, these forests had become more of a monoculture, unable to support or sustain a large variety of animals.

At the same time, I looked around and observed the incredible biodiversity in ponds and wetlands that were surrounded by mixed-wood forests of pine, spruce, fir, and aspen. This was the habitat of the beaver family along the Miette River, and, in fact, they had created much of this habitat. From my wanderings in the outdoors, one other aspect of this environment struck me. Why were there fewer active beaver lodges in the Athabasca and Miette river valleys when compared to decades before, as evidenced by the number of old abandoned beaver lodges and dams?

Perhaps the beaver had not fully recovered from the fur trade era when tens of millions of beaver pelts from North America were shipped to Europe? Historical records indicate that beaver were trapped in the Athabasca River Valley within what is now Jasper National Park for several decades by early explorers, travellers, and then fur traders after the establishment of Jasper House in 1813. The fur trading post was built by the North West Company and later amalgamated with the Hudson's Bay Company in 1821.

Was it the absence of wildfires over the past century that had had an effect on the growth of aspen stands, which provide the staple diet of most beaver? Were traditional wetlands simply drying up, resulting in beaver relocating to more favourable habitat? Was an unnaturally high population of elk due to a lack of predators out-competing beaver for forage? Elk are chiefly a grazing animal but had resorted to browsing on aspen and willow species as a source of "starvation feed" in the Athabasca River Valley in the middle half of the 20th century after they had overgrazed grassland habitats. Could there be other reasons for the apparent decline in beaver over the last half-century that I was not aware of? It would be several more years, after I had finished my post-secondary education and worked in the field, that some of these questions would be answered for me. One thing I clearly understood as I scrutinized the environment around me in the late 1960s was that nature is dynamic and often difficult to understand. The environment is constantly evolving as a result of both natural processes and human activity.

As I entered high school, I also became more aware of the increasingly fragmented ecosystem in the montane area of Jasper National Park. The montane area is the relatively warm, dry habitat along the valleys of the Athabasca and Miette rivers. Wildlife species occur in abundance within the mix of coniferous forests interspersed with smaller deciduous forest stands, grasslands, and various wetlands that comprise the montane. Also squeezed into this relatively small area of the park is the townsite of Jasper, the CNR, Jasper Park Lodge with its expansive golf course, the Yellowhead Highway, an airfield, two large campgrounds, a power station, a pipeline corridor, a waste transfer station, a sewage waste plant, several tourist bungalow camps, picnic sites, and numerous trails. Clearly, wildlife in the park was not only affected by the activities of humans and various management control programs but also by the alteration of prime habitat and in some cases the permanent loss of the habitat that they relied on for movement corridors, food, shelter, and solitude.

◆ ◆ ◆

During our last couple of years in high school, my friends and I began seeking new adventures in areas of the park we hadn't travelled before, often further away from the main valley corridor. I realized that the pursuit of outdoor recreational activities would give me additional skills and knowledge required for a career with Parks Canada. Mountain climbing was becoming a popular sport across North America and we took up the challenge. I also bought a wood-canvas canoe so we could experience our mountain home from a different perspective.

We spent an increasing amount of our weekend and holiday time backpacking into wilderness areas. Jasper National Park spans 11,228 square kilometres of broad forested valleys interspersed with grasslands, subalpine slopes, alpine meadows, rugged mountain ranges, and wild rivers. We were eager to explore as much of our wilderness backyard as possible by way of extended overnight backcountry trips.

I often paired up with my school buddies, John Kofin, Pat Paul, or Richard Ireland for trips, depending on who was available. We had various summer jobs in Jasper during the early 1970s that often prevented all four of us from getting together at the same time, but we did find more opportunities to backpack as a group during the late spring and early autumn months. Within a four-year period, we hiked nearly every established backcountry trail in Jasper and ventured into many of the more remote, seldom travelled areas of the park.

We experienced many memorable wildlife sightings and encounters in remote and wild areas of the park. We faced harsh weather and demanding conditions that taxed our endurance and pushed our limits. Our more challenging trips took us into rugged areas without defined trails or any trails whatsoever. These trips frequently involved dangerous river fords, high elevation mountain ridge crossings into hidden valleys, and back-breaking bushwhacks—all requiring a great deal of route finding skills over difficult terrain.

Many of our more remote backpacking trips took us into areas that only a few people had explored before. In fact, the location and general description of some of these routes were passed on to us by a few of the old-time horse outfitters, guides, and park wardens we knew in Jasper, some of whom had pioneered the routes through the deep wilderness areas.

We were experiencing nature in the raw, something few people do today, or can even imagine. We were very fortunate to have been raised in this environment, but at the time, we never thought much about it. Our wilderness adventures were just something that we did—it came with the territory and with our passion for exploring. When we sat by an evening campfire at the end of a long day in some remote mountain valley far from any other humans, we felt the primeval spirit of the wilderness, and we became part of it.

In August 1973, Pat Paul and I took our longest backcountry trip—a 173-kilometre, 10-day hike along Jasper's North Boundary Trail. We began our hike at Celestine Lake on the eastern end of the trail and trekked west over the Continental Divide into British Columbia at Mount Robson Provincial Park. The last 22 kilometres of the North Boundary Trail through the provincial park contain some of the most spectacular scenery in the Canadian Rockies.

When we walked across the Continental Divide between Alberta and British Columbia on the ninth day of our journey, the towering north face of Mount Robson, the highest mountain in the Canadian Rockies at 3954 metres, came into full view. Experiencing that view for the first time takes your breath away. As the mountain often captures cloud on even the clearest of days, it is rare to see its upper reaches of snow, rock, and ice. Pat and I experienced one of those rare days. The brilliant white snow and ice on the north face and summit ridge stood in stark contrast to the deep blue of the sky. At the base of this magnificent mountain, massive tumbling glaciers spilled into the milky green waters of Berg Lake. We had experienced countless soul-stirring wilderness moments during our many backcountry treks—but this one was special.

Pat and I continued along the shoreline of Berg Lake for an hour, then set our backpacks down beside the trail not far from a horse outfitter's camp tucked into a small stand of trees. The outfitter's clients were out somewhere on a day hike. We walked over to the horse corrals and stroked the manes of a few horses that came up to us alongside the rail. Walking back to our backpacks, we pulled out our lunches, sat down with our backs against some trees, and gazed up at Mount Robson. The monarch of the Rockies was in a blaze of glory. To this day, our conversation is etched in my memory. We talked about our trip over the North Boundary Trail and how it represented a culmination of our many adventures together in the wild before we moved on to college and our careers. It was the end of an era for us and for many of our friends who had begun to leave Jasper to follow their dreams. While resting in the idyllic setting and easing our sore muscles from nine days on the trail, we discussed our ambitions.

Pat planned to take the Forestry Program at the Northern Alberta Institute of Technology (NAIT) in Edmonton in September. I was enrolled in the Biological Sciences Program at NAIT the following year to obtain the academic requirements required for an entry level position as a national park warden with Parks Canada. Looking at the horses in the corral and thinking about the long trek we had just made through the northern wilderness of Jasper reinforced my ambition to become a warden. I would first have to complete my post-secondary education, acquire a few years of related work experience, be granted an interview, and then place in the top ten of hundreds of applicants to attain an entry level park warden position at whichever national park in western Canada had available vacancies. Little did I know that our adventure over the North Boundary Trail foretold a journey I was to make in seven years' time when I would travel its length on horseback as a park warden.

CHAPTER FOUR

Bird Songs, Scats, and Animal Tracks

In January 1976, a few months before I completed the Biological Sciences Program at NAIT, Parks Canada posted a competition for seasonal park warden positions in western Canada. Although I knew that my chances of getting a position fresh out of college were next to nil, I submitted my resume.

Two weeks later I learned that I had not been granted an interview for a seasonal park warden job that summer. There were fewer than 10 seasonal positions available in Canada's western national parks for the summer of 1976. I was one of over 700 applicants that were turned down. I knew that competition for the few available jobs would be just as strong in the years to come.

Not long after applying for a park warden position, I enquired about employment opportunities with the Canadian Wildlife Service (CWS) for the upcoming summer. Job vacancies with the CWS were scarce for recent college and university graduates, so I was surprised to learn that there were a few job openings for a biophysical inventory project in Jasper and Banff. I submitted my resume to Don Karasiuk, lead biologist for the Jasper inventory team, and kept in touch with him until I graduated from NAIT in May 1976.

A few days after returning to Jasper, I received a phone call from Don informing me that I was hired as a wildlife technician with the CWS to work on the inventory project in Jasper called *Ecological (Biophysical) Land Classification of Jasper National Park* (hereinafter referred to as the "Biophysical Inventory"). I was thrilled, realizing that I was very fortunate to find work with an agency that would give me some of the experience and knowledge required to eventually work for Parks Canada. My job started on June 1.

The Biophysical Inventory marked a new era in scientific studies and inventories that greatly added to our understanding of the distribution and abundance of wildlife in the park. As well, it enabled us to associate animal species with different habitats encompassing climactic regions, landforms, soils, and vegetation groups. It was initiated by Parks Canada in 1974 and conducted jointly by the Canadian Forestry Service, Agriculture Canada, the Alberta Institute of Pedology (natural soil science), and the Canadian Wildlife Service. The CWS component of the Biophysical Inventory was a complete inventory of all plant, mammal, bird, reptile, amphibian, and fish species in the park. Previous inventories and studies in the mountain national parks covered only individual or small groups of species in localized environments.

The Biophysical Inventory in Jasper and Banff national parks was completed in two stages. Biologists divided the park into 124 different habitat types called "ecosites." These ecosites were based on vegetation types and specific physical environmental factors, including weather, elevation, degree and facing direction of slope, soil groupings, and drainage characteristics. All ecosites were given a unique designation, and then were charted (diagrammed) on a series of aerial photographs that covered the two parks.

The second stage of the Biophysical Inventory consisted of the wildlife inventory that I worked on. The methodology for the wildlife inventory was based on the premise that the numbers and abundance of each animal species found in each of the 124 ecosites would generally be the same, no matter where the ecosite was located.

The Jasper Biophysical Inventory wildlife team I worked with included Don Karasiuk, Geoff Holroyd, Linda Cole, Duane Sept, Dave McIlveen, and Jim Salt. We were based out of the townsite in 1976 and completed most of our inventory work that year around the northern end of the park. In the summer of 1977 we moved to Tangle Creek Camp, a permanent camp set up for Parks Canada workers near the Columbia Icefields at the south end of the park. On occasion we assisted the Banff Biophysical Inventory team members working in the northern reaches of that park. Half of our work involved day hikes into inventory sites and the other half involved wilderness work in the backcountry. To maximize our time in the backcountry, we contracted Yellowhead Helicopters to transport our team and gear into remote base camps.

We used a wide variety of methods to collect data on the seasonal abundance, distribution, and habitat characteristics of all the species of mammals, birds, amphibians, and reptiles in Jasper. This included scat counts and analysis, track counts, a variety of sight-count surveys, live trapping/release of small mammals, and sound surveys of birds such as breeding bird and nocturnal owl surveys. We also did an in-depth analysis of numerous surveys undertaken by the Warden Service and various biologists in past years.

Determining bird populations in the park was one aspect of the inventory I found fascinating, largely because it was beyond my understanding as to how my gifted colleagues differentiated the various calls of the 305 bird species that make their home in, or migrate through, Jasper National Park.

A total of 168 of the 305 species of birds found in Jasper breed and nest there—of which only about two dozen are permanent residents. The other 137 species migrate through, stopping for various periods to feed and rest. Of the 168 species of nesting birds found in Jasper, 94 are songbirds (such as warblers, sparrows, thrushes, chickadees, flycatchers, and vireos). Although it was largely songbirds that my colleagues inventoried along the breeding bird transects, they also knew the calls of the other bird species. All birds have calls, but most are not as musical as the songbirds.

Breeding bird surveys were completed along 500 metre transects in the early morning hours during the spring breeding season when the birds are most vocal. Don Karasiuk and Geoff Holroyd were masters at identifying not only the species of each bird that was singing along the transect lines, but approximately how many birds of each species were within the defined parameters of the survey. Don and Geoff, along with other dedicated birders across Canada, learn the songs by spending thousands of hours listening to birds. When they hear a bird singing, they search it out and identify it, then remember each song.

Congenital hearing loss in both ears and a partial degree of tone deafness made it very difficult for me to distinguish between musical notes. Learning the English language had been difficult enough for me; differentiating one bird song from another was pretty well an impossible task. What's more, I had contracted a severe inner ear infection when I was a child, which further reduced my hearing in one ear to near deafness.

I, of course, had always been aware that my hearing was compromised. This really hit home the first day I joined Don and Geoff on a breeding bird transect. In a mixed wood conifer forest on a mountain slope above the Maligne Valley, we took out our notepads, stood still, and listened. There was very little wind, no rain, and we were far away from human noise disturbance—an ideal morning to hear the birds. Within three minutes, standing at the first survey location, Don and Geoff heard the songs of eight to ten different species and had also noted the approximate numbers in each group. I heard two, perhaps three, different bird songs and had no idea what species had made them, how many were in the groupings, or even in what general direction they were coming from. I was dumbfounded. By the time we finished all the transect survey points, Don and Geoff had identified more birds than I had in my entire life.

I experienced a huge learning curve during the two summers and one winter that I worked in the park with the Biophysical Inventory team. The information we obtained from our field studies and data collection increased my knowledge not only of birds but also of the distribution, abundance, and seasonal movements of ungulates and carnivores. I gained a much greater understanding of small mammal species; learned to identify almost every plant species in the park; and in the end, was able to identify all but a few bird species in the park—by sight, not song.

What purpose does the knowledge obtained from natural resource inventories and studies serve? Using the Biophysical

Inventory in Jasper and Banff as an example, the data gathered in this comprehensive study of soils, landforms, vegetation, and wildlife provides baseline information to assist park managers, biologists, and wardens in resource management decision-making. The information gathered by the Biophysical Inventory and historic studies is also used for baseline data by researchers and university students undertaking in-depth studies on specific components of the ecosystem. The Biophysical Inventory is more than a list of the living and non-living components of the mountain environment; it allows a glimpse into the structure, function, growth, and distribution of plants and animals in the Rocky Mountains, the ecological relationships between them, and the habitats they live in.

Data obtained from the Biophysical Inventory is valuable to biologists and resource managers beyond the borders of the mountain parks and Canada. For example, researchers evaluating the alarming worldwide decline in migratory songbird populations over the last several decades can compare historic bird data to present-day population counts. From knowledge of the winter range, summer range, and migratory routes of each bird species, researchers can then assess the degree of disturbance the birds encounter in each habitat. Protecting the vast majority of birds that nest in Canada but overwinter in areas as far away as the southern U.S., Mexico, Central America, and South America is a daunting task. Wildlife has no borders, hence the protection of many species requires international cooperation to preserve natural habitat.

With the ever-increasing stresses humans are placing on our natural environment—including the effects of human activities, the misuse, overuse, and in many cases the total destruction of some habitats and the concurrent loss of many species—it is imperative that we understand the ecosystems surrounding us. As the most destructive being on Earth, the onus is on us to acquire a thorough knowledge of our environment and the burden we place on it. We have no choice but to take appropriate measures to mitigate our impact on the planet. We cannot protect and preserve that which we do not understand. It is the knowledge that comes from biological research, studies, and inventories that gives us the tools to manage wisely.

The usefulness of natural studies and inventories goes well beyond the practical purposes of applying the knowledge gained from them to resource management protection and preservation practices. The insights are invaluable for educational and park interpretation purposes. It is especially gratifying to share our knowledge with school children, university students, and park visitors so they can appreciate and understand nature and learn how we can all help to protect and preserve our precious blue planet.

◆ ◆ ◆

As our wildlife-related work for the Biophysical Inventory in Jasper and Banff was winding down in the autumn of 1977, the Jasper Interpretive Service asked Dave McIlveen and me to record the bugle of a bull elk for one of its programs. Every year, from September to October, the park interpreters give presentations on elk at the Whistlers Campground amphitheatre. These presentations are of particular interest to park visitors staying at the campground as elk frequently travel through the general area during the mating (rutting) season.

During the rut, mature bull elk follow groups of cows. The bulls bugle to challenge their rivals and to attract the attention of the cows. The distinctive bugle, beginning with a resonant, high-pitched squeal and ending in a succession of grunts, is an iconic sound in the Canadian wilderness, akin to the howl of the wolf or the call of the loon.

Rival bulls strut around and assess their opponents' antler size, physique, and prowess. When two rivals confront each other and neither backs down, they engage in antler sparring. A serious battle of fairly evenly matched bulls can result in severe injuries to at least one combatant. When taking a break from the heat of battle, bulls paw at the ground, forming a slight depression in which they urinate and then roll. The urine soaks into their hair and gives them a distinct smell to attract cows.

A mature dominant bull in his prime usually defends a herd of cows, proclaiming them as his harem and mating with each in turn. Other large bulls defeated in battle, or smaller bulls too young to do battle, spend most of the rut on the periphery of the harems watching the commanding bull with obvious frustration. This, however, is not always the case, as was made clear by an event I witnessed a few days before Dave and I set out to record a bull elk on tape.

While completing some inventory work near Wabasso Lake, I encountered a mixed sex/age herd of approximately 35 elk. The dominant bull was attempting to herd his harem of about 15 cows away from several other bulls in a small open meadow surrounded by a forest of aspen trees. As I knelt down and quietly watched from the edge of one side of the forest, the dominant bull veered away from his harem and gave chase to a challenging bull. When both bulls disappeared into the cover of the surrounding forest, a young bull on the sidelines streaked into the harem, cut a few cows away from the group, and hightailed into another corner of the forest—taking the cows with him. The remainder of the herd scattered into the forest, leaving me alone looking at an abandoned meadow with the musty smell of bulls in rut hanging in the cool air. Not being able to see what drama was unfolding in the canopy of trees, I imagined that the young bull had his day in the shade, surrounded by brilliant autumn colours.

As to the request by the park interpreters to record a bull elk bugling, Dave and I jumped at the opportunity. I suggested we try a location I knew beside the Athabasca River several kilometres north of the townsite. The mixed pine/spruce forest interspersed with patches of open meadow was a prime elk rutting area. We walked to the site and set up our parabolic microphone and tape recorder under the hanging boughs of a large spruce tree next to a small meadow. We waited for about an hour without hearing or seeing any elk. Then, just as dusk was approaching (a prime period for rutting activity), we heard a single bull elk call out from the forest. He was out of our sight, 200 or more metres away in a moderately dense thicket of trees on the opposite side of the meadow from us. We waited several more minutes as the bull continued to call without a response from challengers. He appeared to be alone. We agreed it was time for us to answer his call.

Using a homemade elk bugle that I had fashioned from some flexible pipe, I took a deep breath and gave my best imitation of a bull elk in full rut sounding the call for a challenger. Dave chuckled at my feeble attempt at proclaiming male domination, but seconds later the bull answered back. I glanced over at Dave, gave him an all-knowing look, puffed up my chest, and continued to exchange calls with the bull. My calls went on for at least a half hour, the bull slowly getting closer to us between each exchange. As darkness descended, he finally broke through the forest cover 30 metres away. We let out a collective gasp—the bull was huge and carried an enormous rack of antlers. His posture displayed a powerful sense of confidence and authority. We wondered why a bull of this size wasn't escorting a large harem and thought perhaps he was slightly past his prime to do battle with smaller but fitter younger bulls.

Dave turned the tape recorder on and pointed the parabolic microphone at the bull. Seconds later the bull gave out a piercing bugle. Then Dave had an idea, and he motioned me to put my bugle down. He backtracked the tape and played the bull's own call back to him. The result was frighteningly dramatic; the bull stiffened his body, glared in our direction, and gave out a bugle that shattered the wilderness. He paused for a few seconds and then made his way straight towards us, head held high, alternately grunting and taking deep throaty gulps of air. I felt the hair rise on the back of my neck as my senses went on high alert.

Dave and I threw the microphone and recorder under the tree and dove for cover. Naturally, we chose the same side of the tree trunk to cower under. Moments later, the bull was upon us, crashing through the low hanging boughs of the spruce tree. Towering above us, he took deep breaths of air while swinging his head back and forth, taking in our scent. In a grand display of frustration and anger he thrashed the boughs directly above our heads to shreds with his antlers. All the while, Dave and I kept stumbling over each other as we crawled around the tree trunk each time the bull circled toward us. Minutes passed and the boughs, which had given us some cover from the direct impact of the bull's antlers, were being thinned out. Our protective roof was disappearing.

Finally, the bull pulled up his head and stood still. All was quiet except for the sound of our pounding hearts and the deep breaths of an angry animal. Steam was rolling up from the bull's back and the pungent smell of sweat, rage, and rut was heavy in the air. Dave and I remained in a frozen position hugging the tree trunk until the bull slowly retreated back across the meadow and into the darkened forest. Letting out a collective deep breath, we grabbed our gear and headed home—we had our bull on tape.

I must caution the reader that calling for bull elk with a bugle during the autumn rut is not only a dangerous activity but also illegal in national parks; non-compliance can result in a heavy fine. The Warden Service granted us a one-time use permit to record the bugle of a bull elk on tape for park interpretive (educational) purposes. Bugling to attract bulls can seriously disrupt the social function of an elk herd and cause undue stress for the bull, not to mention possible serious bodily harm to the human bugler foolhardy enough to attempt to imitate their calls.

CHAPTER FIVE

All Along the Watchtowers

In the early spring of 1978, Assistant Chief Park Warden Bob Haney told me that the Warden Service would be hiring a two-person crew over the summer months to assist in trail work and help wardens with various projects. Julia Paterson (whom I later married) and I were hired. I had met Julia at Maligne Lake during the summer of 1974 when she was working in the cafeteria and I was working as a tour boat operator. Since then, Julia had gained a lot of hiking, backpacking, climbing, and canoeing experience and she was as enthusiastic as I was to work outdoors for the summer.

We assisted whichever wardens required a helping hand with particular projects or everyday work as developments occurred. We became especially involved in wildlife and fisheries management. We also served as a two-person trail crew responsible for clearing and maintaining day-use trails in the frontcountry (high visitor use areas). At times we teamed up with other park trail crews to construct footbridges over creeks and clear trail re-routes around areas washed out by spring flooding.

We were also fortunate to get in two backcountry trips, each a week long, flying into areas and completing trail work that the backcountry trail crews had not worked into their schedules. For me, these flights into the backcountry became the first of many with pilots Gary Foreman and Todd McCready of Yellowhead Helicopters during my Warden Service career in Jasper. Gary and Todd logged many thousands of hours of flying time for Parks Canada over two decades. They ferried park crews and heavy loads of supplies into backcountry locations, flew wildlife surveys over dangerous terrain, worked under demanding conditions during forest fires and prescribed burns, and pulled off incredible rescues with teams of wardens in extreme weather conditions. They were masters of the aircraft they piloted, expertly balancing on the edge of safety and disaster. Our lives were in their capable hands.

Our term positions that summer were to have lasted until the end of August, but extra funding gave us the option of working an extra few months. Julia had college commitments in Edmonton, but I had no specific plans for the autumn and was thrilled when Bob offered to extend my position until the end of October. Bob put together a crew to remove old telephone line along portions of the South Boundary trail.

◆ ◆ ◆

In 1916, the government had begun building single strand telephone lines to connect the Park Headquarters Office in town to a few of the outlying warden stations in the lower Athabasca River Valley. By the late 1930s, the Headquarters Office was connected by a forestry-telephone system to over 30 warden cabins, many of which were deep in the backcountry along the North and South Boundary districts. The line, constructed alongside backcountry trails, was suspended from trees by porcelain insulators at a height of about five metres. In open lower valley meadows and alpine areas devoid of trees, poles were cut, peeled, and skidded by horse to the site.

Once the telephone system was established between the warden cabins, line maintenance became an important routine job for backcountry wardens. High winds could topple enough trees across the telephone line to put a warden to work for several days. The tools and equipment needed to repair phone lines were a necessary part of the gear the district wardens kept in their pack boxes, carried by their pack horses wherever they went. Included in the line repair kit was a pair of climbing spikes made from L-shaped steel shanks that attached from just below the knee to the bottom of the ankle and then around the bottom of each boot. The climbing spikes were secured to each leg with heavy leather straps. A sharp metal spike on the inside edge of each shank was lightly embedded into the trunk of the tree to secure the warden's feet as he climbed. The kit also included a heavy leather climber's belt with loops to accommodate tools, and a large metal ring at each hip from which a second belt could be passed around the tree or pole. The warden leaned back on this belt while completing repairs on the line. This tree and pole climbing equipment is still used by arborists and loggers today.

Beginning in the late 1940s, experiments on various very high frequency (VHF) and single side-band (SSB) radios were conducted. None of these radios worked very well, more often than not failing to transmit over the vast distances and rugged mountain terrain between the backcountry warden cabins and park headquarters. In the late 1960s, a new generation of SSBs was introduced, but it took another decade before most cabins were equipped with these radios. Although they were somewhat more reliable than the prototypes, atmospheric conditions frequently interfered with clear broadcasting signals.

By the late 1970s, wardens were left with a slowly deteriorating forestry-telephone system as a back up to the unreliable SSB radios. A full half century after the first single strand telephone lines had been strung between warden cabins and headquarters, the wardens still could not count on a dependable communication system to contact their colleagues. Then in 1978, with the expectation that technology would soon improve the reliability of SSB radios, we began dismantling the forestry telephones.

The removal of the old forestry telephone line was met with mixed emotions by many of the wardens who had worked in the early and mid-20th century, but it was now time to dismantle the system and replace it with the SSB radios. We understood the significance of the line to the wardens' communication system; it was the only way they could touch base on a daily basis to exchange information on trail conditions, wildlife movements, and the whereabouts of backcountry users. This was especially important in the autumn when wardens exchanged information relating to the movement and activities of hunters along the park boundaries; the objective was to deter poaching within the park. As many hunting camps are located just outside the park boundaries—"the province" side of the boundary as we call it—a large number of the warden cabins in the mountain national parks are situated close to concentrated areas of wildlife and nearby hunting camps to facilitate monitoring of both the hunter and the hunted.

The telephones also provided backcountry wardens with a means to keep tab on what was going on in the frontcountry areas of the park, including park headquarters. Most importantly, the forestry telephone was a lifeline. Over the years, this link between warden cabins and the town saved the lives of backcountry users and park staff alike. The seriousness of numerous occurrences was mitigated due to the ability to immediately report incidences to park headquarters, resulting in a quicker response time.

Our backcountry telephone line removal crew was tasked with dismantling 49 kilometres of line, in stages, between the Medicine Tent and Jacques Lake warden cabins. We used these two cabins, along with the Rocky Forks and Grizzly warden cabins between them, as our home bases. Our crew included Matt and Frank Burstrom, sons of Park Warden Alfie Burstrom. Matt had spent the summer working as a park patrolman. Frank and another member of our crew, John Niddrie, each supervised a park trail crew whose members were from the Saddle Lake Cree Nation Reserve in Alberta. Jim Suttill, who had just finished working on a park rehabilitation crew reclaiming abandoned garbage dumps and construction camps, also joined us. Peter Michaux, a high school buddy of mine from Jasper and a member of another trail crew in the park, rounded out the crew.

Gary Foreman flew us, along with our supplies, into Medicine Tent in early September. The supplies included a large spool mounted on a frame, used to coil the long strands of telephone wire into rolls. Wearing our climbing spikes, we climbed each tree or pole that supported the line and unhooked the line from the insulator. After doing this every 100 metres or so, we cut the line into manageable lengths, then rolled these lengths onto the wheel. We slung the heavy rolls over our shoulders and carried them to one of two drop-off areas, either the nearest warden cabin or cleared locations where the helicopter could pick them up later. The work was extremely tiring and, one might think, tedious. But we were working in remote wilderness surrounded by magnificent mountain scenery. We loved the project, the hard physical labour, and the camaraderie.

One highlight of our trip was the sauna we constructed next to the creek behind the Rocky Forks warden cabin. John and Frank got the idea from the Saddle Lake Cree. The Cree erected sweat lodges at their work camps along the backcountry trails as part of a spiritual ceremony. Their ceremonial sweats were an important cleansing that embodied mind, body, spirit, and heart. Just as important to the Cree members of the trail crew, the sweats were a social occasion, a bonding between themselves and whomever they worked with or welcomed into their ceremony. In part, it became a bridging of cultures.

John had been honoured to be included in the Saddle Lake Cree's sweat lodge ceremony and described it like this: "One of the first things that was erected when we flew into a backcountry area to work was the sweat lodge. River rocks were heated in a wood fire until just about glowing and then placed inside a small canvas tent, and a small amount of sweet grass was placed on the hot rocks. After a short prayer, we breathed in the sweet grass smoke and then poured water over the rocks. The heat and steam were incredible. We also had fun with it, trying to outdo each other to see who could last the longest. We could literally smell burning hair. It was amazing to be part of it."

Our sauna at Rocky Forks (out of respect for the First Nations, we did not call it a sweat lodge) consisted of a tarp spread over a wooden frame. After dinner each evening, we built a hot fire over a bed of rocks next to the sauna. We let it burn until only embers remained, then with a shovel carried the rocks into the middle of the sauna. Next, we brought a bucket of water into the tent, tightly closed the tarp, and ladled the cold liquid onto the superheated rocks. The result was a very hot and purifying steam bath. When we could no longer stand the heat, we spilled out of the tent and plunged into a pool in the cold creek. Over the course of an hour, we repeated our trip from sauna to creek and back several times. After the long days of hard physical labour, followed by the cleansing effect of the hot sauna and cold creek plunges, I slept dead to the world at Rocky Forks.

We reached Grizzly warden cabin by the beginning of October and began removing the last of the 30-kilometre stretch of telephone line between Grizzly and Medicine Tent. Matt joined us on the trail between Grizzly and Rocky Forks warden cabins with his riding horse and two pack horses. The pack horses were a godsend, assisting us in the packing of wire to the drop-off points. Once we had finished removing the final stretch of line up to Grizzly, we started working towards Jacques Lake.

While we worked in the area around Grizzly warden cabin, we were reminded of an event that had happened there 41 years previously. In June of 1937, Park Warden Ed McDonald was returning to Grizzly warden cabin from Rocky Forks warden cabin with his riding horse, two pack horses, and his dog Willie. About one kilometre from the cabin, Ed's riding horse sensed a grizzly just off the trail and responded by violently twisting its body 90 degrees and coming to a direct halt. Ed was ejected straight up from his horse and then, as one of his boots remained in the stirrup, was jerked abruptly downward and onto the ground, landing hard on his shoulders. As his horse spun around in a distraught state, Ed, hanging by one stirrup, felt a powerful blow to his hip; his horse had inadvertently kicked him. As his foot came out of the stirrup and he doubled up with pain, he could hear his three horses galloping up the trail towards the cabin. Not yet aware of the grizzly, he was puzzled as to why his usually calm riding horse had shied so violently.

When Ed was able to compose himself, he tried to stand up but was quickly on his back again; his pelvis was shattered. Lying on his back, he looked up and saw the single strand telephone wire strung between the trees leading to the cabin—his lifeline to help. Ed realized that he'd have to crawl to the cabin. Slowly and painfully, he began crawling on his elbows, his dog Willie by his side. After a few metres he saw the very large and easily discernible grizzly tracks crossing the trail.

Ed continued to crawl, inching his way along the trail and pulling himself along by grasping tree roots or the edges of rocks, or sometimes just using his fingertips. Willie walked in front of Ed, bristling and growling at the bear. Ed, with his face close to the ground, was unable to see anything, but he could hear the crackling of twigs as the grizzly moved alongside them. Then Willie began to bark and back up while holding his tail high. Ed, petrified with fear, pressed his face to the ground and didn't move.

But the bear kept its distance. After a few minutes, Willie calmed down. Ed, still not able to see the bear, continued his crawl. Several hours later, overcome with exhaustion and in excruciating pain, Ed, with Willie by his side, finally reached a small creek not far from the cabin. Ed crawled through the creek. It was here that he thought the grizzly decided to leave them. Shortly afterwards Ed reached a small open meadow—he had arrived at the cabin. The horses were grazing peacefully nearby with their packs still on. They must have wondered why Ed had taken so long to arrive and take the burdens off their backs. They would have to wait a few more days.

Ed had great difficulty getting the door of the cabin open, and once inside was not able to reach the old wooden crank telephone hanging on the wall. Eventually he improvised a way to lift himself up onto a chair and ring Warden Charlie Matheson stationed at Maligne Lake. Fortunately Charlie was near the phone and heard the ring that would save Ed's life.

A rescue party led by Warden Frank Wells took two days to get to Grizzly warden cabin. It took a few more days to transport Ed out to Jasper. He was carried from the cabin to Medicine Lake on a stretcher suspended between two horses, a distance of approximately 30 kilometres. Ed spent over a year in an Edmonton hospital where he was rehabilitated before returning to work in Jasper.

◆ ◆ ◆

I joined my brother as a towerman/patrolman in May 1979. (The dual gender term "person" was not then in use). Gary had been working with the CNR for several years but took a break from the railway during the summers of 1976 to 1979 to work with Parks Canada. Gary was stationed at Signal Fire Lookout and I was stationed at Geraldine Fire Lookout. This turned out to be his last year in Jasper before moving out to the west coast with his wife Sandi.

Parks Canada had begun erecting fire lookouts in the mountain national parks in the 1940s. It was a time when fire management meant fire suppression. All fires, whether caused by humans or by nature, were to be extinguished at all costs. But in the late 1970s, with the increasing awareness of the value of fire to natural processes, the lookouts were slowly being phased out.

Park towermen/patrolmen weren't required to staff the lookout towers 24/7 as the fire lookout staff had in the past. Instead, their duties involved assisting park wardens in patrolling both frontcountry and backcountry areas. The fire lookouts were used as a home base only during periods of extreme fire hazard.

Three fire lookouts were still operational in Jasper during the summer of 1979. Devona Fire Lookout was situated on a ridge above the confluence of the Snake Indian River and the Athabasca River. The tower overlooked a vast panorama of the eastern portion of the Athabasca River Valley in the park. Signal Fire Lookout, perched on a knoll near the top of Signal Mountain, overlooked the town of Jasper and the convergence of three river valleys: the Athabasca, Miette, and Maligne. Built in 1941, it was the first operational fire lookout in the mountain national parks. Geraldine Fire Lookout was situated on a bench below Whirlpool Peak, with views up the Whirlpool Valley towards Athabasca Pass, down the Athabasca River Valley toward Jasper townsite, and up the Athabasca River Valley towards the Columbia Icefields.

Two other lookouts, Bald Hills Fire Lookout at Maligne Lake and Palisades Fire Lookout on the shoulder of Pyramid Mountain, had been decommissioned several years earlier. By the early 1980s, all the fire lookouts in Jasper had been decommissioned. The dirt roads to these lookouts are now used as hiking and biking trails.

Besides assisting the wardens with their various duties as I had the previous year, I spent much of my time patrolling picnic sites, highway viewpoints, lakes, and trails in and around the Geraldine Lakes and Athabasca Falls area. I always welcomed the opportunity to assist and talk to park visitors in the busy high use areas—public relations was an important part of the job.

I also jumped at every chance I got to patrol the backcountry in my area: the wild and remote upper Whirlpool Valley to its headwaters at Athabasca Pass and the heavily used Fryatt Valley to the south. My duties included checking on and assisting backpackers, monitoring bear and other wildlife activity, and performing minor trail work. Another purpose of patrolling these areas was to gain a thorough knowledge of the terrain, wildlife, and natural hazards in the assigned district. This knowledge was invaluable when responding to emergencies such as wildfire, wildlife incidents, lost or injured hikers, trail washouts due to heavy rainstorms, or any other type of incident that cropped up when park visitors, unfamiliar with the terrain or the recreational pursuits they set out to enjoy, found themselves in difficulty. From a preventive standpoint, a broad understanding of the district that towermen/patrolmen were responsible for patrolling allowed them to provide accurate information to park visitors *before* they embarked on their journeys.

As the busy summer tourist season winds down in Jasper at the end of August, park wardens begin to gear up for another season—the autumn hunt along the boundaries of the park. Hunting is not allowed in national parks in Canada, but it is in most of the newer national park reserves, where traditional hunting rights have been granted through agreements with First Nations groups.

Hunting is a traditional autumn activity for thousands of outdoor recreationalists in Alberta. One of the prime hunting areas is along the eastern slopes of the Rocky Mountains that meet the boundaries of Jasper, Banff, and Waterton Lakes national parks. Many hunters set up base tent camps on the province side of the national park boundaries. They access the camps by horse, on foot, or in a few cases, by all-terrain vehicles (ATV's). Many of these camps are within an easy day ride or walk to the park boundaries, and some are only minutes away. Hunters can access much of the eastern slopes adjacent to the Jasper National Park boundary from Willmore Wilderness Park (a provincially managed park where hunting is allowed) to the north of Jasper, and south to the headwaters of the Brazeau River along the shared boundary with the White Goat Wilderness and Banff National

Park. This boundary extends over 300 kilometres. Hunting season usually opens in the last week of August and closes the last week of November. Most autumn hunters seek deer, moose, elk, mountain goat, and bighorn sheep. Other fur bearing and carnivore species are hunted at various times throughout the year.

In the second week of September 1979, my supervisor, Park Warden Gord Anderson, made arrangements for me to fly into Wolf Pass to spend 10 days on boundary patrol. Park Warden Brian Wallace, in charge of backcountry operations, had horse-packed a tent camp from Willow Creek up the valley to Wolf Pass a few days before.

Park patrolmen performed the same job as a warden in the backcountry with the exception of law enforcement. Because they didn't have law enforcement training, patrolmen could not arrest or charge a person for an infraction committed under the National Parks Act. Patrolmen were still responsible, however, to observe, record, and report national park offences in order to pass the information to the nearest warden. The public relations duties that both patrolmen and park wardens were responsible for, and that related to law enforcement, were collectively called "preventive patrol"—a proactive approach to prevent the violation of park regulations (such as poaching) by meeting with and talking to hunters, or by merely having a presence in the area. This was a vital part of boundary patrol during the autumn hunting season.

Wolf Pass is nestled between a series of five mountain ridges of the Bosche Range, which separates the lower reaches of the Snake Indian Valley to the west from the Moosehorn Valley to the east. The park boundary winds back and forth between four of these ridges, which are separated by three passes: the subalpine elevation Wolf and Grindstone passes, and the treeless alpine Laura Pass. Picturesque alpine basins sloping up to a combination of gently rolling and rugged rock ridges make for prime bighorn sheep and mountain goat habitat. The Notch, a deep rock canyon, cuts between the two easternmost ridges and opens up into the headwaters of the Moosehorn Valley. Hunters access the Moosehorn Valley from various points along the eastern front ranges of the Rocky Mountains. Most of the larger hunting base camps are situated around Moosehorn and Busby lakes, three kilometres east of The Notch. Trails lead up from these camps to smaller camps situated within one or two kilometres of the park boundary in the Wolf Pass area.

I tracked the movements of bighorn sheep and mountain goats during my 10-day stay in the tent camp. Within a few days of being flown into the camp, I hiked through The Notch and met a few groups of hunters around the horse camps in the Moosehorn Lake area, letting them know I was around. Each day, I spent a good part of my time hiking up to the various ridges above the passes, keeping an eye on the area. Most of the hunters I met were familiar with the area and heedful of where the boundaries lay.

On the second last day of my stay at Wolf Pass camp, I hiked up high onto a rolling alpine ridge between Wolf and Grindstone passes where there was a commanding view of the boundary in all directions as it zigzagged from one ridge to the next. As I approached the highest point of the boundary, I spotted three hunters sitting smack on the boundary between the park and the province. They were very surprised to see me, and as I talked to them it was clear that they had intended to cross the park boundary with their rifles. It was their first time hunting in the mountains and they had spent the morning hiking up to the ridge from their base camp at Moosehorn Lake. Despite the fact that they were sitting right under the posted boundary marker, they claimed they had no idea where they were. We ate lunch together and I pointed out the boundary delineations on their map. We sat chatting for an hour or so before they headed back toward their camp.

Later, as I was walking back along the ridge, I watched a herd of about 20 goats traverse a series of rock ledges 40 metres below the summit of an unnamed mountain across from Grindstone Pass.

Suddenly, a flash of brown veered from the deep blue sky above the summit and took aim at a group of five goats: a golden eagle dropped one wing and banked slightly as it barrelled down on a kid goat. With outstretched talons, it caught some hair and muscle on the back of the goat, knocking it back towards the cliff face. The kid stumbled on the steep rock but kept its footing. I saw several small rocks hurtling down the face of the mountain, dislodged by the rest of the group as they scrambled off exposed ledges and tucked themselves up against the side of the rock face. Most of the kids instinctively pressed against their mothers' flanks. The eagle turned and slowly flew past the watching herd before it gained height and dropped out of sight over the other side of the summit.

Soon afterwards, the goats resumed their traverse, but in a more deliberate and wary manner. A few minutes later, the eagle appeared over the summit and attacked again. The nanny goats, now vigilant, kept their kids close and once more held tight against the rock. The element of surprise was gone. The eagle was unable to pass close enough over another kid to knock it off balance before it had to twist its two-metre wingspan away from the mountain face. This scenario repeated itself several times over the next half hour, and each time the eagle was unsuccessful in its bid to either knock or haul a young kid off the steep rocky terrain. I had heard and read of eagles knocking goats and sheep off steep slopes and then feeding on the carcass after their plunge to death. In other instances, eagles have been observed sinking their talons into a small kid or lamb, carrying it a few metres into the air and then dropping it, sending it hurtling down a cliff face to its death on the rocks below.

Back at my tent camp that evening, I discussed the day's events with Warden Wes Bradford on the SSB radio. Wes was at Brazeau warden cabin, 85 kilometres away on the southern end of the park. He had experienced some interesting wildlife sightings that day and he related his story in detail.

Wes had been monitoring several groups of hunters camped in the province along the eastern side of the Brazeau River not far from the warden cabin. He was particularly concerned about two hunters from Red Deer who were looking for sheep and elk. When the hunters had questioned Wes earlier in the day as to where the park boundary was, their attitude suggested that they wouldn't hesitate to poach if they could get away with it. Most of the elk were in the park on the west side of the Brazeau River (which delineates the park boundary at this particular location). They were in full rut, the bulls making their whereabouts known with their frequent bugling.

Tom McCready and Floyd Coleman, working with the Warden Service as a cabin maintenance crew, were staying with Wes at Brazeau while completing some repairs on the cabin. After dinner, Wes mentioned that he wanted to check on a few groups of hunters, in particular the two hunters from Red Deer. Tom asked to join Wes and they set out for the nearby slopes of Chocolate Mountain, to a knoll that offers an excellent view of the terrain above and the valley below along the Brazeau River.

Wes and Tom had just sat down upon reaching the knoll when Tom spotted a sow grizzly with two big sub-adult (two-year old) cubs feeding on alpine vegetation across the Brazeau River on the slopes of Longview Mountain. Looking through their binoculars, they spotted nine bighorn sheep rams resting on the slopes above them and 11 mountain goats crossing a high alpine basin to the east. As they adjusted their gaze downwards, two mule deer bucks wandered out of the timber below their lookout, feeding as they ascended the slope in their direction. Moments later, numerous bull elk started to bugle from the river valley below, each challenging rival bulls for dominance in the herd. Shortly afterwards, a large dominant bull elk with a harem of cows and their calves appeared in a meadow directly below. Ten minutes later, a smaller bull appeared from the forest and strode into the meadow. The larger bull, accepting the challenge from the other bull, chased him around the meadow for half an hour to keep him away from the cows. Finally, while the harem looked on in quiet contemplation, the dominant bull retained his position by chasing the eager young bull away.

As Wes and Tom watched the spectacle of wildlife from their vantage point, Tom noticed that the elk were becoming alert and agitated. Wes thought that perhaps the two hunters he had been keeping tabs on had crossed the Brazeau River to try and take an elk inside the park. Indeed, as they sat talking about it, the hunters appeared. But not the two-legged variety. Seven wolves from the Aztec pack gave the elk herd a challenge—of life or death. The wolves appeared from the edge of the forest at a fast trot and broke into full chase as the elk herd began to scatter. The wolves pursued the elk across the meadow and into the trees as they fled downriver, eventually out of sight from Wes and Tom. Wes was familiar with these wolves; he had located their den site on the lower slopes of Mount Aztec earlier in the year and had been watching them all summer. The human hunters never appeared that evening.

As they started descending from the knoll on Chocolate Mountain, the sun began to set and spread an autumn orange glow over the valley. Tom had many years of horse outfitting and trail guiding in the wilderness behind him and he knew the significance of their observations that evening. He turned to Wes and commented that as a young fella, he'd have to put on a lot of distance and be damn lucky to have another evening like the one they had just witnessed. A grizzly family, bighorn sheep, mountain goats, mule deer, bull elk bugling, an elk harem, two sparring bull elk, a pack of wolves, and a brilliant sunset—all on display from one lookout.

CHAPTER SIX

End of an Era – From Bush Lore to Biology

When my seasonal park patrolman position finished in the autumn of 1979, I expressed interest in managing a backcountry district for the upcoming year with Assistant Chief Park Warden Bob Haney. Bob discussed my request with Chief Park Warden Don Dumpleton, and by the spring of 1980, Bob gave me the fantastic news that I'd be assigned to Blue Creek District for that season. I was ecstatic; I would be responsible for overseeing 950 square kilometres of wilderness in the heart of the North Boundary of Jasper National Park.

◆ ◆ ◆

Most of the park wardens I knew while growing up in Jasper had been hired in the 1940s and '50s. They were largely a mix of mountain guides, trappers, bushmen, ranchers, or outdoorsman coming from backgrounds that required skills to survive and work in nature. Some of them were World War II veterans, and many of the wardens before them had been veterans of World War I. Until 1969, the wardens were assigned to one of 14 districts in Jasper National Park.

Eight of these districts had a mixed component of frontcountry (along the various roadways in the park) and backcountry. Wardens working out of these districts lived in government accommodation spaced along the park roadways. One district, the Townsite (also referred to as Jasper) District, consisted of frontcountry in the high visitor use area close to and including Jasper townsite. Most of the Townsite District wardens lived in town and worked out of its main office.

Five of the districts were strictly backcountry, each between 540 and 1170 square kilometres of wilderness that one had to patrol and be responsible for. During the very early years of park establishment, park wardens stayed in tents, tepees, or rudimentary log shelters, most of which did little to keep out the wind, rain, cold weather, or wandering animals. By the 1930s each district had a solidly built district headquarter cabin with more rudimentary shelters as patrol cabins. The patrol cabins extended out into adjacent watersheds and valleys from the headquarter cabins.

Although backcountry wardens spent much of their time patrolling on foot, travel between their district cabins was mostly done on horseback during the late spring, summer, and autumn months. These wardens lived full time in their districts, making only occasional trips into town each year. Travel in winter required snowshoes or backcountry touring skis.

All the park wardens started out as generalists in their respective districts. They were responsible for enforcing national park regulations, providing information to park visitors, monitoring wildlife, dealing with wildlife/human conflicts, working with other agencies on various research studies and inventories, fighting forest fires, and responding to public safety incidents. Public safety responsibilities included monitoring safety hazards, advising park visitors of safety risks and precautions, assisting park visitors with injuries, responding to highway accidents, searching for lost or overdue hikers and missing children, and responding to recreational accidents. The latter included mountain climbing accidents, avalanche search and rescue, water related search and rescue, and general response to any accident or incident involving outdoor pursuits such as hiking and skiing. The job responsibilities of backcountry wardens involved much the same as those in the frontcountry, with the exception of highway accidents. In addition, they maintained trails, backcountry campsites, and cabins.

Although they were generalists, all wardens were mostly proficient in one or two aspects of the job. When they worked alone (and they usually did) they managed the various tasks or situations as they occurred. From basic field training and by working together, all the wardens were aware of each other's different areas and levels of expertise. In an emergency such as a forest fire or a rescue that required teamwork and multiple tasks, the wardens worked together to get the job done.

In January 1910, very little training was available to Lewis J. Swift when he became the first game guardian in Jasper National Park. In April 1923, Dominion Park Inspector Howard Sibbald organized a convention of supervising wardens (early chief park wardens) to exchange knowledge and experiences. This set the stage for annual training courses in the Rocky Mountain national parks, where the main focus was fire prevention and suppression. Over the years, the training sessions began to include enforcement procedures, firearms training, first aid training, the use and care of horses, and basic public safety training.

As road access into the mountain parks improved and visitation increased, accidents became more frequent. Wardens began public safety training in earnest during the early 1950s. Very few of the wardens had any form of mountaineering training or skills; in fact, many had never skied or climbed a mountain. Parks officials recognized the wardens' shortcomings regarding their ability to perform mountain rescues. With this in mind, Walter Perren, a Swiss mountain guide, was hired to implement a public safety program.

By the 1960s, wardens were well trained in public safety standards. They kept current with procedures and equipment, in some cases making advances in search and rescue techniques, which by the latter part of the decade would place Parks Canada as a leading rescue organization in North America. The wardens also kept up with the traditional aspects of their training, such as horse care, backcountry travel, firearms use, firefighting, and law enforcement.

Many park managers, however, began to question whether Parks Canada was keeping pace with what they believed was the pre-eminent role of the National Park Warden Service—resource management. Parks Canada continued to emphasize "protecting people from the park" (public safety) and providing visitors with the means to enjoy the parks, but was it keeping pace with advancements in environmental protection to "protect the park from people"? The effective protection and management of national parks requires a comprehensive understanding of park resources, the ecological processes controlling and influencing them, and the human impact on these resources. The accelerated development of the environmental movement throughout the late 1960s and into the early 70s generated a profound awareness and understanding of the environment. Resulting advances in the fields of biological and ecological sciences gave impetus to a significant shift in the way Parks Canada applied resource management practices in the national parks.

The era of predator control programs, ungulate culls, bear management (before garbage control), fisheries policies geared towards anglers, and forest fire suppression applied without full understanding of their impact on the environment was coming to an end. But it was through the application of these programs that park managers and wardens had, over the years, gathered the knowledge required to lead the way to a new age of environmental protection and conservation. The wardens hired in the 1940s and '50s began their careers with a mix of bush lore and the ability to pack one horse and ride the other; many did not have the opportunity to finish high school and only a few had any post-secondary education. But with continual on-the-job training and field experience, they developed skills that enabled them to improve the management of park resources and to stay current with the rapidly developing field techniques that came about with advances in science and environmental management.

Wardens in the mountain parks had to adapt to further significant change in the late 1960s: the move away from the District System to one of centralization. This period first involved the move to an Area System in which the former districts were basically combined into about half as many management areas. The growth in tourism had resulted in a large increase in frontcountry issues and events. Park managers in Jasper National Park wanted a larger contingent of wardens available in or near the townsite so they could respond effectively to matters of law enforcement, public safety, and resource management. District wardens stationed throughout the lower valley corridors remained in government housing but often had to report to town at the beginning of each workday.

Wardens who had previously worked in backcountry districts year round faced the most significant change; their backcountry postings were reduced to six months, from the first of May to the end of October. They spent the remainder of the year working out of town or from warden stations located along the highway corridors, with only occasional winter trips into the backcountry.

In 1975, a further move towards centralization was established with what became known as the "Function System." An assistant chief park warden headed each of the four newly established functions—law enforcement, resource management, public safety, and administration. All park wardens and warden support staff in Jasper switched over to working within one of these four functions. When I started with the Warden Service trail crews in 1978, I worked under Abe Loewen. Abe was the assistant chief of the Administration Function. As the name implies, Abe took on much of the administration and finance duties. He also supervised the trail crews and assisted the other three assistant chiefs with their function operations. Duane Martin headed the Law Enforcement Function. I worked under Duane in 1979 as a patrolman before joining up with Bob Haney in the Resource Management Function in 1980. Toni Klettl headed the Public Safety Function. The Administration Function eventually went by the wayside as it was incorporated into the other three functions. We also had an excellent group of administrative clerks who were always there to make our work easier.

The transition from the old District System to the Area System and finally to the Function System was a time of enormous change within the Warden Service. Park wardens had to switch from long careers as generalists to concentrate on one specific aspect of the job, and some of the older wardens found it very difficult to adapt to the Function System. They had worked mostly alone in their respective districts, and even when sharing with other wardens, they often worked different shifts. A sense of pride and individualism came with doing things their own way. They developed strong personalities. Now they were being asked to spend less time in their former districts. Taking on a specialty meant working more often as a member of a team and going to whichever location demanded attention. Morning meetings in town became common, yet many wardens still lived in outlying districts, and this took them away from many of their district responsibilities. The transition was slow.

A few of the older wardens adapted very well and found their niche within one of the functions created in 1975. Alfie Burstrom was a good example of this. Alfie had excelled in all aspects of the job and was particularly adept at understanding and handling animals. In 1970, Alfie, still a district warden, got a jump-start on the approaching Function System with the help of an individual soon to become an iconic member of the Warden Service in Canada. His name was Ginger; his father was a big German shepherd and his mother was half coyote.

Ginger started his life as the runt of a litter of 11 pups belonging to Warden Gord McClain. Gord gave his last remaining pup (Ginger) to Alfie, thinking he would make a good family dog. It so happened that the Warden Service at this time was beginning to recognize the need for a search and rescue dog. Alfie saw potential in Ginger.

The RCMP had been using dogs to assist them in their investigations since the early 1900s. They were occasionally called out on mountain search and rescues but did not have the same training and skills in mountaineering as park wardens. Sending an RCMP officer onto an avalanche prone snow slope to search for buried victims, without proper safety equipment or awareness of the risks, was very dangerous.

So park managers took steps to establish a dog-training component within Parks Canada's public safety program. Willi Pfisterer and Peter Fuhrmann, both hired by Parks Canada in 1968 to oversee the public safety training programs in the mountain parks, worked with the RCMP to incorporate a Swiss avalanche dog training standard into the RCMP manual. Alfie and Ginger were subsequently sent to the RCMP training facilities in Innisfail, Alberta.

Ginger initially had to be assessed as to whether he would qualify for the training program. In their book *Guardians of the*

Peaks: Mountain Rescue in the Canadian Rockies and Columbia Mountains, retired Park Wardens Kathy Calvert and Dale Portman note that, "Before (Ginger) even got started, he had three strikes against him: first, he was relatively small for a police working dog; second, only one out of 80 dogs made the cut; and third, Ginger's heritage was in question. His pedigree simply wasn't in keeping with the RCMP's penchant for training purebred German shepherds. Coyotes were not considered."

However, Ginger made the cut, went through a four-month training session with Alfie, and graduated. Alfie became the first professional avalanche dog handler in North America, and Ginger soon demonstrated he was much more than an avalanche rescue dog. Alfie worked with Ginger in locating lost children, searching for missing backcountry enthusiasts, helping with cases of poaching, and assisting the RCMP in tracking persons engaged in criminal behaviour. Although Ginger's work started out in public safety, he extended his discipline by using his sensitive nose for law enforcement purposes. In effect, although primarily a search and rescue dog, Ginger aided Alfie in bridging the gap between what was soon to become two separate functions in the Warden Service in the mid-1970s: public safety and law enforcement. Alfie and Ginger set the standard for future Parks Canada dog handlers and their canine partners in search and rescue. In return for the duo being accepted into the RCMP training program, Parks Canada assisted RCMP dog handlers in expanding their search and rescue capabilities.

Norm Woody, in the final years of his career, also slipped into a specialist role, becoming one of the wildlife management wardens within the Resource Management Function. Norm was instrumental in perfecting the use of wildlife immobilizing drugs and equipment and led Jasper's bear management program for many years.

Alfie, Norm, and Toni Klettl, along with many of the other wardens nearing retirement, were given an additional responsibility as they adjusted to the newly created Function System—that of training my generation of wardens. We graduated from programs in the various science disciplines that would serve us well in the changing role of the Warden Service. But we needed our older peers to mentor us and to pass on the skills, knowledge, and wisdom that were just as, if not more, valuable than academic training.

It was never clear whether the Function System ever intended to take wardens away from being generalists. The idea was to have wardens concentrate their duties primarily on one function at a time: law enforcement, public safety, or resource management. We all loved the generalist aspect of the job—even as we were leaning towards specialization in one function. And frankly, that was the way we wanted it. The workings of the Function System, in fact, did not apply to wardens who remained in backcountry postings. As they worked mostly alone in remote areas, and therefore were required to work as generalists, the District System still applied to backcountry areas for another two decades. It would take another 25 years before transition within the organization resulted in the establishment of strictly formalized specialist positions.

CHAPTER SEVEN

Horse Sense and the Diamond Hitch

Park Wardens Lawrence Baraniuk, Doug Eastcott, and Rick Ralf were scheduled to join me on the North Boundary of the park in 1980. Lawrence, my immediate supervisor, was assigned as the North Boundary Coordinator. Doug was assigned to Smoky River District on the western end of the North Boundary. His district started at the boundary with Mount Robson Provincial Park in British Columbia and covered all the territory up to Snake Indian Pass to the east. Blue Creek, my assigned district, spanned from the west side of Snake Indian Pass to Deer Creek. Rick rounded out our North Boundary crew. His district, Willow Creek, bordered Deer Creek to the west and the boundary of Jasper with Rock Lake Provincial Park to the east. Willmore Wilderness Park bordered the northern boundary of all three districts.

Park Warden Darro Stinson was the South Boundary Coordinator. Park Warden Rod Wallace was assigned the Brazeau District, which takes up much of the southeast area of the park north to Cairn Pass. Jean Stoner was only the second woman appointed to a park warden position in Jasper. She was assigned to the Rocky River District, which ran from the north side of Cairn Pass to Beaver Lake warden cabin near Medicine Lake. Bette Beswick, the first female warden in Jasper, was hired two years earlier in 1976.

John Niddrie, one of my partners on the telephone line removal crew on the South Boundary in 1978, rounded out the list of backcountry personnel for 1980. John, who like me, was a patrolman working his way up to become a park warden, was assigned the Tonquin Valley area. Although smaller in size than the vast boundary districts, Tonquin was very busy. The valley was always popular with backpackers, climbers, fishing groups, and horse outfitting parties.

Our first order of business was to join Senior Horseman Denny Welsh at the Maligne Horse Range to participate in a weeklong horse training session and have our horses assigned to us. This government horse range is located near the Maligne River, one kilometre upstream from its confluence with the Athabasca River. Denny was responsible for the general management of the horse range which included the handling, care, and feeding of 65 head of horses.

During our training session, Denny explained what was expected in the general care and handling of horses from a Warden Service perspective. Denny's instruction was based on tradition and knowledge passed on by early wardens from the beginning of the national parks system in 1885. These early wardens relied on their horses as much as we rely on the automobile today. Their horses were part of their family, or in the case of many wardens in the earlier years of park establishment, the *only* members of their family. We were expected to uphold all the horse handling skills and traditions of our predecessors.

An important part of horse care includes how to treat cuts, strains, bruising, and common ailments that might occur in the backcountry. We were also taught the famed "diamond hitch," a centuries-old lashing technique used to secure loads to a pack horse. There is evidence that the hitch, or at least early variations of it, was used as far back as remote antiquity in Asia and Africa on a variety of pack animals including horses, mules, and camels.

When packing a horse, the first step is to secure the pack box with a rope to the bars or hooks on each side of the pack saddle. A duffle bag filled with light gear, such as clothes and bedding, is then placed on top of the boxes. Next, a canvas tarp is spread over the boxes and duffle bag. A long cinch rope is used to tie the diamond hitch. The end of the rope that is attached to the cinch is thrown up and over the pack boxes and then under the horse's belly. This cinch is tightened up against the front saddle cinch. The free end of the rope is then brought up over the boxes and tarp and tied with a series of loops, knots, twists, weaves, and hitches that would baffle any onlooker. If done correctly, a final pull on the rope creates a symmetrical diamond shaped knot on the top and center of the tarp. The diamond knot is then tied off and the remaining end of the rope tied in a series of loops or chains. A diamond hitch is harder to learn than to explain, and believe me, it is something that one must practice in order to fully comprehend it. Once we mastered the hitch, we recognized that it is actually simple in design and ingenious in how it keeps a packed load in position on the back of a horse.

The next phase of our training was learning how to cold shoe a horse. Cold shoeing requires the shaping and fitting of a horse's metal shoe without the use of a forge. As a practicing farrier, Denny was responsible for shoeing all the horses, a time-consuming and strenuous job that he often did alone. Backcountry horses were shod every six weeks or so depending on the extent of rough mountain terrain they had travelled.

We learned the basics of shoeing so we could replace shoes in the backcountry if necessary. We checked the horse's hooves each day, as it was not uncommon for a horse to loosen and throw a shoe. If we noticed a loose shoe before it detached from a horse's hoof, it was a relatively easy process to tighten it. If the horse, however, threw a shoe and we were unable to find it, it was a laborious process to fit a new shoe in the backcountry without the proper tools. Fortunately, a shoeing kit, spare shoes, and the all-important anvil to use for shaping shoes were kept at most district headquarter cabins.

Throughout our training session, Denny kept a discerning eye on our progress, evaluating what combination of three horses he'd assign to each of us. Denny had the uncanny ability to match the disposition of each horse to the experience and handling skills of the person that would be responsible for its care.

At least one horse assigned to each district had to have spent considerable time beforehand in that district. Those horses would lead the others to the best grazing locations and help guide the warden throughout the district, whether a trail was well defined or a rough undefined route with no marked path. (Horses have an incredible memory for recalling each twist and turn of every trail or route they have travelled).

At the end of the training session, Denny assigned me three horses, all geldings: Hep and Help, both dark bay Thoroughbreds, and Ernie, a big sorrel Belgian-Thoroughbred cross. Denny told me that all three horses could be ridden or packed. With one look at Ernie, weighing in at 700 kilograms of rippling muscle power, I knew he'd be a great pack horse. As it turned out, I always packed Ernie, as my riding saddle didn't fit properly over his broad, hulking frame. Throughout the season, I alternated packing Hep and Help as my second pack horse, using the other as my riding horse. It didn't take me long to realize that the four of us were a great match.

CHAPTER EIGHT

Snake Indian Territory – River of No Return

In the third week of May, a week after our training sessions with Denny, Lawrence and I packed up our horse gear at the Maligne Horse Range and drove north out of town and onto Celestine Lake Road. We headed towards Seldom Inn warden cabin at the road's terminus for the start of our first 17-day patrol on the North Boundary of the 1980 season. Denny had driven my horses, Hep and Help, and Lawrence's horses, Izzy and Hawk, to Seldom Inn in the park stock truck the day before. Denny had arranged for me to pick up Ernie in another three weeks.

As Lawrence and I drove along the 27-kilometre, one-lane, dirt access road on the west side of Jasper Lake from Snaring Warden Station to Celestine Lake, I pondered the history of the lower Athabasca River Valley in the park. Recent findings by scientists estimate that glaciers from the last ice age retreated back from the lower Athabasca River Valley in Jasper around 12,000 years ago.

A mixture of low-lying shrubs and grasses were likely the pioneering species following the retreat of ice. These species would have been followed within a few thousand years by much the same montane habitat we see today in the lower Athabasca River Valley of the park: white spruce forests mixed with open grassland meadows dotted with occasional stands of pine trees. These areas became prime habitat for deer and elk after the glacial retreat from the valley. Bison, no longer found in the park, also roamed the open habitat for thousands of years. The willow, sedge, and deciduous trees that dominated wetland areas along the floodplains of creeks and rivers offered suitable habitat for moose, beaver, fish, and a myriad of bird and small mammal species. Bighorn sheep and mountain goat became well dispersed across the rocky ledges and mountain slopes above the valley. As high elevation areas in the subalpine and alpine zones far above the valley corridor became ice free, woodland caribou and many other wildlife species became established.

The abundant game species brought bears, wolves, and other predators into the valley along with other hunters in the middle prehistoric era—humans. The oldest known archaeological site in Jasper dates back 9,000 years. This site is located in the hilly terrain close to where Devona warden cabin (removed in the late 1970s) once stood on the banks of the Snake Indian River. The historic Jasper House site is located one kilometre east of Devona, not far from the confluence of the Snake Indian River and the Athabasca River at the north end of Jasper Lake.

Lawrence and I parked on the roadside and walked over to a hill overlooking the valley where much of the early cultural history of Jasper began. From our hillside viewpoint, we had a panoramic view of the lower Athabasca River Valley in Jasper, an important eastern corridor where early Aboriginal people from the foothills and plains beyond entered into what is now Jasper National Park.

◆ ◆ ◆

The traditional life of the Aboriginal people was rapidly coming to an end by the late 18th century. The profit made in trading furs to the North West Company (NWC) and the Hudson's Bay Company (HBC) resulted in subsistence living becoming a way of the past. Many Aboriginals, forced into a meagre living (or actually facing starvation) due to the depletion of game species from the advancement of Europeans moving westward, traded furs for goods.

As the fur trade reached the eastern corridor through Jasper, the seasonal movements and territories of Aboriginal cultures had already begun to change. Cree and Assiniboine (Nakoda in their own language, or Stoney, a name given by early Europeans), armed with guns obtained from HBC merchants, pushed west into lands they did not traditionally occupy in search of furs. As these bands approached the Alberta foothills, they pushed the Sarcee to the south. The Sarcee were subsequently pushed further south when the Assiniboine moved into the area around Jasper to trade at Jasper House, established in 1813. By 1817, the post was under the charge of chief factor Jasper Hawes, whose name became synonymous with the post, the national park, and later, the townsite.

The Athabasca River Valley proved to be rich in fur and game resources such as black and grizzly bear, wolf, fox, lynx, beaver, muskrat, wolverine, marten, mink, otter, deer, elk, moose, and bison. Substantial profits from furs enticed other Aboriginals from further reaches of eastern Canada, especially those of Iroquois heritage, to move west. They worked as employees for the trading companies, becoming guides, interpreters, hunters, and trappers. By 1830, when the original Jasper House was moved from Brule Lake just outside the park's east boundary to near the mouth of the Snake Indian River, a unique group of English, French, Métis, Iroquois, Cree, Assiniboine, Shuswap, and Snake (for which the river was named) occupied the area.

The Snake (sometimes referred to as the Snare) were one of the first Aboriginal people to make Jasper home. They came from the west over today's Yellowhead Pass at the western entrance to Jasper National Park. The Snakes were believed to be a branch of the Shuswap from the southern interior of British Columbia. Some accounts, however, suggest they were a branch of the Porteurs from the central interior region of British Columbia.

Several early European visitors to Jasper made reference to the Snake Indians in the accounts of their travels. These included the missionary Father Pierre-Jean De Smet and early explorers Dr. James Hector and Alexander Henry. Henry Moberly, the factor at Jasper House from 1858 to 1861, also wrote about the Snake Indians. They had lived in the area around Jasper House long before the days of the fur trade, perhaps thousands of years before Europeans set foot in Canada. Records indicate that they didn't trade with the HBC to the extent other Aboriginal groups did. They were a peaceful band that avoided conflict and, by some accounts, did not possess the firearms that other Aboriginal groups had acquired through the fur trade.

Disputed areas not controlled by any one Aboriginal group, such as the eastern corridor of Jasper, could be extremely volatile. The early inhabitants of North America occasionally warred, often over scarce food resources and other pressures brought on by contact with one another. The Assiniboines had long been a rival of the Snakes, and numerous minor skirmishes between the two groups had reduced the Snakes to a remnant of their former selves. By 1840, only a small band of approximately 50 Snake Indians remained in the area, camped on the side of a mountain just west of Jasper House along the river that bears their name. This camp was situated in the area below the hill where Lawrence and I now stood.

The Snakes felt safe near Jasper House because the HBC had a reputation for treating the Aboriginals well and for keeping peace amongst the various groups and the Europeans. The Snakes' trustfulness, however, was their undoing. The Assiniboines, camped beside Brule Lake 15 kilometres to the northeast, proposed a meeting with the Snakes to ratify a peace. Both parties were to be unarmed. The Snakes agreed, and the men of the band, leaving their weapons behind, arrived and joined the Assiniboines around the council fire. At a prearranged signal, the Assiniboines drew their concealed rifles and in cold blood shot the members of the Snake band. They then rushed to the Snake camp and massacred the rest of the band with the exception of three young women whom they took captive.

Once back at their own camp they realized that the HBC might become angry at this breach of peace and boycott trade with them. They set out for Fort Assiniboine, over 300 kilometres down the Athabasca River to the northeast. At Fort Assiniboine, a Métis by the name of Bellerose learned that three young Snake women were lying naked and bound in one of the tepees. Whatever may have been the Assiniboines' intentions, Bellerose feared the women would be killed the next day. It is very doubtful the Assiniboines would have gone that far, as it was their practice to adopt captives, treat them kindly, and have them intermarry into their band. Regardless, Bellerose entered the tepee of the young women during the night, cut their bonds, and turned them loose. He gave them a knife and his fire-bag containing a flint, a steel striking plate, and some kindling.

Accounts of the event recorded by Henry Moberly and Alberta historian James McGregor (as passed on to him by Provincial Park Ranger James Shand Harvey) are similar and tell a remarkable story of survival and the adaptability of one of these women. The three women headed back up the Athabasca River to the mouth of the Berland River. Two of the women, taking the fire-bag with them, decided to follow the Athabasca River and were never seen again; presumably they perished. The third woman, named Secak, took the knife and headed up the Berland River. She settled in the Berland Lake area north of Pinto Creek and prepared for winter.

Secak gathered berries and managed to kill a few porcupines, woodchucks, and squirrels. She kindled fire in the primitive way (by spinning the point of one dry stick rapidly in the hole of another stick) and prepared dried meat for the winter. She made a robe from the skin and fur of rabbits and other animals she was able to catch with snares. Incredibly, she was able to eke out a living in the bush through two winters.

During Secak's second summer of extraordinary survival, an Iroquois hunter wandering far from his camp found signs of her activities. He located a small cave with a large pile of firewood stacked inside and hid nearby until she returned. When Secak approached the cave, the hunter could not help but notice her wild state and realized that she must be one of the three young women who had escaped from the Assiniboine camp two years earlier. Secak made a frenzied effort to get away from the Iroquois hunter but he was able to overtake her and brought her back to his camp. She remained with his family for two years before returning to Jasper House and her home territory alongside the Snake Indian River. The factor at Jasper House hired her to help his wife at the post. Two years later she met and married a Shuswap. There is no further account of Secak after her stay at Jasper House. Perhaps she stayed on in the area—if so, she would have been the sole surviving member of the Snake Indians in Jasper.

◆ ◆ ◆

A few decades later, game populations in the valley became very scarce as hunters and trappers in the fur trade eventually decimated these populations. As well, the increase in the numbers of people moving west and relying on subsistence hunting took its toll on the wildlife. After years of minimal trading due to overhunting and trapping, Jasper House was permanently abandoned in 1884, and most of the Aboriginals, Europeans and Métis trading in the area moved on. Elk, never in abundance in the mountain valleys, were on the verge of becoming extirpated, beaver had been nearly eradicated, and wood bison were totally wiped out.

As the fur traders left, other people slowly started to travel through or settle in the Jasper area. These included naturalists, explorers, and a few early tourists that ventured into the park on horseback with outfitters. One of these early outfitters was Walter Moberly, a brother of Henry Moberly. In 1872, Walter was hired by Sandford Fleming (appointed by Prime Minister John A. Macdonald) to find a railway route through the mountains linking eastern Canada to British Columbia. This route was to pass through what would later become Jasper National Park and then over present day Yellowhead Pass into British Columbia. It became one of two routes the railways eventually took through the Rocky Mountains. Walter blazed the trail, but it wasn't until 1911, 26 years after the last spike had been driven in the Canadian Pacific Railway line through Yoho National Park, that the Grand Trunk Pacific Railway line was pushed through to the present day Jasper townsite.

When Jasper was established as a park in 1907, a small community called Fitzhugh began to form near the confluence of the Miette and Athabasca rivers. This became a divisional point for the Grand Truck Pacific Railway in 1911. With the coming of the "iron horse" to the community, a hotel, hospital, store, and railway yards were established. In 1913, Fitzhugh was surveyed, and leases were issued for lots. The town's name was then changed to Jasper. A second railway line, the Canadian Northern Railway, passed through Jasper National Park from the east and established its divisional point at Lucerne Lake near Yellowhead Pass in 1913. The Grand

Truck Pacific and the Canadian Northern were amalgamated into the present day Canadian National Railway (CNR) in 1922.

A new era began in 1922 when the first automobiles to travel successfully from Edmonton to Vancouver via the Yellowhead Pass bounced and rattled along an old wagon trail. A gravel road from Edmonton to Jasper was completed in 1928, bringing with it the first visitors to arrive in the park in relative comfort by "horseless carriage."

The days of Aboriginal people, European explorers, adventurers, fur traders, and other trailblazers who opened up the country through hardship, toil, and grit were now mostly history. Many of these pioneers had relied on their horses—trusted companions that carried them and their supplies into the deep wilderness. The horses' final act on this historic stage was to provide their strength and endurance by hauling supplies and building materials for the construction of the railways and roads that traverse the Rocky Mountains, in effect replacing themselves in the annals of history.

After the arrival of the iron horse and the horseless carriage, small numbers of horse outfitters stayed on in the park or in the foothills to the east. Many of these outfitters blazed new trails into the backcountry, taking their clients into areas likely never travelled by humans before. Other adventurers and horsemen became the first wave of wilderness game guardians—early park wardens in national parks, and park rangers in provincial parks and other protected areas.

The arrival of the Europeans in Jasper National Park and the advancement in means of travel drastically changed the landscape of the Athabasca River Valley. Most of the changes occurred in and around the vicinity of the townsite with the associated infrastructure of roads, buildings, and other facilities required for residents and tourists. The CNR yards created a huge footprint on the terrace above the Athabasca River within the boundaries of the townsite. The depot included sidings, a station, freight and baggage sheds, an ice house, a round house, water tanks, a coal storage shed (for steam engines), sanding facilities, and a large locomotive repair shop.

Changes in the landscape could be seen throughout the rest of the park. This was especially so in the area around Jasper House.

The gravel road from Edmonton traversed the valley across the Athabasca River east of the historic post. Two kilometres downriver and across from the confluence of the Snake Indian River with the Athabasca River, road builders blasted away a large portion of a rock ridge on the lower flanks of Roche Miette to make room for the road that was wedged between the rock face and the river below. The Yellowhead Highway has since replaced the gravel road.

The railway ran through the montane meadows one kilometre west of Jasper House. Devona warden cabin was constructed on the banks of the Snake Indian River in 1928, another kilometre west of the railway and near the location of the Snake Indian massacre.

◆ ◆ ◆

Park Warden George Fowlie began his career just as the Devona warden cabin was nearing completion. George and his wife Peggy, with their newborn son Jim, moved into the new cabin in the summer of 1928. George was assigned the Willow Creek District, deep in the wilderness of the North Boundary, and Devona became their district headquarter cabin. George was given three riding horses and six pack horses. His territory followed the river north up the Snake Indian Valley to his patrol cabins at Shalebanks and Seldom Inn and then on to Willow Creek. From there his patrol area ran further north up Deer Creek to Little Heaven and beyond to the park's northeastern boundary. He also patrolled the Wolf Pass area, east towards the Moosehorn Valley—the next valley over the Bosche Mountain Range from the Snake Indian. Small shelters existed at Little Heaven and Wolf Pass. A local train ran between Jasper and Devona Siding, one kilometre away from the cabin. Other than occasional trips to Jasper for supplies or for George to check in with the office, the Fowlies spent all their time in the district. They covered the district with their horses in the summer months and by snowshoe in the winter.

Park Warden George Busby was the Fowlies' nearest neighbour, stationed at Miette warden cabin approximately 12 kilometres to the east. Busby had begun his career in 1913 and was among the first group of wardens in Jasper to be assigned backcountry districts. He was near retirement and thought park management was pampering the new wardens—George Fowlie included. He told the Fowlies that when he started with the Warden Service, he covered the entire North Boundary from Miette right through to Mount Robson on the border with British Columbia—close to 3,000 square kilometres of wilderness. He was given two pack horses to carry his supplies and equipment, but no riding horse. He slept in rudimentary shelters made of hastily thrown together logs, in a tent, or under the stars. Tough character that Busby.

The only daily contact the Fowlies had with the outside world was the forestry telephone line (when it was not hampered by fallen trees) that connected their district cabin with the park office in Jasper. They got the occasional and welcome company and news from horse travellers and other backcountry enthusiasts passing through the district. When working out of Willow Creek, one of George's responsibilities was to meet all the horse outfitting parties travelling through the park on their way to hunt in the Athabasca Forest Reserve (later renamed Willmore Wilderness Park) to the north. To track their movement while in his district, he broke the park seals on all firearms carried by the hunters before they headed into the forestry reserve, and then resealed the same weapons on their return into Jasper National Park.

The Fowlie family lived the typical life of the year-round backcountry warden. George often patrolled his district alone for weeks at a time when away from his home cabin. When Peggy stayed back at Devona, she had to mind all the needs in and around the main district cabin, tend to any horses left behind, assist travellers making their way through the lower district, investigate reports of wrongdoing or accidents, and respond as best she could to requests from park headquarters. In addition to managing the home cabin while her husband was away in the far reaches of his district, Peggy cared for their young son Jim.

When Peggy, with Jim, joined George on his patrols, she served as his extra pair of hands. She was his wife *and* working partner. The government never paid wardens' wives. *Silent Partners: Wives of National Park Wardens*, an excellent book written by Ann Dixon, the wife of Park Warden Fred Dixon, recounts the stories of many of these pioneering women.

The Fowlie's son Jim spent his first 12 years in the Willow Creek District with his parents before George took a posting in town. Like most children raised in these remote warden posts, he learned to ride a horse not long after he could walk and helped with chores around the cabins. Like the children of many warden families, he began correspondence lessons through the Department of Education in Edmonton when he turned six.

◆ ◆ ◆

Many of the park wardens spent much of their careers working alone (without families) in the backcountry districts. One of these was Bob Jones, a World War I veteran hired in the 1930s. In 1949, after being stationed in Blue Creek District for 13 years, Bob was moved to Devona warden cabin.

Likely the most exciting group of visitors Bob had while at Devona was a large film crew from Hollywood in 1953. Mac Elder, working as a packer and guide for a horse outfitter before joining the Warden Service, recalled riding out to Devona after a three-month wilderness horse trip with a crew of geologists. Riding west out of the Moosehorn Valley, Mac crossed the Snake Indian River and met Bob as he came running over to him from his cabin. Bob appeared very excited, and Mac thought perhaps he was lonely and bushed, having not talked to anyone for a long time. Mac reined in his horse beside Bob and before he could even say, "Hi," Bob breathlessly shouted, "Mac, how was your trip?" Without waiting for an answer and in the same breath, Bob shouted, "You won't believe this—Marilyn Monroe was in my cabin!"

The spectacular scenery in Jasper was a backdrop to many Hollywood movies filmed in the Canadian Rockies between the 1930s and mid-1950s. These included *The Emperor Waltz* with Bing Crosby and Joan Fontaine; *Rose Marie* with Howard Keel and Ann Blyth; and *The Far Country,* starring Jimmy Stewart and Walter Brennan. One of the last movies filmed in Jasper was *River of No Return.* But Jasper wasn't the main attraction in the film;

Marilyn Monroe was the star of the movie, which also featured Robert Mitchum.

Set in the northwestern United States, the movie takes place during the gold rush in 1885. Much of the drama centres around the trials and tribulations Monroe and Mitchum have with Aboriginals, unsavoury prospectors, a cougar attack, and a dangerous river rafting trip down the "River of No Return"—the Snake Indian River. A movie set, including a log cabin and horse corral, was constructed right next to Devona warden cabin. Much to Bob's delight, Marilyn Monroe was given permission by the park to use the cabin as her dressing room.

During the movie's production, many Jasperites, including my grandfather Herb Karran, had the pleasure of meeting Ms. Monroe. As the locomotive shop foreman at the CNR train station in town, my grandfather arranged to have the film crew taken by rail to Devona Siding each day. From there, they were driven on a dirt road to the work site. When the filming was finished in Jasper, Marilyn stopped by the CNR shops and as thanks gave my grandfather a bottle of Crown Royal. He proudly displayed the bottle on the mantel above his fireplace for several months before a group of his friends convinced him they should open it and drink a toast to Marilyn.

The Jasper residents who had the privilege of meeting Marilyn Monroe speak of a gracious, caring, and intelligent woman, certainly not the person she portrayed in the many movies she starred in that reduced her to the role of a sex symbol. Some of the older residents I spoke to sensed that she was overwhelmed, stressed, and unhappy with her life. Marilyn certainly left a part of her spirit and imprint in Jasper, as many residents grieved her very sad and unfortunate death nine years after she starred in *River of No Return*.

Bob Jones met his own fate in December 1954, a year after the movie was made and not long after its release. Bob had made a trip to town to pick up supplies and chat with friends over a beer before returning to his district cabin. Park Warden Harold Elvin, Bob's nearest neighbour 14 kilometres to the west at Snaring Warden Station, was also in town. As Harold was returning to

Snaring, he volunteered to give his friend and co-worker a ride home. A rough road (today's Celestine Lake Road) had been built between Snaring and Devona since the Fowlies were stationed there, making it much easier for Bob to get into town from his district.

When Bob and Harold arrived at Devona warden cabin in the dark, Bob grabbed a bucket and a flashlight to get fresh water out of the Snake Indian River to make coffee. Harold remained in the cabin to start a fire in the wood stove. After several minutes, Harold became concerned that Bob had not returned. He went to check and found Bob's footprints leading to the edge of an ice shelf forming out from the banks of the fast flowing river. Bob was nowhere to be seen. His flashlight, lying on the ice, was still on, illuminating the water as it rushed by the ice shelf. Harold searched frantically for Bob and feared he had drowned. The following morning search parties were sent out to look for his body, but they didn't see any sign of Bob, nor did they find his water bucket. It was surmised that when Bob had dipped his bucket into the river, the force of the water rushing into the bucket had thrown him off balance, into the current, and downstream under the ice of the partially frozen river.

When the warming spring sun began to melt the ice on the river, further search parties were dispatched to find Bob's body but with no luck. Shortly afterward, Brian Jones (no relation to Bob), a helicopter pilot for Trans Mountain Pipe Line, was asked to check the river from the air. Trans Mountain had run a crude oil pipeline through the park two years earlier, placed along a corridor cut between the railway and Devona warden cabin. Brian flew his regular check of the pipeline, then veered off route near the site of historic Jasper House towards the Snake Indian River close to Devona. Within a few minutes he located Bob's body hung up in a logjam in the middle of the river a few hundred metres down from the cabin. Sadly, Bob had taken a real life journey, his last, down the "River of No Return."

The cabin at Devona was occupied by a succession of wardens and their families until 1976, each serving out their stay as guardians of the wild in the district and contributing to the rich and diverse history of the area. That year, park managers decided that the cabin was no longer required as they slowly began the move to centralization, decommissioning several district stations in the process.

◆ ◆ ◆

The sound of a CNR freight train approaching Devona Siding from the east broke the silence as Lawrence and I gazed at the panoramic view from the hillside, a view that spanned a relatively small area of Jasper but was of great historical importance to the park. As I was brought back from my recollection of the historical events of the area, I contemplated the significance of those who had come before us. We are not simply who we are at birth; we are the result of our heritage, of other cultures that have influenced and enriched our lives, and of the past and present connection and interplay with our physical environment. The raw and wild beauty of Jasper National Park still exists—not far from the noise and busyness of the Athabasca River Valley corridor that winds its way through the park—with history around each bend of the river. This history, our connection to the past, gives us an understanding of the present and allows us to ponder what the future may bring. As Lawrence and I left the Devona area and headed to Seldom Inn, I was about to enter a new chapter in my life—living out my dream as a guardian of the wilderness in the high country of northern Jasper National Park. I realized what a great privilege it was to have the opportunity to travel the mountain trails of our ancestors.

CHAPTER NINE

The High Country

When Lawrence and I arrived at Seldom Inn warden cabin, we could hear a horse bell a few hundred metres away in the trees beyond the open pasture. When Denny Welsh had trucked our horses up from the Maligne Horse Range the day before, he had placed a bell around the neck of one of the horses before he released them in the fenced pasture. The bell allowed us to locate the horses when it came time to find them—a daily backcountry task referred to as "jingling."

Lawrence and I each took a halter from the tack shed, opened the gate to the pasture, and followed the sound of the bell to find our horses. Locating horses from the cabins at Seldom Inn and Willow Creek was a relatively easy task in comparison to the other warden cabins in Jasper since these were the only two cabins that had large fenced-in pastures.

At all the other backcountry cabins in the park, horses are turned loose to graze, and generally they must be hobbled when left to graze freely in unfenced backcountry areas. Hobbles are made of leather straps buckled to the lower part of a horse's front legs with a short length of chain attached to each leather strap. They work on the same principle as handcuffs, except the "cuff" is made of leather. They impede a horse's ability to take long strides, which *usually* prevents it from wandering too far at night. However, horses can actually hop with their hobbles on, and when so inclined, they can travel great distances (more on this in a later chapter).

Once we found the horses, we spent the rest of the day getting acquainted with them, checking over our gear, and repairing breaks in the pasture fence. The next morning we were up early to jingle the horses and pack for our trip into Willow Creek. We had arranged to spend most of the first backcountry trip in the Willow Creek District, clearing the trail of trees downed by winter storms and becoming familiar with the area.

I quickly learned that the horses, mostly left to fend for themselves over the winter at the Ya Ha Tinda Ranch—a remote winter range on the banks of the upper Red Deer River along the eastern border of Banff National Park—tend to be a bit on the wild side when they return to the park each spring. The riding horses, mounted for the first time in six months, may feel the need to shake the winter cobwebs, and the unwary warden, off their backs. It's important to be calm but firm with them to prevent their initial skittishness from escalating into an unruly situation. It's also not unusual to have a pack horse patiently wait to be fully loaded, to the last tightening of the diamond hitch, before testing the skill of the packer. Some seem to take great delight in bucking off the packs and scattering the contents. So it was with all this in mind that Lawrence and I, with great care and confidence, saddled and packed our horses for the first time that spring.

Lawrence's horses Izzy and Hawk and my chosen riding horse for the day Hep proved to be fairly calm and amenable when we saddled and packed up. Help was another story. He pranced around the hitching rail making it difficult for us to pack him, and just before we could secure his boxes and tarp with the diamond hitch, he let loose and unloaded the packs. His mission accomplished, he stood and eyed the mess of boxes and gear scattered on the ground with a hint of glee in his eye. Then he walked up to the hitching rail as if to dare us to try again. I wondered if he had been given his name because his caregiver (that would be me) needed a lot of *help* in handling him. This didn't prove to be the case, however, as Help was merely testing my resolve. After we patiently repacked him while calmly asserting our authority, Help accepted his load. He turned out to be a trusted pack horse and a more than reliable riding horse.

As we rode away from Seldom Inn towards the beckoning high country of Jasper's northern wilderness, I envisaged the months ahead. I was thrilled to have the horses as companions and eager for adventure. Although I had ridden and been in the company of horses before and had always been good with animals, I knew that I would have much to learn from our back-country horses. I had to be aware of all the mishaps that could happen while handling them, including the possibility of being kicked.

◆ ◆ ◆

Ten months earlier, in late July 1979, Banff wardens had become concerned when backcountry warden Neil Colgan had not checked in to park headquarters for several days. Missing one or two procedural radio calls was the norm in the backcountry: perhaps the SSB radio in Neil's cabin wasn't transmitting well or he had simply missed calls while out with his horses during the morning and evening radio call-out hours; or maybe he had run into some sort of delay or trouble. Patrolling backcountry areas alone is a dangerous job.

Wardens miss many radio calls. They are usually given a day or two to respond before headquarters becomes concerned. But this time Neil had missed more calls than usual, and search parties were sent out to locate him. Neil had been patrolling the Douglas Lake area located deep in the heart of the rugged wilderness along the Sawback Range of Banff National Park. His last radio call had been from the Sandhills warden cabin approximately nine kilometres north of Douglas Lake.

Neil's horse, Gunner, was found in the pasture close to the cabin, but Neil was nowhere to be seen, nor was Gunner's saddle. The search quickly expanded out from the cabin. It wasn't until the next morning that helicopter pilot Jim Davies and Park Warden Lance Cooper spotted Gunner's saddle on the Douglas Lake trail. Shortly afterwards, Neil's body was located several hundred metres away, close to a stand of trees beside the lake.

Examining the riding saddle left on the trail, Banff wardens pieced together the circumstances of Neil's accident as best they could. It appeared that Neil had dismounted Gunner to adjust the blankets and saddle, slacking off both cinches to do so. What followed is unclear. Gunner must have reacted to something: a movement in the forest, restlessness from pesky horse flies, or a quick move by Neil (perhaps a stumble over a tree root) that startled him. Neil was either kicked or knocked over and stomped on by Gunner, perhaps as he was bucking and spinning as the loosened saddle dropped under his belly while Neil tried to calm him. It appeared that Neil had dropped to the ground with a ruptured kidney and that Gunner had managed to kick the saddle away before turning back toward the cabin. Neil, most certainly aware of the seriousness of his condition and that a search was imminent, was somehow able to make his way down towards the lakeshore where a helicopter could spot him. It was here in the wilds of the Rockies he loved where he scribbled a goodbye note to his family, tucking it into his jacket before the light faded away from his energetic young life.

And what became of Gunner? He was taken out of the backcountry and assessed as to his reliability for continued use as a park horse. In other words, was it safe to be around this horse and could he function as a trustworthy partner for a backcountry warden? Managers in Banff decided to put Gunner down. There wasn't further indication that Gunner might be a dangerous horse, but after the accident they didn't know for sure. No one wanted to be responsible for another warden being hurt or killed. It was a sad decision nonetheless.

◆ ◆ ◆

A few days before Lawrence and I left town for the backcountry, we learned that John Niddrie (assigned the Tonquin Valley area) had asked Chief Park Warden Don Dumpleton if he could get a second riding horse. He planned to have his fiancé, Lise, join him for a few trips in the backcountry. John was granted an extra horse for the season and he eagerly headed over to the Maligne Horse Range to pick it up. Denny Welsh was expecting him. He handed John a halter and pointed out a gelding in the pasture for him to fetch—Gunner!

When Denny had heard that Gunner was going to be put down, he called the park office in Banff and requested to take him.

Denny had known Gunner as a colt and was well acquainted with the mare that foaled him. He insisted Gunner was not a killer. This was a gutsy move, but Denny was an impressive horseman and he was sure he had made the right decision.

John learned that the horse was the one that Neil Cogan had been given. He was told to be careful around Gunner's back feet as he could kick. But then any horse can kick—almost always a reaction rather than a malicious act. Being a novice horseman, John took precautions and was careful around Gunner. He decided to use him as a pack horse and his other two as riding horses.

When John first packed him, Gunner became "unglued" (a word we use when a horse loses its composure and bucks off its packs, resulting in a "wreck"). John repacked Gunner without incident and had an uneventful trip into Tonquin Valley. However, as John brought Gunner up to the hitching rail by the cabin, he became unglued again, resulting in a gallon of paint spilling inside one of the boxes. Much of their food was spoiled and some personal items were damaged. It wasn't long before John and Gunner figured each other out and the wrecks became few and far between. Gunner went on to become a tried and trusted horse in Jasper, used by numerous wardens for many years without further incident.

◆ ◆ ◆

Lawrence and I cleared the deadfall off the trail as we rode north from Seldom Inn to Willow Creek, all the while getting to know the horses and their individual personalities. Hep and Hawk, our chosen riding horses for the day, pranced around a little when we left Seldom Inn, adjusting to having a rider in the saddle again after the long winter. In turn, our pack horses Help and Izzy put on a bit of a show the first half hour on the trail, snorting and puffing in defiance of carrying packs again. But it wasn't long before they settled themselves down.

We arrived at Willow Creek in the late afternoon, wet and tired from trail clearing in frequent showers of rain. The sun was edging out between the clouds as we rode out from the dense lodgepole pine forest, under the overhead gate of the pasture fence, and into the open vistas of the meadows around the cabin. This gate signified what I liked to call the entry point into the high country: the vast wilderness of northern Jasper National Park.

Daybreak Peak, seven kilometres away, dominated the distant panoramic view across the pasture to the north of the cabin. To the west, across the Snake Indian River, the gently rolling summit of Mount Stornoway wedged up against the higher jagged peaks still farther west into Blue Creek District, their summits still draped by the clouds that had brought us rain.

Between the two mountains, Willow Creek and several small feeder streams slowly meander their way throughout the valley before joining the Snake Indian River. The valley contains a pastoral mosaic of lodgepole pine, white spruce, and aspen forest, interspersed with grass and sedge meadows dotted with various species of low lying shrubs. This dreamlike setting viewed from the cabin, home to a vast array of the wildlife species you can expect to see in the mountains, is a favourite destination for park wardens. Many early Jasper wardens began their careers in the lower Snake Indian Valley. Two chose it as their final resting place, their ashes scattered on a low ridge above the creek.

After we unpacked the horses, gave them a treat of oats and turned them loose, I looked out across the valley. I noted a few changes since my 10-day backpack trip through Willow Creek en route to Mount Robson seven years earlier, in 1973, with my high school friend Pat Paul. Willows and other shrubs were slowly taking over many of the grass and sedge meadows in the area. The fenced north horse pasture was now extended to include a sizable pasture to the south called the Bison Pasture. Patrolman Matt Burstrom and a crew from the Saddle Lake Cree Nation Reserve had constructed the new fence around the pasture in the autumn of 1977 to temporarily hold wood bison from Elk Island National Park.

In the mid-1970s, the Canadian Wildlife Service suggested Jasper as a location to re-introduce wood bison into natural areas of suitable habitat as part of a recovery plan to re-establish populations. With only a few isolated pockets of wood bison left in northern Canada and in Elk Island National Park, the Committee on the Status of Endangered Wildlife in Canada (COSEWIC) designated wood bison as an endangered species in 1978. Park management looked at the proposal favourably, as a key conservation goal for Canada's national parks is to reintroduce extirpated species that were once part of the landscape.

The northern portion of Jasper was one of the southern-most ranges of wood bison before their numbers in Canada were reduced to less than 500 animals from estimated numbers of over 170,000 before the days of the fur trade. (Wood bison should not be confused with the much more common plains bison in North America whose numbers dropped to a mere 200 animals from an estimated 30 to 60 million after the arrival of Europeans.)

Early explorers and fur traders reported small numbers of wood bison in the Athabasca River Valley from the eastern boundary of the park to Prairie de la Vache, an extensive meadow 11 kilometres south of Jasper townsite. Bison skulls have also been collected from the valley along the Brazeau River corridor in the southern reaches of Jasper and at various locations throughout the North Boundary.

In his book *Pack Saddles to Tête Jaune Cache*, James MacGregor recounts Vincent Wanyandi's stories of bison hunts in the northern areas of Jasper and around Rock Lake in the Willmore Wilderness. Vincent was a full-blooded Iroquois born near Jasper House about 1850. When Vincent, still a young boy, began hunting with the men, they travelled up the Snake Indian River to the Willow Creek/Rock Lake area from Jasper House to procure game for the fort each year. The older men and the women and children of his band started out several days before the hunters to set up camp. One of their favourite hunting camps was located along the Wildhay River beside Mumm Creek approximately four kilometres downriver from Rock Lake. Vincent recalled hunting bison, moose, and deer.

Vincent described the hunt to James Shand Harvey (interviewed by MacGregor for his book) when Harvey was employed as a provincial park ranger in the Willmore area in 1913. Vincent recalled the hunt as a time of great excitement:

"There were tepees here and there and all over, close together. The fires blazed while the women cooked moose nose and buffalo hump. Ribs roasted by the fire, marrow bones sizzled in the coals—great feasting, happiness, and laughter. All day the women cut the meat into strips and hung them on the drying racks while the little ones fed the fires, which kept the flies away. At night we danced. All night the drums throbbed. The women dried the meat and pounded some of it into pemmican. The saskatoons were ripe and the buffalo fat."

After many days, the band packed its horses and headed back down the Snake Indian River to Jasper House. The dried meat bought many things for them: tea and tobacco, woollen blankets, and needles. Those were good days, but with the winding down of the fur trade era and the eventual abandonment of Jasper House, they were not to last. Before the dawn of the 20th century, the bison were gone. Adam Joachim, a Métis guide and trapper born in 1875, recalled that the last of the bison in the area perished during a very severe winter when he was a child.

Mac Elder remembers coming across seven old gravesites scattered throughout Willow Creek District and adjacent areas of the Willmore Wilderness when he guided horse trips in the area from 1947 to 1956. He also took note of decaying tepee poles, meat drying racks, and other traces of old Aboriginal camps. Like the vast herds of wild bison that were once a staple diet of the earliest inhabitants of North America, the camps have long since vanished: the wood recycled into soil and other camp traces lost in time.

◆ ◆ ◆

In June 1978, as part of a joint venture between the CWS and Parks Canada, 28 wood bison, captured in Elk Island National Park, were reintroduced into Jasper. They were trucked to Rock Lake, then individually crated and flown by helicopter into the bison pasture at Willow Creek. The animals were kept there for 43 days prior to release to prevent the herd from scattering. This allowed the bison to regroup while becoming accustomed to their new surroundings.

With great anticipation, Park Wardens Dave Norcross and Tom Davidson opened the gate to the pasture on the morning of July 22 to let 27 bison (one had died before the release) slowly find their way out. Then Dave and Tom waited...and waited. The bison seemed to have taken a liking to their new home along Willow Creek. With its fresh mountain water, succulent green grasses and supplemental hay, life couldn't be better.

It wasn't until the next morning that the bison slowly passed by the open gate and moved out into the mixed meadow and forest habitat along the Snake Indian River a few kilometres south of the cabin. Dave was given the enviable task of monitoring the movements of the herd. How exciting it must have been for him to track these enormous beasts as they ventured out into the haunts last travelled a century earlier by their kind near the end of the fur trade era.

Over the next few days the herd crossed the Snake Indian River to graze at Grizzly Meadows at the foot of Mount Stornoway, then crossed back over the river and headed towards Deer Creek approximately eight kilometres from Willow Creek warden cabin. The bison then moved on to the meadows around Welbourne warden cabin not far to the west of Deer Creek on the North Boundary trail. Dave spent the better part of one afternoon watching the bison graze contentedly in the meadows before he returned to Willow Creek for the night. It was close to a week since their release. The bison were at home, or so it seemed.

Dave set out the next day and tracked the bison all the way up to Little Heaven warden cabin—a good day's ride from Willow Creek. He saw extensive signs that the bison had fed in the expansive meadows along Mowitch Creek below the cabin. The bison's tracks indicated they had headed further up the Mowitch Creek Valley towards Desolation and Glacier passes, both alpine passes that border Willmore Wilderness.

But where were the bison, and why hadn't they remained in this meadow of abundant forage longer? Perhaps they were on the move, for some reason not content with what we considered to be adequate habitat. A few hours later, as the day was turning to dusk, Dave spotted most of the herd with his binoculars from the open eskers in front of the cabin—small dark forms 11 kilometres away. They were moving across the high alpine slopes of Arcturus Basin at the northern end of the Starlight Mountain Range, near the head of the Mowitch Creek Valley.

Dave was unable to spot the bison from Little Heaven the next morning and set out on horseback to find them. Many hours later he stood alongside his horse looking down the steep shale slopes of a high rocky pass above Arcturus Basin close to Desolation Pass. He was standing on the park boundary. With Jasper National Park at his back, he gazed over the boundary into Willmore Wilderness. His eyes followed bison tracks heading down a steep shale slope into the province.

A week and a half later a herd of 21 wood bison appeared as if out of nowhere on private fields near Grande Prairie. They had travelled well over a hundred kilometres. The herd was eventually rounded up and taken back to Elk Island. What of the six other bison? By the time winter closed in, only two bison were still in the Willow Creek area (the Warden Service later lost track of them) and three others were never found. The sixth bison, a three-year-old bull, found his way down the Snake Indian River and ended up crossing the Athabasca River not far from long abandoned Jasper House. This bull lived for another decade, spending much of its time in the lower Rocky River Valley across the Athabasca River from the historic fort where fur traders relied on bison meat as part of their diet—an ironic ending to a failed attempt at reintroducing wood bison into Jasper National Park.

Why had the reintroduction failed? Members of the CWS and Parks Canada program knew that older re-introduced animals tend to travel more than younger ones and will sometimes head homewards no matter how far that may be. Although the bison herd was mostly comprised of calves, yearlings, and young adults, the reintroduction team had decided that the bison herd should have a few "elders" for stability. The oldest animal, an eight-year old cow, was the leader of the herd and was almost certainly the one that led the rest of the bison away from Willow Creek.

Team personnel had considered leaving the herd at Willow Creek for a few years before taking the adults away and leaving behind the calves brought in with the reintroduction along with the calves that would subsequently be born at Willow Creek. Being their home, the calves would most likely have stayed in the area. But funds were not available to have the bison monitored for several years, or to supply hay over the winter months.

The other burning question was whether the habitat on the North Boundary was still suitable for bison. The accounts of wardens and horse outfitters who knew the area well showed that the vast meadow systems had been reduced to a small remnant of their original size. In 1980, I clearly saw the reduced size of open meadows since I had hiked the boundary in 1973. When I was last at Willow Creek in 2007, the growth of willows and other shrubs overtaking the meadows left some areas almost unrecognizable.

To what degree the change in habitat is a result of human interference is unclear. Certainly fire suppression may have had an effect on the area. Between 75 and 235 horses (the numbers varied each year) belonging to the Warden Service and local outfitters were overwintered in the Willow Creek area from the early 1950s to the mid-60s. Elk, reintroduced into Jasper in 1920, were more abundant on the North Boundary than they are today. What effect did the grazing by horses and elk have on the habitat? According to Mac Elder, there were far more moose in the area in the 1950s and '60s. Moose are largely browsers. Did they keep the shrub species in check in years past? And did the extirpation of bison in Jasper and Willmore a century ago result in an altered landscape over time? Is the change in habitat merely a result of the natural succession of vegetation? Or has climate change influenced the picturesque mosaic pattern of trees, meadow, and wetlands in the valley? There are many questions. The answers will continue to challenge Parks Canada in striving to maintain Jasper National Park in as natural a state as possible.

◆ ◆ ◆

Lawrence and I spent six days exploring several creek drainages and clearing trails in the Willow Creek area. With warming late spring weather chasing the snow line down from the mountain slopes, we headed up to higher country to explore a good part of the remaining several hundred square kilometres that comprised Willow Creek District. We spent several days travelling in and out of the park into Willmore Wilderness, getting to know the boundary areas and outfitter camps that would be busy with hunters later in the autumn. This would serve me well as, come autumn, I would be not only patrolling the boundary of Blue Creek District but also helping Rick Ralf cover areas of the Willow Creek District that border Willmore.

Beginning the third week into our first trip of the season, Lawrence met up with Rick at Willow Creek and I moved on for a three-day stay at Blue Creek warden cabin—my district headquarters for the summer. I had just enough time to complete several maintenance jobs around the cabin and get it in order for the summer before it was time to head out to Seldom Inn for days off.

CHAPTER TEN

The Ancient Wall

During the second week of June, after a few days leave in Jasper, Lawrence and I geared up for our second backcountry stint. I picked up my third horse from Denny at the Maligne Horse Range: big Ernie, the large sorrel Belgian-Thoroughbred cross that would quickly become the real character of my equine trio. Lawrence and I spent two days ferrying gear and supplies with the horses into Willow Creek from the trailhead at Seldom Inn before heading off to Blue Creek. On our way there, we checked out an old den site used by a wolf pack in the early 1970s. The site, now abandoned, was once a hub of activity for a family of pups closely monitored by a young biologist, Ludwig (Lu) Carbyn.

Lu grew up in Namibia, in southern Africa. His father, a forester, instilled the joys and discoveries of nature in Lu when he was a very young boy. Lu spent many hours sitting quietly under a camel thorn tree watching the bird life around a local watering hole. His first article for a wildlife journal, based on observations of cattle egrets, was written when he was nine years old.

After obtaining a master's degree in zoology from the University of Alberta in 1967, Lu worked for the Canadian Wildlife Service. In the late 1960s, Parks Canada proposed a wolf study with the CWS to determine the extent to which wolves were controlling elk populations in Jasper. Park managers wanted to know why wolves weren't doing a better job of it. Elk were still very plentiful in Jasper in spite of having been culled annually for close to three decades. Lu was chosen for the study and sent to the North Boundary.

After much searching, Lu found a wolf den hidden at the edge of a stand of trees encircled by the open grassland and shrub meadows typical of much of the habitat between Willow and Blue creeks. He found a place to cold camp, a term used for setting up a very simple camp—basically a small tent with a minimum of gear and no fire.

Lu was the first in the world to study wolves from what he describes as, "the middle of the pack." This technique, known as habituation, was used by world-renowned primate biologist Jane Goodall during her life-long research on chimpanzees in the Gombe Stream Reserve in Tanzania. Habituation involves being in the vicinity of the animals until they no longer respond to human presence. Once they trust that the human means no harm and will not disrupt their activities, they regard that human, for the most part, with indifference.

Lu found the place near the den, called a rendezvous site, where an adult or two was left to babysit the pups each time the rest of the pack went out to hunt. Over a period of many days, he hiked down the same path from his campsite, sat under the same tree, wore the same clothes, and behaved in the same manner. He stayed under that tree for progressively longer periods until the wolves became used to his presence. Once their curiosity about this strange animal on two legs was satisfied, they lost their natural fear of him. Lu was free to make his observations of this big predator from the middle of the pack. Lu's study employed what he called the "naturalistic method," as this was before the era of using collars to radio track the wolves.

As his study progressed, Lu was astonished at how well this technique worked. He felt incredibly privileged to be in the company of wolves. Lu neither feared nor felt threatened by the wolves in any way. He became part of the wolves' environment; his presence neither disrupted nor altered their behaviour and activities.

Al Stendie, working out of Blue Creek District, and Brian Wallace, stationed in Willow Creek District, assisted Lu during the field study between 1969 and 1972. Al and Brian made many of the logistical arrangements, helping Lu into and out of the study area, and kept in touch with him while he was there. They also assisted by collecting scats for hair analysis to determine what the wolves were eating and monitored the wolves' movements using tracks and incidental observations. They took care to keep well away from Lu's observation area near the den. The number of wolves in Lu's pack fluctuated between 7 and 12 individuals throughout the study period.

The results of Lu's study answered the question as to why wolves had not been adequately controlling elk populations in Jasper National Park. The reasons were obvious to many and confirmed by Lu—wolves were still relatively scarce in Jasper. Over 90 years of persecution (from approximately 1860 to the 1950s) by intensive predator control programs had almost eliminated wolves from the Rocky Mountain national parks. The wolves in Jasper had not increased enough in numbers by the time of Lu's study to have had an impact on elk populations.

Lu's study provided new information on wolf predation and behavioural interaction with elk and other ungulates in an area of high prey diversity in the park. The study also provided baseline data relevant to future wolf research. Lu earned a PhD in zoology based on his study and went on to do further research on wolves in Wood Buffalo and Riding Mountain national parks, and further afield in Poland, Portugal, and Mexico. He is now one of the world's leading wolf behavioural scientists.

◆ ◆ ◆

Lawrence and I searched the general area of the old wolf den for more recent dens without success before continuing on to Blue Creek. We spent much of the next morning making repairs to the equipment and tack sheds. We then saddled our horses and rode up to McClarens Pass—a high alpine pass that cuts through a notch dividing Mount Kelsey from The Ancient Wall. The Ancient Wall is a mountain range that rises up along the Blue Creek Valley from near its confluence with the Snake Indian River to its headwaters at Hardscrabble Pass—one of several high mountain passes that bisects Jasper and the Willmore Wilderness.

McClarens Pass is an important area for mountain goat and bighorn sheep. In the spring, they descend the steep rocky crags to an alpine mineral lick where they supplement their diet with minerals lost during the harsh winter months. Al Stendie and Brian Wallace documented several mineral licks in the Willow Creek and Blue Creek districts in the 1970s. These licks were known to wardens working the backcountry districts for decades but had not been documented for monitoring purposes. Mineral licks are key areas for monitoring ungulate species and predator activity. Cougars, wolves, bears, and wolverine are opportunistic hunters, ever aware of the best areas to locate their prey. Goats and sheep are particularly vulnerable to attack when not in their preferred habitat—steep terrain that gives them quick access to rock outcrops or cliff bands that their pursuers have difficulty navigating.

Mountain goats and sheep stay at a lick for only short periods of time, always wary of predators. Lawrence and I lucked out at the pass. As we ascended through the stunted subalpine fir (krummholz) just below the pass, we spotted a herd of 29 goats—20 adults, 3 yearlings, and 6 very small bundles of fine, white, woollen hair: goat kids only a few weeks old. The kids were likely having their first taste of mountain soil laced with essential minerals for their growing bodies. Not wanting to disturb the herd, we headed back down towards Blue Creek.

The next morning brought grey sky and drizzle as Lawrence packed up for Willow Creek. Not long after he rode out of Blue Creek, the drizzle turned to a heavy rain that lasted most of the day. I spent part of the morning studying the maps in the cabin and marking all the trails in the district on the topographic maps that I would be carrying with me. This included all the undefined routes we refer to as "primitive trails" that are unmarked on printed maps. Aboriginals developed some of these trails; others were blazed early in the 19th century by explorers and horse outfitters. Wardens also established trails in the early years of park establishment. Most of the trails followed rough paths used by animals since the retreat of the last ice age. We travelled these routes to monitor wildlife populations, to access specific sites for studies and research, and to reach high elevation vantage points for monitoring activity along the park boundary during hunting season in the province.

After I completed my mapping, I read through documents, logbooks, and other literature in the cabin relating to information I needed for patrolling and monitoring activities in the district. The most interesting documents were the various accounts left behind by wardens that had managed the backcountry districts decades before—now invaluable historical information.

Four rain-drenched backpackers stopped by in the evening as the rain clouds began to lift. They were staying at Blue Creek campsite a kilometre west of the cabin and planned to head towards Snake Indian Pass the next day. I invited them in for some much appreciated hot coffee and biscuits. We chatted about trail conditions and backcountry travel. They left an hour later, thankful for the chance to dry out their clothes. After the backpackers left, I planned my next trip for the following morning into the upper Blue Creek Valley.

I had conditioned Ernie, Help, and Hep to come in from grazing just before dark by offering them a treat of oats. This way I could see which way they headed before I turned in for the night, making it easier to find them the next morning. After devouring their oats, they headed east towards a meadow along the river a few hundred metres away just as it started to rain.

The rain fell all night and was still coming down when I left the cabin for my early morning horse jingle. I listened for the sounds of a bell from the cabin porch. I heard nothing, which is usually the case. Catching the horses before sunrise is important, as they begin to feed *very* early in the morning and then tend to travel after their predawn feed. Waiting to jingle the horses until after they feed gives them time to wander far from the cabin.

I stepped off the porch and headed east towards the direction of the meadow where I had last seen them after their evening oats eight hours earlier. They weren't in the meadow. I followed their tracks and their fresh piles of manure east for several hundred metres, then back again onto the main trail west towards the cabin. The horse tracks led me right back behind the cabin. I could tell by the shorter distance between their hoof prints that they had slowed their pace—as if tiptoeing. I swear Hep knew that if he walked his normal pace while leading the other horses past the cabin, the motion of his swinging head would sound the bell around his neck. The ponies had given me the slip by making a wide loop during the night, and then sneaking by the cabin without my hearing the bell. I had spent over half an hour looking for them when I could have simply started the jingle behind the cabin and followed their tracks west from there.

So westward I headed, following their tracks. Half a kilometre further, their tracks split off the trail and went into a stand of pine trees and shrubs. The tracks were fresh. This should be easy, I thought. I listened for a bell under the dark canopy of clouds and forest but could only hear the rain. I knew they had to be nearby. I must have walked in a dozen circles and figure eights following their meandering tracks, made as they had walked back and forth while feeding. I did this for about an hour before I finally ended up following the freshest tracks back to the trail where the horses had initially entered the forest. This was crazy! The horses seemed to have vanished.

There I stood, on the spot where I had started from an hour earlier, cold and drenched to the skin with rain running off the front rim of my Stetson and down in front of my eyes as I peered into the dark undergrowth. I listened...and listened...but could hear nothing. I stood several minutes more, closed my eyes, and focused on just listening. A few more minutes went by, and then I heard it—a barely detectable, short and single high note—"ting." Then silence.

I realized that the sound came from just metres away. I took a few steps down the trail and once again strained my eyes looking into the forest. I detected a black form. Hep was standing slightly ahead with his left side facing me, just 10 metres into a thicket of trees, camouflaged by the dull light of the morning. He had moved his head just slightly to follow my movements when the bell had betrayed him. He was now frozen on the spot, following me with his left eye. He knew not to turn his head back towards me again as that would result in another "ting" of the bell. He had a furtive look, knowing I might have heard the bell. I had found their hiding spot. Help and Ernie were standing behind him, also facing away from me. They were glancing sideways as well, not moving a muscle. I could only laugh.

Obviously, they had heard and spotted me coming along the trail an hour ago. They likely sensed it was going to be a day of travel, and like us, horses prefer not to travel in the rain. Several times in the last hour I had walked on the other side of the thicket of trees only metres away from them as I searched in vain. The horses had stood motionless the entire time, watching and listening to me floundering around in the bush.

I disabled Hep's bell by slipping a hole in the end of the leather neck collar over the metal clapper, placed a halter over his head, and untied the hobbles of all three horses. I led the reluctant trio back to the cabin. Two hours later, I had the horses packed and standing at the hitching rail; Hep with his riding saddle on, and Ernie and Help with their packs tightly secured with the diamond hitch. We were all in a spirited mood. The rain had stopped and the sun was edging out behind a few clouds. Our bellies were full with oats, the horses with the raw variety and me with the cooked. And the cabin was cleaned and locked. The four of us were chomping at the bit, ready to go.

I untied the horses, slid my .270 Winchester into the rifle scabbard on the left side of the saddle, and tied my trail axe on the right side. I put one foot in the stirrup, one leg over the cantle, and settled my weight onto Hep's strong back. My daily morning routine on a travelling day was complete. It was another day in paradise as we headed to Topaz warden cabin.

Nine kilometres past Blue Creek we came over a rise on the trail, leaving the heavily timbered forest behind. The upper Blue Creek Valley had captured my imagination for several years and finally it was before me. As the horses rested, I scanned the vista ahead. The upper valley stretched out for 29 kilometres, the valley floor dominated by open shrub and grass meadows and fringed by pine and spruce trees that carry up to the mid slopes of the mountains on each side. Looking up towards the end of the valley far beyond, I could see the terrain rising upwards as it slowly changed from the habitat along the valley floor to subalpine meadows, and then to high barren alpine slopes at Hardscrabble Pass. A ridge extending out from the mountains on the west side blocked my view of the summit of the pass. Rock ledges lead over Hardscrabble Pass into the Willmore Wilderness, a route that only a few horse parties and a handful of backpackers travel each year.

The Ancient Wall, a magnificent saw-toothed escarpment of steep limestone slabs, rises up along the northeast side of the valley floor. Extensive slopes of nutrient rich grasses and wild-flowers carpet the lower elevated terrain at the base of this great walled mountain range. These slopes provide excellent sheep and goat habitat and are home to large herds of both species. Small herds of woodland caribou, drastically reduced in numbers from previous decades, are occasionally seen lower in the valley.

The horses and I continued on, crossed Blue Creek and entered the upper Blue Creek Valley. We reached Topaz warden cabin two hours later. I unpacked and arranged the horse gear and my personal belongings on the cabin porch. The horses had a cool down period before I gave them their treat of oats. I then placed hobbles on each horse, the bell on one, and set them loose.

As the horses munched on grasses close to the cabin, I took my binoculars out of one of the saddle bags and scanned The Ancient Wall rising up from the valley floor above the back of the cabin. I spotted a herd of 19 goats and a herd of 12 sheep grazing a few hundred metres apart on the mid-elevation alpine slopes at the base of the rock precipices. Looking further up the valley towards the alpine slopes below Hardscrabble Pass, I could make out a few more groups of sheep and goats.

◆ ◆ ◆

Years later, Mac Elder explained to me the significance of The Ancient Wall. Mac's story begins with the discovery of crude oil in Alberta. Alberta's economy was transformed when Leduc No. 1 struck black gold on February 13, 1947. Oil and gas soon supplanted farming as the primary industry and the province became one of the richest in the country. Mass immigration followed as billions of investment dollars flowed into Alberta; Edmonton and Calgary doubled their populations within a few years.

The discovery at Leduc No. 1 resulted in a rush of geologists looking to find other Devonian deposits in Alberta. Oil companies sent their geologists to study the exposed Devonian age limestone in the Rockies. They found that the formation and thickness of the Devonian limestone thrust up during the creation of the mountains were similar to the deposit found underground in the newly discovered Alberta oil fields.

Mac Elder began leading crews of geologists into the distant backcountry areas of northern Jasper, into the Willmore Wilderness, and north to Grande Cache and areas beyond in the summer of 1947. He travelled south and east as far as the Clearwater River between Red Deer and the northern portion of Banff National Park. Mac usually had a second horse packer and a cook along with him, a few geologists, and between 20 and 30 horses, depending on the duration of the trip. Most survey trips lasted three to four months. Mac led many of his trips from Devona warden cabin; other outfitters and their guides took similar trips out of the Hinton area. It was a booming business for horse outfitters. There were no roads into these areas and helicopters were in their infancy.

The geologists dashed from one area to the next studying sediment layers, collected rocks and fossils to determine mineral content and origin, took pictures, and looked for abnormalities or certain structural formations in the rock sediments that might lead them to oil deposits. Mac often took the geologists out on horseback in the morning and returned with the horses to pick them up in the evening. Back at the camp area, he minded the horses, tended to camp chores, cut trails, and kept a watchful eye open for wildlife that commonly traversed the same mountain slopes as the geologists.

Mac made a few final trips with the geological survey crews in 1956. Mac had learned a lot in his ten years with the geologists. On one of his latter trips, he took aside the group he was guiding and said, "You know, I don't understand a great deal about the Jurassic, or Triassic, or Cambrian periods like you guys do...hell, I don't even have a good knowledge of the Devonian or Mississippian periods you fellas have been talking about and studying, but I have some advice for you. If you want to know what period of geological history you are looking at and where you might find your oil, just study the wildlife—you'll find the sheep on the Devonian formations and the goats on the Mississippian."

The Ancient Wall was one of the mountain ranges where Mac often observed both sheep and goats when guiding various horse parties along Blue Creek and over Hardscrabble Pass into the Willmore Wilderness. The Ancient Wall complex in Jasper consists of one of the most diverse and abundant above-ground deposits of fossilized ancient sea creatures from the Upper Devonian period in North America. Mac wasn't idle at the survey camps while the crews were roaming the hills: he seems to have discovered the bigger picture looking up from down below. At the very least, it gave him material to weave a good tale. Or was he actually right about the sheep and goats?

And what were the results of those comprehensive explorations carried out by the geologists in the 1940s and '50s? Jasper National Park is protected from oil and gas exploration and development. Geological research, however, has always been encouraged in the mountain national parks. The culmination of the many geologic events that resulted in the grandeur of the Rocky Mountains makes for fascinating study. The knowledge that we have gained from geological studies is interpreted to the visiting public through Parks Canada educational programs.

The effects of oil and gas exploration in Willmore Wilderness Park took a somewhat different turn. Oil and gas leases were awarded in the park and seismic roads were cut into the drainages. Outfitters, guides, hunters, trappers, and other outdoor enthusiasts in Hinton, Edson, and other communities nearby expressed concern that the wilderness would be lost if further resource exploration and subsequent extraction was allowed. They successfully lobbied the provincial government for legislation to protect the area, and in 1959, the Minister of Lands and Forests, Norman Willmore, was instrumental in passing legislation that protected the park and promoted the establishment of the wilderness area for recreational purposes. The park, initially created as the Athabasca Forest Reserve in 1910, was renamed Willmore Wilderness Park in 1965. By this time, pressure from the oil and gas sectors had subsided as no oil of any consequence had been discovered. Their leases expired and nature began to heal some of the scars left behind. There are no new roads and no public buildings in the Willmore and the park remains a designated provincial wilderness area.

◆ ◆ ◆

I stayed over at Topaz the next day and rode Help up the valley to Caribou Inn horse camp, leaving Hep and Ernie in the meadows near the cabin. Contrary to its name, there is no inn here—no pub with cold beer, no comfortable rooms for the night. Just like any other backcountry horse campsite, it is located in a pretty spot to make camp and put up a tent; there are no amenities other than a cold, clear running stream and ample grazing nearby. The campsite, at the base of the subalpine meadows that lead up to Hardscrabble Pass, would serve as the location for my boundary patrol camp in the autumn. Wardens had established tent camps at various locations in the upper Blue Creek Valley for decades. This allowed them to access Hardscrabble Pass and other passes and ridges along the boundary with Willmore Wilderness and to engage in the annual cat and mouse game with unscrupulous hunters looking to bag a trophy bighorn, caribou, or other animals inside the boundary of the park.

I scanned all the slopes, ridges, and terrain features in the area of Caribou Inn with my binoculars before Help and I headed back to Topaz. A most impressive sight in The Ancient Wall is a huge hollowed-out upfold called The Natural Arch. The arch opening, about the size of an average two-storey house, spans a steep gully and a creek that flows from the heights above. A small waterfall tumbles over an eight-metre drop below the opening and ends in a moss-lined pool below the span. On a ridge just to the right of the arch, I spotted a group of 11 mature ram sheep bedded down and chewing their cud. They had arranged themselves facing different directions to cover a 360° area—a strategy they use to keep a wary eye out for predators. These rams remain in a loose grouping together until joining up with the ewes, smaller rams, and lambs during the autumn rut.

After spending the night at Topaz, the horses and I travelled back to Blue Creek. I spent several days in the area erecting new trail signs, repairing small bridges and wood corduroy, exploring nearby drainages, and meeting and talking with the summer's first wave of backpackers. My orientation into a few of the more travelled areas of both Blue Creek and Willow Creek districts was coming to a close. It then took a few days to ride to Seldom Inn warden cabin where I left the horses behind to graze in the pasture. From there, I drove down Celestine Lake Road and into town for four days off before gearing up for another 17-day backcountry trip.

CHAPTER ELEVEN

In the Company of Wolves

I drove back to Seldom Inn on July 8 and found my horses waiting at the hitching rail. Rick Ralf had jingled the horses for me. Rick had ridden from Willow Creek the day before to spend some time with three members of the CWS Biophysical Inventory team (the project I had worked on in 1976 and 1977). The team was winding down its work in the park. I caught up with the progress it had made the past two seasons, then packed for Willow Creek. I rode to Blue Creek the next day, meeting several hiking groups along the way. The summer backpacking season was in full swing.

I spent most of the summer travelling between cabins, working out of each one for a few days before moving on to the next. My chainsaw was always top-packed on one of the pack horses and my axe was at hand, tucked under one side of my riding saddle. There was always trail work to attend to: clearing trees, replacing corduroy, building and repairing bridges, and constructing new hitching rails at horse camps and bear poles at horse and hiker camps. I also tended to ongoing maintenance around the cabins and to the daily care of the horses. The horse tack required constant care, and repairs. I honed my horseshoeing skills as the rough and rocky terrain loosened many a shoe. I checked the horses' shoes every day, tightening loose ones by clinching the shoe nails against the hoof wall. The horses slipped a shoe now and again, requiring me to shape and nail a new one in place. Amazingly, all of the shoes I re-shod held until Denny was able to replace them. Lawrence, Rick, and I met Denny at Seldom Inn warden cabin every six weeks to have the horses re-shod.

I always took pleasure assisting and chatting with the backpackers I encountered on the trails or at one of my cabins. Most were hiking the entire length of the North Boundary trail from either Seldom Inn or Rock Lake to Mount Robson, a distance of 173 kilometres. A few ventured off onto more remote trails. Packing enough food for trips longer than a week is always a fine balance for hikers as they need abundant calories to sustain them for long strenuous days but must keep their packs to a reasonable weight. Dry food such as oats or pasta or freeze-dried food is essential.

Wardens working the backcountry districts have the luxury of packing almost any food that they normally eat. The horses can comfortably carry 30 to 40 kilograms of supplies in each of their two pack boxes. Fresh food can be kept for weeks in the cabins that have small root cellars. For cabins without cellars, food (especially meat) can be wrapped and buried in a barrel of oats. One or two old 45-gallon oil drums are kept at warden cabins to store oats for the horses. Fresh meat can last a week or more during the summer months and much longer during the autumn in these barrels.

Ageing meat can be preserved a few days longer by immersing it in a pot of water, vinegar, and salt. By far the best roast I ever ate had been aged this way before I cooked it with vegetables in the wood stove at Blue Creek. The meat was unbelievably tender and tasty. I gorged myself, and then wondered how to keep the leftovers as I was planning to travel to another cabin the next day. Not five minutes later there was a knock on the cabin door.

A group of three boy scouts and their leader, tenting at Blue Creek campsite, stood on the porch and muttered something about food. They must have smelled my roast from the campsite, a kilometre away. They tried their damnedest to look like they hadn't eaten in a week, until one of the scouts opened his mouth and said it was their third day on the trail and they still had plenty of food left. With the looks the other two scouts gave him, I thought for sure this party would be going back to civilization with one less scout and a tribunal on its hands.

I thought it best to invite them in. These were growing boys and no amount of freeze-dried food was going to sustain them for long. Wardens have never had a policy of supplying food to back-country travellers other than perhaps a biscuit or two over a cup of coffee or tea, but some of this delicious roast was doomed for waste unless I shared it, which I did. The scouts had a better back-country treat than they could ever have imagined. Apparently, a few more scouts were back at the campsite, so I wrapped up the rest of the roast and vegetables for them. I trust the food got as far as the camp.

With all the backpackers that passed through the area over the summer, I was somewhat surprised that there were no major safety or first aid issues that year. Usually, a fair number of hikers come unprepared in one way or another. Common mistakes are a lack of food, improper clothing, or a forgotten piece of necessary equipment such as fuel for a mini camp stove or the stove itself.

◆ ◆ ◆

I had learned a great deal from my horses by the end of the summer of 1980. It didn't take long for them to figure me out; but it took a little more time for me to figure them out. With dispositions as different as every human's personality, they constantly kept me engaged with their antics.

Every year or two, district wardens fell dead trees to provide fuel for the wood stoves and heaters in the cabins. Most main cabins in each district have a skid harness to enable a large horse to skid the limbed trees. Ernie, with his Belgian blood, was the designated skidding horse on the North Boundary. I was eager to learn the skidding process. Lawrence had skidded wood using horses a few years previously and he met up with me at Blue Creek later in the summer to bring in wood. We felled several trees along the trail behind the cabin and cut them into lengths that Ernie could pull. We then brought out all the necessary rigging from the tack shed, dusted it off, and sorted it out. Ernie had been trained by Denny Welsh to skid wood and we rigged him up without a problem.

Ernie had a lot of character, and when in the right mood could be spirited and mischievous, always in a manner that made me shake my head and laugh. I led Ernie out behind the cabin, hooked up a log with the skid chain, and brought him into the yard where the other horses were resting and watching what was to become a show. As we approached the wood shed, Ernie lifted his head, glanced at the other horses, and took a few prancing steps. Before I knew it, the reins were ripped from my hands and Ernie was tearing around the yard in circles with the heavy log kicking up dirt and dust behind him. This got the other horses going, running in all directions, doing their best to avoid Ernie with his out of control log. A mule deer doe appeared from the edge of the forest, intrigued by the raucous performance. Ernie was thoroughly enjoying his show of power until he tried to circle around one of the hitching rails. He made it around the first post—but the log didn't. Shattered pieces of strong and sturdy hitching rail flew in all directions.

The show was over. Ernie came to an abrupt stop and the other horses settled down. The deer, startled by the collision of the log with the hitching rail, had retreated into the trees. After the dust settled, we calmed Ernie down. He had had his fun and was satisfied with his antics. We straightened out his rigging, got him going again, and had no trouble skidding a few more logs. We didn't have time to finish, however, as we had to construct a new hitching rail.

The following morning we travelled to Hoodoo, my westernmost district cabin. The next day Lawrence carried on from Hoodoo and headed off over Snake Indian Pass to meet up with Doug Eastcott in Smoky River District. I spent most of the day at Hoodoo felling trees and working with Ernie skidding the logs to the cabin. The job proceeded without a hitch. Ernie knew what was expected of him and worked exceptionally well. The show back at Blue Creek had been just that; now he was prepared to do some serious work. In fact, Ernie took tremendous pride in skidding; I was taken by how he took to the job with very little guidance from me. Denny Welsh had trained him well.

A few days later I was back at Blue Creek where Ernie and I finished skidding the wood required for the remainder of the year and into the next season. Several days afterwards I met Rick Ralf at Welbourne warden cabin, and with Ernie we brought in a few years' supply of firewood.

Other than their occasional bouts of stubbornness or amusing antics, I appreciated the horses' unwavering willingness to carry riders or pack loads over rough terrain and long distances and through whatever weather nature threw at us. The horses also impressed me with their brute strength. They constantly reminded me that the best way to handle them through a bout of stubbornness was with my head and heart, and not with my strength. The horses did so much and asked for so little: fair treatment, kindness and compassion, ample rest, good grazing meadows, and two treats of oats per day.

◆ ◆ ◆

One of my highlight trips over the course of the summer was with Smoky River District Warden Doug Eastcott. I rode from Blue Creek to Hoodoo in early August, stayed overnight, and met Doug at Snake Indian Pass the next day. Doug had made the long journey from Mount Robson over several days, staying in a few of his patrol cabins along the way. We rode back to Hoodoo together from the pass. The next morning we packed our camping gear and left for a four-day trip into the remote headwaters of the Snaring River and the southern fork of the Snake Indian River, a seldom-travelled route. Our main focus during the trip was to assess the presence of caribou in the area. In recent years, very few caribou had been observed in the park's northern reaches. Because their numbers had declined over several decades, we wanted to determine if there were any small herds in the upper Snaring River watershed.

The first three days of our trip involved rough slogging through dense growth on lower elevation slopes and pleasant riding over three high alpine passes. The last day took us down the southern fork of the Snake Indian River, around the south and east shoulders of Mount Simla, and back to Blue Creek warden cabin. We spent many hours travelling through vast open alpine meadows where we expected to see small herds of caribou during these warmer months. We saw only one lone female and very little sign of others, indicating their numbers may have dropped in this area as well.

We did, however, have a wildlife encounter that made up for the dismal lack of caribou sightings. We camped close to Idalene Lakes (three small subalpine lakes) our first and second nights. On the second day we left the horses to graze and hiked up to Comoy Pass. We were walking along the rolling alpine tundra when a very light coloured wolf appeared from over a low hummock approximately 150 metres away. The wolf was heading straight towards us but had its nose to the ground so failed to see us. We crouched to the ground, concealing ourselves behind a small hummock a metre higher than the surrounding terrain. If we had remained standing, we knew it would have bolted to avoid a close encounter. A lower profile would be less threatening to the wolf while also giving us the opportunity to observe it.

We remained still for over a minute. The wolf didn't appear and we thought it may have deviated from its path. We waited several more seconds, then slowly rose and peered over the hummock. Just as we were rising up off our knees, the wolf came into full view not more than 20 metres in front of us. We froze. The wolf stopped dead in its tracks, clearly alarmed and bewildered. It stared at us for several seconds, taking a read to establish whether or not we were a threat. Remaining otherwise motionless, it moved its head upward, straining to get our scent. Then abruptly it took a few quick strides several metres to our right, stopped, looked at us again, and then glanced to the rear. Bounding along not far behind, four bundles of playful energy materialized. The wolf was a female with four small pups in tow.

When the pups saw us, their reaction was completely different from their mother's. They were tremendously curious, yet cautious. The female moved off to our right side in an attempt to direct the pups away. The pups, still curious about the two-legged animals they had never seen before, bounded towards us, stopping almost at our feet. The female became extremely agitated and began pacing back and forth. She gave a warning bark and then a few short howls. The pups responded immediately. But instead of joining their mother, they trod up onto a small ridge, about 50 metres from her. They stood there, whined, and then gave their best youthful imitations of the haunting howl their species is noted for. Their mother barked a few more times and howled back at the pups. They remained where they were while she took a few more minutes to survey the area and scrutinize us. Her decision made, she loped over to the pups and led them back in the direction from which they had come. We watched the family until they were slowly lost from view in the rolling alpine tundra two kilometres away.

We wondered why the female was so far away from her pack. The pups, at approximately three months old, would normally be closer to their den site and to other members of their extended family. I also wondered about her creamy-white coat, a rarity in wolves, excepting the all-white arctic wolves of the far north. All four pups were developing multi-coloured coats, the striking combination of white, grey, black, and light umber tones common to wolves in the Rocky Mountains. Many other wolves in the Rockies have black or near black coats.

I had a few other encounters with lone wolves that year while on foot or with the horses. With each encounter, the wolf invariably stopped, stared curiously for a few seconds, and then was gone as quickly as it had appeared. I frequently heard wolves howling in several locations throughout the district and often saw their tracks on the trails. On a few occasions I came across their fresh tracks when jingling the horses in the early morning.

My next encounter was the most thrilling of the year. Later in the autumn, when Julia joined me for a few weeks, we left the horses at Blue Creek and hiked up the trail to McClarens Pass. Halfway up the trail we heard a movement in the trees and turned our heads just in time to catch a glimpse of a deer's rear end moving quickly away in the dense undergrowth. Moments later, as we ascended a steeper section of the trail, a large wolf suddenly appeared, rounding a bend in the trail at a run. It almost slammed into us with the momentum it had coming downslope. If we had been quick enough, we could have reached out and touched the wolf, but before we could catch our breaths it was gone, seeming to vanish into the forest. Julia and I stood for a minute, exhilarated by this amazing encounter.

Unbelievably, only seconds later, a smaller wolf came barrelling down the same trail. When it saw us, it too swerved into the forest at the last second. Like its companion, it was gone as quickly as it had appeared.

We continued on to McClarens Pass, observing just one caribou and a single nanny goat and her kid on the slopes nearby. There were no fresh animal tracks at the lick Lawrence and I had checked two months previously. After lunch, we began our journey down, and I kept thinking of our incredible encounter with the two wolves.

A few hundred metres from where we had run into the wolves and sighted the deer, we came across a large piece of liver lying beside the trail. It was fresh, the blood still moist. The wolves had had a successful hunt that day.

After examining the liver, we continued down the trail. There was no need to look for a carcass and disturb the wolves any further than we might have already. I was left wondering what chain of events had led to one of the wolves abandoning the flesh. Why near the trail? Did the wolf drop the meat when it sensed us coming, and why? Why was it carrying the flesh away from the carcass? We had seen two wolves on the way up to the pass—were there more? And how did the events of the wolves' successful hunt unfold? Many questions, yes, but I didn't need to know the answers. Understanding how the drama—the struggle and the conquest—unfolds can diminish the mystery.

Being in the company of wolves and having the opportunities to observe this mystical, mysterious, and magnificent icon of the northern wilderness, so besieged by myths and false legends over millenniums, always filled me with intense wonderment—but never fear.

CHAPTER TWELVE

Caribou In Crisis

For the backcountry wardens, bighorn sheep hunting season marks the first unofficial day of autumn, usually the last week in August. Hunting season for most other species opens around the middle of September. In 1980, the autumn hunting season in Willmore Wilderness was open to sheep, mountain goat, woodland caribou, deer, elk, moose, wolverine, wolf, coyote, and black bear.

Many hunters travelled with guided horse parties. Most of the licensed outfitters and their guides were well known to us as they had been in the business for many years. A few of them took outdoor enthusiasts for trips in both Jasper and Willmore Wilderness in the summer and switched to guiding hunters in Willmore and other areas in the province during the autumn hunting season.

Rick Ralf, Lawrence Baraniuk, Doug Eastcott, and I kept an eye on hunting activity in our respective districts from the last week in August to the end of October. Several wardens stationed in the frontcountry for the summer came in for 10-day stints to help with the hunting season patrols. We usually worked alone, each of us stationed at one of our patrol cabins along the boundary, separated by a mountain range or two. We set up tent camps at various sites along the boundary within Willow Creek and Blue Creek districts. These camps allowed us to patrol boundary areas that were otherwise too far away to adequately patrol on a daytrip from one of our cabins. Moving the tent camps from one location to another kept potential poachers guessing as to where we were located. The other wardens and I were in daily contact with each other via the SSB radio. We punctuated our lone vigils along the boundaries by pairing up on occasional overnight trips into Willmore Wilderness Park for more direct contact with hunting parties.

All wardens had Alberta Game Guardian Appointments that granted limited law enforcement authority under the Alberta Wildlife Act on provincial land outside the boundaries of Jasper. We could investigate hunting infractions, check for hunting licenses, and enforce some of the regulations under the Act. But we were not authorized to search, seize, or arrest a hunter committing an offence outside the park as this was under the jurisdiction of the Alberta Wildlife Act.

These appointments enabled us to be the eyes and ears for Alberta Fish and Wildlife officers, as their ranks were stretched too thinly to adequately patrol all backcountry areas on a weekly basis.

Those who hunted illegally had no qualms about poaching an animal inside the park or hunting outside it without a license or animal tag. Most hunters respected the wilderness and took issue with those who didn't. Apart from our own patrols, law-abiding hunters were a major deterrent to poachers, serving as the "neighbourhood watch" of the wilderness. Many hunting camps were situated very close to Jasper's northern, eastern, and southern boundaries. Hunters in those camps closely observed one another's activities and reported suspect activity.

◆ ◆ ◆

According to the hunters we encountered in 1980 with legal kills, bighorn sheep were the most sought after big game species in Willmore Wilderness Park. Relative to their population, a very large number of caribou were hunted in the wild areas not far from Jasper's northern boundary. Ten caribou were taken out of the province within Willmore Wilderness, seven of them shot within a 15-kilometre radius of the Jasper-Willmore boundary. Two of these were taken just outside the boundary line. We wondered how many caribou were left.

I was shocked to learn that woodland caribou hunts were still allowed. Very few caribou had been observed in the northern reaches of Jasper over the last few decades. Woodland caribou populations had been on a downward spiral throughout Alberta.

For centuries, most of Jasper's population of caribou along the northern boundary has migrated out of the park in winter.

They travel over the high passes into Willmore and beyond to areas north and west of Grande Cache in Alberta and into British Columbia. Their main source of winter-feed is terrestrial lichens in old growth forests.

Wardens stationed in Jasper's North Boundary districts in the 1920s estimated that 200 to 300 caribou roamed the area. Mac Elder reported the North Boundary population in the late 1940s and early '50s at between 150 to 200 animals. Mac remembers Bob Jones (Blue Creek Warden from 1937 to 1949) reporting large herds of caribou. Bob told Mac that he once followed a wide swath of caribou tracks leaving Jasper early one winter for the old growth forest farther north. The compacted caribou tracks were so numerous that he could easily walk on top of the deep snow without snowshoes. By 1980, park wardens estimated that only 50 caribou inhabited the northern regions of Jasper.

Caribou population trends throughout the rest of Jasper roughly paralleled those of the northern regions of the park. Data compiled from wardens and a study by CWS Biologist John Stelfox estimated between 800 to 875 caribou resided in Jasper over the summer months from 1915 to 1940. Stelfox's data and Warden Service reports indicated caribou numbers had dropped to 435 by 1974. By 1980, the Warden Service estimated there were only 150 to 200 caribou left in Jasper.

I saw only 10 caribou in the six months I patrolled extensive areas of Jasper's northern wilderness in 1980. Five of the sightings were of a single animal only; one sighting was of a female and calf at Snake Indian Pass. My last sighting was of three caribou near Hardscrabble Pass during the provincial hunting season. Although my incidental observations of these caribou were not by any stretch a population estimate, they clearly suggested an enormous decline in woodland caribou in Jasper compared to the observations recorded in wardens' journals decades earlier.

Woodland caribou in Jasper National Park have declined further since the estimate of 150 to 200 in 1980. The last caribou survey results from the three southern herds in the Tonquin, Maligne, and Brazeau areas in 2014 gave maximum estimates of 38, 5, and 8 caribou respectively. The population of Jasper's northern area is unknown but expected to be fewer than 50 animals. Some of these caribou still migrate beyond the park boundary into the province during the winter months. This would place the 2014 population of woodland caribou that spend at least part of the year in Jasper at no more than 101 animals.

The southern three herds of caribou in Jasper do not face the same pressures from industrial development as the northern herds do on their winter range outside the park. However, the snow plowing of secondary travel roads in Jasper has created a predicament for the southern herds. With their long legs and snowshoe shaped hooves, caribou are well adapted to life in deep snow, giving them a distinct advantage over their predators. Wolves have difficulty travelling in deep high elevation snowpacks and usually avoid these areas. Roads cleared for cross-country skiers and snowshoers, who then hard-pack trails into higher elevations, give wolves easier access into areas that would otherwise be inaccessible to them. Park managers have instituted winter seasonal trail closures in some of these areas to keep wolves away from critical caribou winter habitat and lessen disturbance from backcountry enthusiasts.

Vehicle collisions on the main highway corridors present another hazard. Collisions on the Icefields Parkway were responsible for 13 caribou mortalities from the Brazeau herd in a 15-year period from the late 1980s to 2003. There have not been any caribou deaths along the Icefields Parkway since 2003. Reduced speed limits and visitor awareness of vehicle–caribou collision zones along highway corridors frequented by caribou have been in place for over a decade.

Two factors that threaten the survivability of woodland caribou in the mountain national parks cannot be controlled. Permanent snow patches have been retreating since the last ice age. Woodland caribou in the mountains venture onto alpine snow patches between times of foraging during the warmer days of summer to avoid biting insects and to thermoregulate body temperature. As these snow patches slowly recede from the landscape, it is unclear how important they are to caribou. The second factor is the rising treeline in the Rocky Mountains. The treeline on many of Jasper's subalpine slopes has extended 30 to 50 vertical metres in the last 25 years. The mountains are slowly losing their alpine areas—important summer feeding grounds for caribou and a multitude of other animals.

Climate change is altering the face of the mountains. Some believe this is simply an evolutionary state and woodland caribou may be on their way out, making efforts to save this species fruitless. Other wildlife experts are more hopeful. Either way, there is no doubt climate change is altering our forest and mountain ecosystems.

Jasper is not the only mountain park to experience a decline in caribou numbers. In Banff National Park, an estimated 25 to 45 caribou in the 1970s to '80s dropped to less than 10 caribou by the mid-90s. These caribou frequented the upper Siffleur River, Pipestone Pass, and Clearwater Pass areas in Banff's northern reaches. Only five caribou remained in the Banff herd in 2009. Tragically, they were all killed in an avalanche.

The demise of the caribou herd in Banff remains more of a puzzle than the decreasing numbers in Jasper's herds. The Banff herd was not threatened by industrial development as it ranged in the park or in the Siffleur Wilderness near Banff's northeastern boundary. Some of the same natural factors that have affected Jasper's herds likely accounted for the extirpation of the herd in Banff.

Two herds of woodland caribou with a portion of their range in Mount Revelstoke and Glacier National parks in British Columbia have plummeted from approximately 100 animals in 1994 to fewer than 16 in 2012. These herds may soon be extirpated, as these parks are not large enough to protect caribou habitat from the increasing pressure of land use in the Columbia Mountains region. The Committee on the Status of Endangered Wildlife in Canada (COSEWIC) listed woodland caribou as an endangered species in the Central Rocky Mountains region in May of 2014.

Woodland caribou numbers in Alberta outside of the national parks have plummeted in recent years as well. The Alberta government did not abolish caribou hunting in the province until 1981. Declining caribou populations in the province (outside of the mountain national parks) were reported as far back as 1929. In 1937, an Alberta government report acknowledged declines in caribou in areas where logging companies operate. It wasn't until 1978, however, that provincial biologists, in conjunction with various conservation groups, began to establish a caribou management plan for Alberta. Other than ending the caribou hunt, recommendations from these groups to protect and restore caribou numbers by managing industrial development were ignored. Now, close to 35 years later, after numerous reports, consultations, plans and promises, little has been done to protect Alberta's caribou from further decline.

The chief cause of woodland caribou decline in Alberta is habitat loss and disturbance from logging, mining, and oil and gas development. The many roads, cut blocks, seismic cut lines, and pipelines from these resource extraction activities have opened up vast areas of recreational land where caribou are harassed by all-terrain vehicles and snowmobiles. Many caribou have met their fate on highways in vehicle collisions. Legal killing of caribou (before the hunt was suspended in 1981) has taken its toll on populations already under duress from industrial development.

Although caribou have coexisted with wolves for many thousands of years, wolves have been criticized for preying on caribou outside the park. Just as plowed roads and packed ski and snowshoe trails in Jasper have allowed wolf packs to travel farther and wider than before, the vast network of snow-packed and cleared open roads, cut lines, and trails used in the province allows wolves greater access to caribou wintering grounds.

Alberta only adopted a plan for woodland caribou recovery in 2005. Shockingly, the control of wolf populations has been the focus of caribou recovery. Little or nothing has been accomplished in the way of habitat protection and restoration, and industrial development continues without sustainable land-use guidelines. The Alberta government slaughtered 841 wolves north of Jasper National Park between 2005 and 2012. A total of 579 were shot from the air, 108 were trapped, and 154 were poisoned by strychnine-laced bait—the same poison that has been used to kill thousands of wolves in Alberta and throughout North America for over 150 years. Strychnine is a barbaric poison that progresses painfully from muscle spasms to convulsions to suffocation over a period of hours. It is especially lethal as it kills any animal feeding on poisoned bait or baited carcasses. During the seven-year Alberta government wolf control program, 36 coyotes, 31 foxes, 6 lynx, 8 marten, 4 weasels, 4 fishers, and 91 ravens were reported to have suffered a cruel death from strychnine-laced bait. Many more animal deaths were certain to have gone undetected, and therefore unreported.

Researchers have determined that the wolf control program has had little to no effect in stabilizing the threatened caribou herds, yet the Alberta government has continued the slaughter, killing about 100 wolves each year since 2012. Wolves are being used as a scapegoat while the complex ecology of vast ecosystems is ignored. Killing wolves is an attempt to take the focus away from the real problem: continued habitat destruction by unbridled industrial development in critical caribou wintering grounds.

CHAPTER THIRTEEN

Moose Madness

Julia joined me for my final trip of the 1980 season in October, a 24-day trek along the entire North Boundary. Denny Welsh paired her up with Indian, a pinto coloured, Thoroughbred/Quarter Horse gelding. Julia and I spent the last week of boundary patrol in the upper reaches of the Blue Creek Valley. A gathering snowstorm that signalled the end of hunting season throughout higher elevations followed us down from Hardscrabble Pass.

We travelled down valley to Blue Creek for a few days before heading west towards Mount Robson for the remainder of our trip, taking the same route Pat Paul and I had backpacked seven years earlier. We cleaned and closed down all the cabins in the Smoky River District as we passed through. During our last two days, we stayed at Adolphus warden cabin, not far from the towering north face of Mount Robson. We had made a number of memorable wildlife sightings over the two weeks since leaving Blue Creek, but our last day in the wilds with our horses was especially eventful.

Shortly after dinner on our first night at Adolphus, a massive bull and two cow moose walked past the cabin window facing the hitching rails and the salt block we had put out for the horses. Either the moose had seen us arrive earlier in the day or they had been alerted by the horse bell. They knew from experience that a salt block would magically appear with the arrival of horses. The two cow moose licked the block for a few minutes while the bull stood nearby at the edge of the woods, uttering short, deep throated grunts; it was the end of October, the middle of the moose rut season. The cows, which are usually more vocal than the bulls during the rut, ignored the bull and were silent as they savoured the salt. The horses were off grazing up valley out of sight.

The next morning we watched the three moose wander about on a thick willow-vegetated slope across the valley from the cabin. We could hear the bull bellow from time to time and the cows' longer, deep nasal, bovine-like calls. When I checked the horses shortly before dark, I found them in a meadow below the slope where the moose had been in the morning. Big Ernie was standing still and stiff legged, focusing his attention on the slope. The other horses were grazing not far away. I couldn't make out the moose in the dim light of dusk but I heard the bull grunt a few times. This really captured Ernie's curiosity. He took a few comical hops towards the slope, holding his head high, as if wanting to challenge the bull. Just as quickly, he turned tail and hopped back to his original position. He repeated the scenario a couple of times, unsure whether to be fearful or bold.

Although Ernie likely outweighed the bull by a couple hundred kilograms, I wouldn't have wanted to witness the bull challenge him. Rival bull moose sometimes have fierce fights during the rut, and this bull had a huge set of antlers. Ernie only had his wits, and they seemed to be somewhat frazzled by the show of authority the bull was displaying up on the hill. The interesting situation with the bull was that he was courting two cows. Bull moose are polygamous, but usually remain with only one cow at a time. I led Ernie away from his fixed gaze on the slopes and took him over to the other horses. I told to him to behave and then found my way back to the cabin in the dark.

We were awakened in the wee hours of the night by the bull moose grunting behind the cabin. I looked up from the bed and saw one of the cows, silhouetted by the moon, pass by the window. I rolled over, hoping Ernie and the rest of the ponies were not on the bull's mind.

Morning dawned with a heavy late October frost. It was a clear, cool day. The north face of Mount Robson was still dark against a backdrop of light blue sky at sunrise when I went to jingle the horses. This was our last day in the backcountry for the year and I took my time searching for them. The air was crisp and the valley was quiet except for a family of mountain chickadees bringing in the morning with song. I found the horses close to where I had left them. There was no sign of the moose.

Back at the cabin I gave the horses their oats, brushed their coats, saddled them, and put the salt block away in the tack shed. I left Hep and Indian, our riding horses for the day, at one hitching rail, and Ernie and Help at the other. We ate our breakfast, cleaned up, and packed our gear one last time into the pack boxes and duffle bags. The last two chores in our routine were mopping the floor and closing the shutters. We always left the door unlocked until we were ready to leave.

I packed Help and then moved over to the left side of the rail to pack Ernie. I finished the diamond hitch, checked all the loops, twists and knots, then lowered my head to check the saddle cinches. Julia was standing next to me holding Ernie's halter shank. Help suddenly shuffled his feet and jerked his head up. His eyes and ears were riveted towards the woods on our left. Then Ernie lurched forward and turned his attention to the same spot. Without warning, the three moose came charging out of the trees and into the yard. Ernie panicked and crashed into Help's right side, pulling the halter shank from Julia's hand in the process. One of his back hooves came down twice on my right foot. Despite the steel-toed rubber boots that I was still wearing (I routinely switch to my dry riding boots just before leaving the cabin), I felt the impact of Ernie's hoof crash down on my toes.

I grabbed Ernie's halter shank off the ground and hung on tight. The moose bellowed and snorted as they darted back and forth around the yard between the two hitching rails, the cabin and the tack shed. Hep and Indian, still tied to the other hitching rail, were frantic. They made attempts to break away from the rail but could not loosen the knots I had tied with their halter shanks. Ernie pulled me around in tight circles at our rail as he followed the movements of the moose while Julia tried to calm Help down. The bull then crossed the yard and made a pass close to us. Ernie made a quick lunge toward the bull, inadvertently slamming me against one of the hitching rail posts in the process. I was sure my big horse wanted to take him on. The bull circled around us before joining the cows at the edge of the woods across the other side of the yard, only 20 metres away from Hep and Indian at the other rail.

Help, Hep, and Indian settled down somewhat but remained tense and uneasy, their attention fully focused on the three moose. Ernie remained agitated, puffing and snorting, still pulling my arm back and forth while I hung on to the halter shank. It seemed that he was trying to decide whether he should duel with the big bull or stay his ground. After a minute, he calmed down somewhat and the moose ceased their ranting behaviour. All three stood at the woods' edge, faces forward, glaring at us. Julia and I looked at each other dumbfounded, and a little shocked. I said something like, "What the hell was that all about?"

Then we both commented that we should make as quick an exit as we could. I told Julia to stay beside Ernie and Help while I switched boots. I hurried over to the cabin, changed from the rubber boots (my right foot was red and sore from being stomped on by Ernie, but no broken bones) to my riding boots and locked up. I grabbed the various items that go into our saddlebags off the porch and my rifle—the last things we pack—and headed over towards Hep and Indian. The moose remained standing in the trees near them.

My approach set the moose off on another crazy rant. Once again this unnerved the horses, resulting in the same frightened reactions as before. They bounced around like giant pinballs, held by their short halter leads at the hitching rails as they constantly shifted their body positions to follow the frenzied movements of the moose. In the midst of the foray, we made a final quick check of the saddles and cinches, untied the horses, and made haste. As we rode out into the meadow away from the cabin, I looked back. The cows were pacing back and forth between the tack shed and the hitching rails, and the bull, not far from them, was violently tearing the bark off a young spruce sapling with his antlers.

I have no idea what precipitated the strange display from the moose. Obviously the rutting hormones coursing through the bull's body and the cows being in estrous had a lot to do with their behaviour. But what accounts for the crazed exhibition at the cabin? The cows were certainly interested in the salt block that I had put away earlier. Perhaps the bull was trying to lead the cows away from the yard and maybe even from big Ernie, if he thought the big horse might have been a challenger for *his* cows.

Other than a sow grizzly with cubs, moose can be the most dangerous animal in the Rocky Mountains. Approaching or running into a cow moose with a young calf, or a bull moose in rut, can be very dangerous. I feared for our and the horses' safety throughout that bizarre incident.

We left the valley to the moose, rode out past Berg Lake, down through the Valley of a Thousand Falls around the base of towering Mount Robson, and out to the Mount Robson Visitor Centre on the Yellowhead Highway. Lawrence had a stock truck waiting for us at the backcountry staging area near the visitor centre. As we drove to Jasper I was already missing the backcountry. I also lamented the loss of the horses for the season—they had become my tried and true companions.

CHAPTER FOURTEEN

Bear Management by Bullet

Since the arrival of European settlers in Canada, human disregard toward bears has often resulted in tragic outcomes for the bears. The records of the number of bears killed from the inception of Jasper National Park in 1907 up until the 1950s are incomplete. Hundreds were put down, mostly due to the predator control programs that ended in 1954, but also as a result of problems the bears ended up getting into due to their reliance on human food.

By the late 1950s, national park officials had made some headway in their efforts to deal with bear-human conflicts. An amendment to the National Parks Game Regulations made the touching, feeding, or enticing of bears illegal. Education and awareness programs began to get the message across to visitors that feeding bears along roadsides and in campgrounds was dangerous; many people had suffered claw and bite injuries from bears attempting to reach or grab proffered food. Visitors became aware of the negative consequences of these practices for the bears. In addition to their obvious conditioning to human food and the problems associated with it, an increasing number of bears suffered serious wounds or death from collisions with vehicles along park roadways.

In the 1950s, the use of trailer-mounted culvert bear traps for capturing "problem bears" became a management tool at the disposal of park wardens. A bait of meat or fish was set on a treadle at the closed end of the trap to attract a bear. When a bear walked into the trap and stepped on the treadle, the door at the front of the trap slammed shut. The bear was then transported elsewhere in the park and released. This was usually a short-term solution as most bears, having a home range as most animals do, would return within a few days. On many occasions, released food-conditioned bears discovered other easily accessible, unnatural food sources on their way home. This food source was often found in park campgrounds, outlying bungalow camps, or garbage dumpsites. Essentially the problem bear was shifted from one area to another. Every bear that failed a couple of trapping/relocation attempts ended up looking down the barrel of a warden's rifle.

By the mid-1960s, the feeding of bears was drastically curtailed. However, bear/garbage management problems continued. In Jasper National Park, the inadequate storage of household garbage in town alleys and the lack of bear-proof garbage containers at campgrounds and picnic sites remained unresolved issues. Moreover, the partial incineration of garbage in dumps could not keep up with the onslaught of waste from the increasing number of tourists. Park wardens in Jasper were still killing a dozen or more garbage-conditioned black bears annually.

The bear/garbage problems came to a head in Jasper in August 1965 after a serious grizzly mauling at Maligne Lake. A sow grizzly with four young cubs attacked a Brewster's Lodge staff member returning from a hike in the late evening near the garbage dumpsite used by the lodge. The sow seriously mauled the young man. His female friend, who was not attacked by the bear, ran back to the lodge to get help. Park Warden Mac Elder, who was at his warden station across the bay from the lodge, was summoned.

Mac rushed to the scene with Stan Kitchen, a horse outfitter working for Brewster's Lodge. When they arrived at the dump it had begun to rain and darkness had fallen. There was no sign of the injured man or the bears. After checking the perimeter of the dump with the vehicle headlights and a flashlight, they finally located the injured man's motionless form in some bushes. Fortunately, the sow grizzly and her cubs had left the area.

The man had multiple injuries and had lost a lot of blood. He was taken to Seton General Hospital where his condition was stabilized by Jasper's local surgeon Dr. George Betkowski (renowned for his trauma skills and surgical expertise) and his medical staff. He was later transferred to Edmonton for long-term care. Mac recalled, "The bear got a hold of the young chap pretty bad...tore up his scalp, broke his cheekbone, took out one eye, chewed up a hand, and bit and tore deep gashes in one thigh. I've seen people that were dead from accidents in the park—unrelated to bears—that sustained far fewer injuries than he had. I visited him in the hospital in Edmonton...he was in recovery for about a year after that. He was a good lad; no one deserved the mess he got into."

The man's family sued Parks Canada. The government won the case, but paid for medical expenses, court proceedings, and other costs related to the man's injuries in an agreement that the case not be appealed. The man later credited Mac and Stan for saving his life. To this day, Mac believes it was a miracle they found the victim before he succumbed to his wounds.

Along with other wardens and park staff, Mac was upset and frustrated that many of the bear/garbage management problems in the park were taking so long to resolve. The wardens understood, however, that a tremendous amount of government funding was required to build the infrastructure and purchase the equipment needed to deal with waste disposal at park dumpsites.

A committee was formed to deal with the issue and dozens of unfenced, open-pit dumpsites that had existed since the park's establishment were ordered closed. All the dumpsites scattered throughout the park were closed by 1970 and a centralized garbage dump—the Palisades Landfill—was opened near the Yellowhead Highway seven kilometres northeast of Jasper townsite.

A heavy-gauge chain link fence was built around the landfill to keep bears away from the food waste. A landfill operator buried the waste daily to reduce odours and monitored the gate into the site. His job responsibilities included keeping the black bears from entering the landfill via the open gate. Grizzlies generally kept well away from the dumpsites and human activity during daylight hours; at night the gate was closed and locked to keep out the grizzlies.

It didn't take long, however, before the grizzly bears found a way into the landfill each evening by simply tunnelling under the fence. Black bears then located the tunnels (or dug their own) to access garbage during the daylight hours. Once they made it into the landfill, it took little effort to excavate the buried garbage.

Keeping black bears away from the landfill gate during the day was one matter, but chasing them out of the landfill as they entered multiple tunnels under the fence on a continual basis was not an official part of the landfill operator's job—nor was it safe. Attempting to chase grizzlies out of the landfill at night would be problematic—inviting certain death. Parks Canada had to come up with a better solution to keep the ever-resourceful bears from breaching the fence.

In September of 1973, park managers obtained funding to provide an additional barrier to prevent bears from tunnelling underneath the Palisades Landfill. It just so happened that I was employed at the time (five years before being hired by the Warden Service) by a construction company that had received the contract to install the barriers. I worked on a four-man crew building large concrete pads around the outside perimeter of the landfill fence. The concrete pads extended two metres out from the fence and were attached to the lower links by a series of metal hooks and strong steel cables. On the first day of the job, when I looked at what work had to be done with the materials at hand, I expressed my concern to the other members of the crew and our foreman that the bears would find a way to move the concrete pads, or simply dig under the pads in the same way they dug under the fence—with strong muscles, big paws, and long claws. This wasn't rocket science. They replied that I was only 19 years old and had never worked in the construction business, so what did I know? Well...I did know a little about bears.

When we started our work early each morning, we noticed fresh bear tracks entering and exiting the landfill from the various tunnels under the fence. The grizzlies had developed the habit decades before at the old dumpsites, and more recently at the landfill, to leave before sunrise, or at least before human activity disrupted their feeding activities each morning. Our construction activity during the day kept most black bears away from the site. When we were near job completion, we noticed that the bears had already started to re-excavate some of the tunnels we had filled in and blocked with the concrete pads.

We finished laying the pads and securing them to the fence with the hooks and cables by the middle of October, which was roughly the time the bears would be spreading out from the area and looking for winter denning sites. We continued to work at the site for a few days after laying the last pads to complete some finishing work and to clean up the area. On the second last day of the job, we did our early morning check of the site by walking along the fence's outside perimeter. I was eager to see what the bears had accomplished in their attempts to re-gain access to the landfill. We came across a few more uncompleted tunnels before we rounded the last corner of the fence. Then our eyes caught a bulge in the fence and we walked over to investigate. I couldn't believe what we saw; during the night a grizzly had simply torn through the heavy gauge link fence to enter the landfill. I was always mindful of the incredible power of these animals but this was totally unexpected. No one knew that a bear could tear through a metal link fence of this gauge. I could imagine a bear bending the links to some degree but never breaking them.

The landfill fortification effort proved to be only partially effective. Maintenance staff kept busy repairing breaks and tears in the fence and filling in tunnels that the bears dug under the concrete pad. Other bears moved on, supplementing their natural diet with garbage waste whenever the opportunity presented itself. Two years after we completed the partially effective pad structure, I was to learn firsthand the extent that food-conditioned bears go to in order to obtain human food.

◆ ◆ ◆

During the 1975 Thanksgiving long weekend, I took a break from my studies in the Biological Sciences Program at the Northern Alberta Institute of Technology (NAIT) in Edmonton and returned home to do some hiking. I set out with my Jasper high school buddy John Kofin early in the morning for a day hike into Geraldine Lakes. These lakes are set in a narrow high-elevation valley surrounded by mountains rising above the Whirlpool Valley to the northwest and the Fryatt Valley to the southeast.

When we pulled off the main road near Athabasca Falls and turned into the trailhead parking area, we saw a shocking scene of damaged vehicles. Three cars, parked overnight by backpackers, appeared to have been senselessly wrecked by vandals. But then we took a closer look. All around were fresh grizzly tracks. The offending bear had left a signature of muddied paw prints and claw marks all over the cars. The side-front wheel fenders of a Volkswagen Beetle were torn away from the chassis. One tire was slashed, flattened in seconds by the grizzly's long claws. An outside doorframe of a small Ford was torn out and folded over like a lid on a tin can. A Pontiac Strato Chief sustained the most interesting damage of the three. The bear had smashed the driver's side door window, leaned through, and torn the front seat to shreds. Lying on the passenger side seat was a *You are in Bear Country* pamphlet. This Parks Canada pamphlet includes descriptions of black and grizzly bears, bear facts, a brief summary of precautions to take in bear country, and how to avoid unnecessary encounters, such as leaving unattended food in vehicles.

The grizzly, in a rage, had pounded the vehicles like a boxer would a punching bag. The front of the Volkswagen was parked beside a trailhead signpost. Nailed to the post was a "Bear Warning" sign recently put up by the Warden Service to notify hikers that a grizzly bear had been frequenting the area.

The bear was a large boar that had acquired enough celebrity to be bestowed a name: "Jaws" (even though his paws and claws did most of the damage). Jaws' legacy of destruction had begun a year earlier when he honed his break-and-enter skills on warden cabins in the Whirlpool Valley.

In October 1974, Park Wardens Gord Anderson and Ron Chambers began a patrol to Athabasca Pass from Tie Camp warden cabin at the end of Moab Lake Road. This small cabin, used as a staging area and base camp for horse trips into the Whirlpool Valley, is situated in the area of the original Tie Camp, a lumber camp operated in the early 1900s that supplied ties for the building of the two railways through Jasper.

From Tie Camp, Gord and Ron rode 12 kilometres up valley where they spent their first night at Middle Forks warden cabin situated in the forest near the confluence of the Middle Whirlpool and Whirlpool rivers. The next day they set out for Kane Meadows, 19 kilometres further into the subalpine below the towering glaciated peaks of Mounts Kane, Evans, and Hooker. A small 4 x 4-metre bubble-shaped fibreglass shelter had been flown into Kane Meadows a few years earlier to serve as a patrol hut for wardens travelling in the upper Whirlpool Valley.

A few hours out of Middle Forks, Gord and Ron emerged from the forested area and out onto the Scott Gravel Flats, a wide gravel plain between opposing mountain ridges. The Whirlpool River meanders down the middle of the plain, dotted with shrub willows and small stunted spruce trees. As they reached the middle of the flats, Ron picked out a channel of the river he thought might offer some trout for dinner. Ron dismounted and gave his horse to Gord to lead. Gord continued to ride along the main river channel, roughly paralleling Ron's course as he walked along scouting for a good fishing spot in the side channel.

When Ron was about 200 metres away, Gord spotted a large grizzly coming down the channel on a collision course with Ron. Ron was unable to see the grizzly over the stunted spruce. Gord had a panoramic view of the scene from his saddle—the grizzly bearing down on Ron, both human and bear unaware of each other. Gord quickly turned the horses towards Ron and the bear to intersect their paths. The grizzly spotted Gord and the horses and made a hasty retreat into the tall timber of the nearby mountain slope. Ron heard, but never saw the bear crashing up the slope. They left the area to the grizzly and continued on their way.

Several hours later, they arrived at Kane Meadows and found that the grizzly had demolished the small fibreglass shelter. The grizzly had torn off the door on one side of the shelter, completely ransacked the inside, and then had taken out the entire wall on the other side of the shelter as he tried to get his large mass through a small window. Gord and Ron spent a cold, fearful, and restless night sleeping under the stars.

Not set up to camp, they decided to forgo their trip to the pass and headed back to Middle Forks warden cabin in the morning. The bear had beaten them to it. Fortunately, he had departed before the men arrived but not before he had left a large hole in the cabin where the door once stood. The bear had torn apart the inside of the cabin in much the same way he had demolished the

Kane Meadows shelter. He had punched out two windows and clawed apart the roof of the cabin near the stovepipe. Wardens usually leave their rifles outside in the tack shed at night, along with the saddles and assorted horse gear. That night, though, Gord and Ron snuggled up with their firearms. They were kept awake by a steady breeze circulating into the cabin through the punched out windows, the gaping hole in the roof above the stove, and the large opening that was once the cabin door.

The next morning, Gord and Ron, now deprived of sleep for two nights, rode back out to Tie Camp only to find that the grizzly had beaten them to that cabin as well, destroying part of it and ransacking the inside just as he had with the other two. Jaws had completed his sweep of the Whirlpool Valley, leaving the cleanup and repairs to the Warden Service.

Jaws was already well known by the town folk in Jasper, and of course the Warden Service, by the time he started breaking into vehicles. He was one of the many grizzly bears that spent much of their time feeding in the park's garbage dumps. After the closure of the open pit dumpsites in the late 1960s and the fortification of the fence around the Palisades Landfill in 1973, Jaws searched elsewhere for the human food he had become accustomed to. After cleaning out the warden cabins in the Whirlpool Valley in 1974, he discovered that he could find groceries, coolers, lunch boxes and the like in vehicles. Jaws then busted into vehicles in the Athabasca River Valley, eluding all the traps and snares set by park wardens for his capture.

Jaws was finally caught in a culvert trap at the same trailhead where John and I had witnessed the damage he had inflected on metal, glass, and rubber. He weighed in at 326 kilograms—a very large grizzly. Although he had no history of aggressiveness towards people, Jaws, sadly, was destroyed out of concern that he might turn his fury onto something other than heavy metal. He was one of the many bears (black and grizzly) destroyed during the slow process of resolving the park's garbage issue, an unfortunate but necessary period of adjustment for bears conditioned to human food. For Jaws, his was a tragic ending in the prime of life.

CHAPTER FIFTEEN

Breaking Bears' Habits

I applied for the biannual park warden competition in the early spring of 1981. A few months after the tests and the interview, I learned that I had made the list of candidates to be offered a position. Nine years after graduating from high school with my goal set on becoming a park warden, I had finally made it. My post-secondary training in the biological sciences, two years of employment with the Canadian Wildlife Service, three years working as a park patrolman, and more than two decades of intensive outdoor activities that gave me the skills to pursue a career as a guardian of the wild, had finally paid off. Success at last!

In addition to the fantastic news that I would become a warden, I was going to begin my career in my home park—Jasper. I was ecstatic! I remained with the Resource Management Function, which was headed by Assistant Chief Park Warden Bob Haney, with whom I had worked as a patrolman when I was in the Blue Creek District in 1980.

On my first day as a park warden in 1981, I was immersed in the ongoing problem bear issues in Jasper. Wardens, frustrated in dealing with bears searching for improperly stored food in campgrounds, begging for handouts along highways, and scavenging for garbage throughout the park, had run out of options for managing the crisis. Far too many bears had been killed for far too long.

With the closure of Jasper's open pit dumpsites and the partial success of keeping most bears away from Palisades Landfill (some were still finding ways to breach the fence and concrete pad structures), many black bears conditioned to human waste returned to their old food sources: campgrounds, bungalow camps, and garbage containers in Jasper townsite. The predictable result was more black bear-human encounters. Grizzlies, preferring to stay away from areas of human settlement, generally kept out of trouble. However, they still frequented the Palisades Landfill and occasionally broke into garbage containers—mostly at night and on the fringes of human settlement.

With the increase in undesirable black bear-human encounters and a solution to the park's waste containment and disposal problems largely unresolved, park managers applied to the National Parks Branch in Ottawa in 1980 for additional funding to help resolve bear/garbage issues. Ottawa, in turn, requested a report summarizing the history of bear management in the park and its relation to waste disposal issues and human safety. Additionally, we were tasked with creating Jasper's first Bear Management Plan.

Norm Woody, Gord Anderson, John Woodrow, and I, with assistance from other wardens in the Resource Management Function, completed the report summarizing the history of bear management in the park and the Bear Management Plan by May of 1981, in time for implementation that summer. The plan outlined the implementation of short and long-term strategies for waste management. Other components included public awareness and education programs; effective law enforcement strategies; measures to reduce highway and railway mortalities; a bear monitoring and reporting system; area closure and warning guidelines; handling and trapping measures; guidelines for the use of immobilizing drugs; and further research on bear biology and human disturbance of bear habitat. The plan's final component was an outline of the funds required to implement each proposed measure.

The completion and implementation of the Bear Management Plan was a significant milestone that ushered in a new era of resource management under the umbrella of an integrated system called the "Conservation Planning Process." Traditional resource management practices such as predator control programs, elk culls, forest-fire suppression, and problem bear management were now understood to be totally ineffective in managing the park's resources.

Other plans followed the Bear Management Plan in the next few years, including backcountry management, wildlife monitoring, vegetation and fire management, and a plan to reduce wildlife mortalities along the park's transportation corridors. Budgeting for future resource conservation activities was dependent on the timely completion and regular updating of these plans and the many that followed. Objectives in each plan had to be periodically updated in response to changing park mandates due to continuing pressures from development in and outside the parks, human activities, and the growing understanding of ecosystem interrelationships. The Conservation Planning Process recognized that continued studies, inventories, and monitoring of park resources were an absolute necessity in expanding our knowledge of an ecosystem that was constantly changing and evolving as a result of natural processes and human activities.

In the past, resource management activities had been carried out on an ad-hoc basis, often without adequate knowledge of how the consequences of each management action would affect the environment. The Conservation Planning Process became our guideline to managing and protecting the park's resources using an integrated, reasoned course of action.

◆ ◆ ◆

We began implementing the new Bear Management Plan in late spring of 1981. The first step in putting the plan into action was to set up a daily monitoring system whereby all park staff reported bear observations and issues to the Park Warden Office. All outlying bungalow camp operators, as well as hotel, motel, and restaurant operators in town and Jasper residents, were asked to do the same.

This monitoring system, simple as it was, formed the basis of how we acted on all bear issues and on waste management. It enabled us to track individual bears that had become reliant on garbage as a source of food. We tranquilized them and attached coloured, number-coded tags to their ears. The fate of each bear was determined on an individual basis. Usually, if a bear had been trapped or immobilized twice and moved to remote locations in the park, and then had subsequently returned to its unnatural food habit a third time, it was destroyed.

Public awareness and education were an essential part of the bear plan. We worked with park interpreters to set up education programs and spent considerable time talking to park visitors, especially during evening and night patrols in the campgrounds. The message we wanted to make clear was that leaving food unattended and feeding bears was detrimental to the long-term survival of the animals, as well as unlawful and dangerous.

Meanwhile, the issue of inadequate food waste disposal in town was still unresolved, and Parks Canada drafted a new set of regulations to create a more effective system of food waste disposal within townsites in the national parks. It stipulated that residents and commercial establishments must use approved curbside containers or facilities to store food waste before scheduled pickup. These had to be constructed so as to be bear proof. Law Enforcement Warden Terry Damm was assigned the task of promoting the new regulations in the townsite that summer. As Parks Canada was still in the transition period of establishing bear proof waste containers, Terry's job was more of a public relations initiative than a strict law enforcement position. We had to be very careful seeking compliance with these regulations as Parks Canada had yet to develop its own bear proof garbage container. In a technical sense, Parks Canada could be viewed as being in violation of its own regulations regarding adequate storage of food waste—we had to get our *own house* in order.

Upon obtaining additional funding in 1981, we tried out two means of improving waste management. The first was the purchase of Haul-All bunker style waste containers. These large containers, the size of a small car, used hydraulics to unload food waste into a specifically designed loading hopper on a garbage truck. These fully enclosed containers were made of steel panels and had covered self-locking steel door latches. Several dozen of these large containers were placed in a few campgrounds, replacing some of the older garbage bins. Before the bunker system was brought in, the park had experimented with a long succession of different types of food waste bins over the years, but none could withstand the power and intelligence of bears that either broke into the containers or figured out how to unlock the mechanisms on the various bin doors.

We had high hopes for the second initiative: the installation of electric wiring around the Palisades Landfill fence. Twenty-two grizzly bears had frequented the landfill the previous summer and a small number of black bears also fed at the site. These bears were still finding ways to breach the fence and concrete pad structure around the landfill. The electrified wiring was installed in May. To our relief, it worked.

Black bears began their yearly treks into town from their hibernation sites in late April and by the middle of June the usual issues with garbage surfaced. One of the first bear incidents we dealt with involved a sow black bear and her two young-of-year (born the past winter) cubs. The cubs were in the latter stages of weaning and quickly learning the garbage habit.

Although the sow was keeping her cubs well away from people and there were no reported public safety concerns, we decided to move them out of town. She was not a bear we had dealt with before. Norm Woody and I tranquilized the sow and cubs and relocated them to the Shale Banks area along the old dirt fire road between Celestine Lake and Seldom Inn warden cabin, 53 kilometres from the capture location in Jasper townsite.

Translocations are almost always a short-term fix, and in this case, the bears were back in town three days later. They had walked at least 53 kilometres. I could hardly believe those small cubs could walk that distance in such a short period of time. We had hoped that they would take a few weeks to return (if they returned at all), giving the sow a chance to teach the cubs the many natural edibles available to them in the wild. We kept a close watch on them for a few weeks. Surprisingly, the bear family stayed away from town and outlying campgrounds for most of the remainder of the summer.

Unfortunately, a desirable outcome for bears that relied on human food rarely occurred. Most sows that structured their family's feeding habits around human food waste met death by bullet. Wardens are reluctant to destroy cubs unless absolutely necessary. Black bear cubs usually do not become independent until they are well into their second year of life. If the mother is killed before this time, the cubs have an uphill battle for survival. The problem becomes greater if the family is spared and the cubs become conditioned to human food waste and then pass their addiction onto the next generation. Decisions are never easy when dealing with wildlife-human issues.

A few weeks after Norm and I relocated the sow with two cubs, I encountered another sow with three young-of-year cubs alongside the Icefields Parkway a few kilometres south of town while on patrol early in the morning. There was little traffic and I watched the family for several undisturbed minutes before they moved into the forest. I read the number on her red ear tag with my binoculars and checked a list of bears that had been handled in previous years. She had been handled twice and had a long history of feeding on garbage and unattended food in Whistlers Campground, six kilometres south of town. The cubs, not much bigger than a medium-sized dog, romped around, wrestled, and tripped over one another in comical play as their mother fed on vegetation. Their very young lives were pure joy and wonder and absolute innocence. I drove back to the office, apprehensive and fearful for their future.

A week later an attendant at Whistlers Campground reported that a black bear with three young cubs had been into some of the older style garbage containers. I found them walking along the perimeter road at the back of the campground and was disheartened to see it was the same family—the sow was back to her garbage habit, passing it on to her cubs. I sounded the PA system air horn on the truck's roof rack. They scampered into the woods but I knew they would be back in the campground before too long. I wasn't looking forward to the inevitable.

Over the next several days, campground staff and other wardens and I tried our best to encourage clean sites and frequent food waste pickup. Whistler, however, is a huge campground of over 800 sites. We couldn't be everywhere, all the time. A few other solitary black bears had claimed other areas of the campground as their territory. The sow with the cubs had staked out a large portion of the campground as her family's real estate. She became a public safety concern as a result of her protectiveness when it came to her cubs and their food source. Management made the decision to destroy the family.

Four of us headed out to Whistlers in two trucks from the Park Warden Office with the necessary tools to carry out the terrible task. Our mood was sombre. We located the family roaming through one of the tenting areas. The sow spotted us from a long distance away. Recognizing our trucks and sensing what was coming, she scurried her cubs off to the perimeter road, intent on getting them safely into the forest away from the campground. We fired a few loud cracker shells in their direction, which resulted in the sow giving notice to her cubs to quickly climb the nearest aspen tree. This was exactly what we intended her to do. They immediately responded to her call. The sow paced around the tree with worried glances at her cubs and furious glares at us. We had them where we needed them; she wasn't going to leave her cubs.

Now we had to carry through with the dirty deed. I can't adequately express my feelings of betrayal. After all, we were supposed to be protectors of the wild.

The small cubs climbed 8 to 10 metres up the tree, dug their claws into the soft bark of the trunk, hung on, and whined for their mom. The sow remained at the base of the tree, ready to defend her cubs where she thought they were safe. But it wasn't necessary to get any closer to the tree; we raised our rifles from 20 metres away. Her life was instantly cut short. We then took aim at the cubs. They met their fate and dropped from the tree—joy, wonder, innocence—life—gone in a flash.

We dragged the sow and carried the cubs out of the forest, extremely remorseful and angered at the fate of the black bear family. We were thankful for only one thing—that we had carried out this sickening task away from the eyes of the public. We solemnly lifted the four bears into the back of one of the trucks and left the area. I don't recall a single word said between my riding partner and me on the way back to the Park Warden Office. We were absolutely distraught. Our silent, dark moods changed when we arrived at the office. We were enraged at having to kill the sow and her cubs and we confronted our managers and peers. We exploded in anger and an extremely heated exchange of words ensued. But there was no one to blame and no one to take the heavy load of frustration off our backs. Once our heads cleared, we realized that it was unfair to direct our outrage at our fellow workers; we were all in the same boat.

We were impatient with the slow progress of the waste management issue in our otherwise beautiful park. Looking back, I know many of us were on edge that summer of 1981. The superintendent and various managers in the park were doing a credible job of following up on the advice of the wardens and other park staff to resolve the problems. As usual, we required money to clean up the mess, but the funding was slow in coming. In the meantime, we knew there'd be more unpleasant days ahead.

Garbage conditioned bears kept us busy most of the summer. We responded to 180 complaints or incidents and had to put down 14 black bears. Although this was 14 too many bears for me, it was almost half the number (27) that had been killed the previous year.

The monitoring system was key to the operational success of the 1981 bear management program. There had never been an effective daily bear reporting system that allowed us to respond to complaints and problems quickly prior to this. Our public education and awareness programs were factors in reducing conflicts between bears and park visitors. Progress was also made in gaining the cooperation of commercial establishments to improve their food waste storage facilities. Some even purchased the new bunker style containers.

The two greatest advances made with the bear management program in 1981 were the success of the new experimental bunker style containers and the electrified fence at the landfill. There was not a single incident of a bear gaining access into any of the new containers; they proved to be 100 percent bear proof. This was a phenomenal achievement in bear/garbage management. The electrified fence at the Palisades Landfill also proved its worth in deterring all black and grizzly bears that attempted to breach the fence or bury tunnels underneath it.

◆ ◆ ◆

I worked for the Resource Management Function again in 1982, and once again we responded to bear/garbage related incidents on a daily basis. Most of these incidents involved bears accessing the many old garbage bins that had not yet been replaced by the bear-proof containers. We ended up killing only 5 troublesome black bears in 1982, compared to 14 in 1981 and 27 in 1980. There were now fewer problem bears, due to the replacement of garbage-addicted bears by younger bears born into the population that weren't taking on the habits of their predecessors. This was a clear indication that the combination of measures initiated under the Bear Management Plan had decreased bear-human conflicts. By the end of the 1982 season, the placement of more hydraulic bunker style containers at various locations in the park further reduced the availability of human food waste. The electrified fence at the landfill continued to work flawlessly—not a single bear gained access to the dump.

Overall, we were extremely thankful (and very fortunate) that the transition period during which black and grizzly bears had to adjust to the decreasing availability of human food in the early 1980s did not result in a single major bear-human incident. There were more observations of bears wandering around the high visitor use areas than in previous years as they adjusted their feeding patterns. The bears, true to their nature, avoided humans as much as they could.

The access bears had to human food waste in the townsite, however, was still a major issue. The commercial establishments were making efforts to comply with new regulations that stipulated bear proof bins. Town residents lagged far behind. How could you blame them? What was bear proof anyway? Parks Canada had not yet been able to develop or find a supplier for bear proof bins that fit residential requirements.

As a result of the largely unresolved issue in dealing with food waste in town, the bear situation was much the same as it had been when I was a kid. Bears were still wandering the back alleys every night and stories of their antics were still being talked about at the Post Office (a common meeting place for town residents) each day, as they had been for decades past.

◆ ◆ ◆

The initiatives implemented under the Bear Management Plan during the 1981 and 1982 summer seasons were pivotal in resolving 75 years of conflict between bears and humans in Jasper National Park. With the successes of the electric fence at the Palisades Landfill and the public awareness campaign, park staff and management turned their attention towards conclusively resolving the waste management containment issue.

More hydraulic bunker style containers were installed in the campgrounds in 1983; once again they proved their worth in foiling the attempts of bears to access food waste. In light of the success of these containers, park management committed to install them throughout all campgrounds and high visitor use areas in the park as funds permitted.

The main issue left to resolve was a long-term solution to the townsite garbage problem. The implementation of a standardized residential garbage containerization system within the townsite began in 1984 with the phasing in of the large hydraulic bunker containers. These containers were placed at the end of all alleyways in town.

Smaller style bins that did not require the need for large waste pickup were also tested throughout several areas in the park. These smaller bins, the size of waste containers town and city dwellers leave at their curb for pick up, are easily unloaded by hand into a garbage truck. Both container models continued to be bear proof for the first couple of years. But then, to everyone's astonishment and disappointment, bears learned how to open the container lids.

This troublesome issue came about just as we thought we had the bear/garbage issue solved once and for all, not just in Jasper but also in other parks with established bear populations. The lids had a round knob the size of a standard doorknob. Bears that learned to master what we thought were secure containers stood on their hind legs, placed the doorknob between their paws, gave it a twirl to disengage the locking mechanism, opened the lid, and then reached in and pulled out their meal. Did we really think we could outsmart them?

This issue culminated in Jasper in 1985 with an incident that could have proven fatal. A family (mother, father, and two young boys) had just finished eating a peaceful lunch at the Palisades picnic site in early October. Preparing to pack up and leave, the father picked up their garbage and headed for the large hydraulic container a short walk from the picnic table.

As he approached the container, he heard moaning and groaning and scratching sounds coming from inside. He was startled and perplexed by the sounds because the container was closed. Whoever (or whatever) was inside could not get out. Thinking that perhaps foul play had taken place and an injured person was inside, he called out. There was no response. He imagined the person might be so badly beaten up that he or she was not able to call out—or was there a domestic or wild animal inside? And if so, how did the animal get in the garbage bin? The father wisely refrained from opening the lid. While he stayed at the site, his family drove to Jasper and notified the RCMP.

The police in turn called the Park Warden Office asking for assistance. Rick Ralf and Wes Bradford responded to the call and met an RCMP officer at the picnic site. They saw garbage strewn around the front of the container, indicating that a bear had dragged the refuse out of an open lid, and they heard the moaning, groaning, and shuffling from inside. Rick and Wes could also smell the bear, and when they checked around the frame of the lid, they found grizzly hair. The silly bear had opened the lid, reached inside the bin, and grabbed some leftover food. Not satisfied with what it could reach, it had somehow squeezed its massive body through the opening and ended up at the bottom of the container, with the lid closing and locking shut behind.

Rick and Wes determined that as the bear had been assisted by gravity in getting through the small door opening, it was unlikely that it could pull itself out. They gave Waste Crew

Foreman Ross Pigeon a call over the radio and asked him to attend. Ross parked his garbage truck alongside the container and hooked up the hydraulics that lifted the bin, dumping the refuse and the surprised bear onto the ground. As soon as the bear was on its feet, it was off into the woods like a flash.

The opening on these otherwise bear-proof containers had to be modified so that bears couldn't deposit themselves inside. A phone call verified that the container company was already working on this. Shortly after this incident, a second-generation container was developed with covered latches. Even though the bears could have eventually figured out the new latch mechanism, they could never get their clawed paws up into the latch. Problem solved.

By 1986, the bear proof containerization system was completed in the townsite residential areas. Jasper businesses (in town and throughout the outlying bungalow camps) were allowed to phase into the system through a business licence agreement. The park was totally "containerized" by 1989.

By 1990, the major cause of bear-human conflicts—bear access to human food—was virtually eliminated. The standardization of garbage storage and disposal throughout all residential areas and at all commercial and park facilities was complete, and the electrified fence around the Palisades Landfill continued to keep the bears out of the pit. Roadside bear feeding became an issue of the past and unattended food at campgrounds was greatly reduced. A new system of food storage was devised whereby a steel cable-pulley arrangement, strung over bear poles secured high between two trees, allowed backcountry hikers to safely store bagged food away from bears' reach at night or while they were away from camp. Bear proof food storage lockers were installed at many large group camps in the high visitor use areas and walk-in storage lockers were built in some of the campgrounds.

In 1992, a waste transfer station was completed at the site of the Palisades Landfill. All garbage collected in Jasper is initially hauled to the transfer station on a daily basis. From there, it is transferred to a regional landfill near Hinton. Jasper residents, in cooperation with Parks Canada, began recycling and composting in the early 1990s.

The number of bear-human encounters that have resulted in injuries to park visitors has decreased significantly since the intensive efforts in the 1980s to reverse the long-term trend of conditioning bears to human foods and food waste. Between 1973 and 1980, black bears injured 19 park visitors. Fortunately, most injuries were minor and involved scratches or bites to various parts of the body. All injury incidents involved human-food-conditioned bears seeking food waste, improperly stored food in campgrounds, or roadside feeding by passing motorists. There have been only two reported black bear inflicted human injuries in Jasper National Park since 1981.

Interestingly, neither of these injuries involved human-food-conditioned bears. The first attack, in August 2004, occurred a few kilometres west of Jasper townsite. A 13-year-old boy was fishing at a beaver pond with some friends when a black bear emerged from the forest and pursued him. The black bear inflicted minor injuries on him as he jumped into the pond to avoid it. His friends, in the meantime, went for help. The boy swam across to a beaver lodge and the bear followed, inflicting bite wounds as it caught him on the lodge. He jumped into the pond again and swam across to the beaver dam, with the bear in pursuit. Once on the dam, the boy tore off his bloody t-shirt hoping it would distract the bear and started walking back to town on an old dirt road. The bear was distracted by the discarded t-shirt and gave up its pursuit. The boy was very lucky to have received only minor injuries. The bear was found on the beaver dam shortly afterwards by park wardens and shot. Its behaviour was ruled as a predatory attack, exceedingly rare for a black bear.

The last attack in the park occurred in August 2006 near Jacques Lake, when an off-leash dog lured a black bear out of the woods and back towards its owners, a man and woman. In the melee that followed, the bear, in a purely defensive move to avoid the woman after almost colliding with her, bit her in the thigh. The incident ended when the bear, no less frightened by the encounter than the hiking party, climbed a tree to avoid further confrontation. The woman received two non-serious puncture wounds. The death of the young girl at Sunwapta Bungalows in 1958 (mentioned in Chapter 1) remains the only black bear inflicted human fatality in the history of the park.

Despite the grizzly bear having a reputation as the most ferocious and dangerous mammal in North America, grizzlies have killed only two people in the past century in Jasper National Park. Until the Maligne Lake dumpsite mauling incident, there was only one other case of a recorded grizzly attack in the park. The incident involved a mauling that took place in 1929 in Tonquin Valley, a vast area of subalpine and alpine meadows and a popular backcountry camping destination for hiking and horse parties. The victim was Park Warden Percy Goodair.

Percy was stationed at Maccarib Creek warden cabin, situated on a knoll with a commanding view of the turquoise coloured waters of Amethyst Lakes at the base of the towering Ramparts. The Ramparts are ominous, steep-faced mountains that join together much the same way as the buttresses of a dark castle. Each adjoining peak of this massif has been given an appropriate name—Drawbridge, Redoubt, Dungeon, Bastion, and Parapet. Thunderbolt, Blackhorn, and Throne peaks rise high above the south end of the valley, guarding its entrance like massive stationary sentinels.

When Percy was not heard from for several days, Park Warden Alec Nelles led a horse party along Portal Creek from the Athabasca River Valley to the summit of Maccarib Pass, and from there, down towards the subalpine meadows in the Tonquin Valley. Snow had fallen for two days prior to their departure, leaving behind a thin blanket of white throughout the landscape. As the party approached the cabin, they didn't see any human footprints in the snow. Percy's horses were grazing in the nearby meadows and the saddles and other riding gear were laid out on the cabin porch. A half-cooked meal was found on the stove inside the cabin. Percy's belongings were arranged in a way that showed he had intended to return a short time later after checking the whereabouts of his horses.

Percy's body was eventually found in an area of krummholz within a short walking distance from the cabin. It appeared that he had jumped over some downed timber and come face-to-face with a sow grizzly and her cub that had bedded down. Percy had been mauled by the sow and died from the severe wounds. He was buried on a high bluff behind the cabin, which has since been dismantled. His gravesite overlooks the great peaks of the Ramparts.

The second incident involved a British couple that was attacked in 1992 at Portal Creek campsite located on the Portal Creek trail, one of two maintained trail systems leading into Tonquin Valley. As the couple were pitching their tent, a grizzly walked into the camp area. The couple ran from the bear, prompting it to give chase. The woman climbed a tree but the bear was able to grab her hiking boots and pull her to the ground. Her husband distracted the bear, enabling her to flee. The bear, however, chased him and he was seriously mauled and killed. He was found with injuries to his head and torso and part of one leg had been eaten. Park wardens later killed the bear. The woman sustained non-life threatening injuries.

There are seven recorded incidents of non-fatal injury related attacks by grizzly bears in Jasper. The grizzly attack at the dumpsite near Maligne Lake in 1965 was directly related to improper waste disposal. Three years later, a sow with cubs attacked a Jasper horse outfitter and his two clients in a remote backcountry location. This incident is discussed in a later chapter. Three other attacks, one in 1969 involving injuries to three hikers, and two in 1972 resulting in injuries to three hikers, were by grizzly bears that were very likely (though this was not conclusively proven) conditioned to human food waste. Injuries to the hikers were not serious.

Two other grizzly attacks resulting in non-fatal injuries involved cyclists. One was a male cyclist who surprised a sow and her cub at very close range on a park trail in 1992. The sow turned on him, attacked, and hastily delivered a few bites and tears with its claws before it fled with its cub. The man's injuries were not serious.

The most recent grizzly attack occurred on May 24, 2014. In the early evening, Etienne Cardinal was mountain biking on a trail near Cottonwood Slough on the Pyramid Bench when he heard a terrifying roar and turned to see a massive grizzly bearing down on him. The bear reached Etienne in a few seconds and hit him hard on his back, knocking him off his bike. The bear pushed him to the ground and bit into the pack on his back. Etienne crouched down and covered his head with his arms, expecting a vicious mauling. But it never came.

Etienne turned around to see the grizzly running away up the hill behind him. A moment later a cloud of capsicum spray overcame him and he was left blinded and choking for 20 minutes. Unbelievably and with incredible luck, the grizzly had bitten into a can of bear spray inside Etienne's pack, getting a mouthful of powerful capsaicin. Etienne had then breathed in the remainder of the spray left hanging in the air.

Etienne, a Parks Canada employee, was able to call a co-worker for help on his cell phone. He received four minor lacerations between his left shoulder and hip and a sore back—an extremely fortunate outcome.

Except for a few isolated incidents, black and grizzly bears roaming the park today have largely reverted back to natural feeding habits in the wild, ending a period of close to a century of intensive management directed towards human food-conditioned bears. Park staff from Jasper and other national parks with bear populations continue to work hard to ensure that the history of improper handling, storage, and disposal of food that led to the destruction of many hundreds of bears does not repeat itself.

CHAPTER SIXTEEN

Horse Tales

Every autumn, wardens working in the frontcountry were given the opportunity to take one or more backcountry shifts to assist with autumn boundary patrol. Needless to say, I eagerly anticipated the autumn wilderness sojourns in the years I was not assigned to a backcountry district.

In early September of 1981, Denny Welsh set me up with two horses, Harvey and Lucky. Denny drove me to Devona, we unloaded the horses and gear from the trailer, and within an hour I was in the saddle for a 10-day stint patrolling the park boundary. Harvey took me across the Snake Indian River with Lucky in tow carrying the packs. We set out for Moosehorn warden cabin situated in the upper reaches of the Moosehorn Valley 23 kilometres away.

On the second day of the trip, the horses and I travelled to the park boundary at Moosehorn Pass and over into the provincially managed Rock Lake-Solomon Creek Wildland Park. Several hunting camps are located around Moosehorn and Busby lakes just outside the Jasper boundary.

Once we crossed the boundary marker at Moosehorn Pass, the trail became more rutted from decades-long horse use, and more recently, all-terrain vehicles. I recall thinking how fortunate it is that these vehicles are not allowed in Jasper National Park. Three hunters with five horses and one all-terrain vehicle had recently pulled into a camp on the north shore of Moosehorn Lake. I chatted with them awhile and then moved on to Busby Lake where I checked in on a long-established horse outfitter from the Hinton area. His party was sitting out the wet weather; it had rained the day before and was not letting up.

The outfitter's party included two wranglers, a cook, and two American hunters who were after bighorn rams. I was graciously offered tea and biscuits in the warm cook tent. We discussed hunting for over an hour while Harvey and Lucky waited out of the rain under the boughs of a large spruce tree. I then returned to the Moosehorn warden cabin after checking out other established hunting camps, all unoccupied.

The next morning I saddled the horses and left for Wolf Pass warden cabin. Once again, we travelled up valley over Moosehorn Pass into the province and onwards to Moosehorn and Busby lakes, checking on the hunting parties along the way. From Busby Lake I turned west and began the ascent to Wolf Pass via The Notch. This is the route I travelled on foot when patrolling down into the Moosehorn area from the tent camp near Wolf Pass that I patrolled out of in 1979. The Notch, a steep walled canyon, cuts through the eastern ridges of the Bosche Range. A rocky trail following alongside a small creek crammed between the canyon walls ascends westward towards Wolf, Grindstone, and Laura passes.

From The Notch, I continued up and around a corner of a subalpine slope that leads to a ridge separating Wolf Pass from Grindstone Pass. I rode back across the boundary into Jasper National Park at Wolf Pass. I noticed week-old horse tracks, indicating that hunters had been on the province side of the two passes, but I didn't observe any recent activity or meet anyone. From Wolf Pass, I traversed down a slope through semi-open spruce and fir forest for a few kilometres beyond the old boundary tent camp to Wolf Pass warden cabin. The cabin had been built in 1980 to replace the tent camp.

After unpacking, I turned Harvey and Lucky loose to graze for the remainder of the afternoon and set out to crisscross several ridges between Wolf and Grindstone passes to monitor sheep and goat herds and check on hunting activity. When I returned to the cabin in the early evening, I found the horses' tracks had headed up the valley. Later, just as it was getting dark, I checked their whereabouts. They were dozing in a small meadow beside a creek about half a kilometre up the valley, having had their fill of grasses for a few hours. I examined their hobbles to ensure they were tight and secure and checked that the bell on Lucky was fitting properly.

When I left early in the morning to look for them, I found their tracks 30 metres from the cabin, heading westward down the valley to a large meadow in the opposite direction from where I had found them the evening before. They had walked right by the cabin in the middle of the night without me hearing them. Wolf Pass is a difficult area to find horses during the morning jingle. They like to feed in the large meadow at the base of a densely forested mountain slope. Most horses had a habit of climbing high up onto the slope during the night for further feed and rest. We don't know why they like to travel so far and high, as there is plenty of feed in the meadow. On other occasions the horses preferred to head north down the trail towards Willow Creek warden cabin. Horses can travel a long way with hobbles; it just takes them a little longer to get where they're going.

Off I went towards the meadow. The horses were nowhere to be seen, but very discernible tracks led up the mountain slope. Five hours later, I was back at the cabin without the horses. I had followed their tracks up and down, high and low, and many times sideways across that damn slope. I could see from their track patterns that both still had their hobbles intact. I was glad of that. I also checked the trail leading down to Willow Creek, but they hadn't headed out that way.

I had a quick lunch and set out for the slope again. Sure enough, there they were, fairly high up the slope and tucked into the trees. It was Lucky's bell that led me to them. Both horses greeted me with a short nicker, as if saying "Hello!" and looked at me as if asking, "Where have you been?" They were close to an area I had checked earlier, but they had likely been resting under the trees at the time or I would have heard the bell.

Six and a half hours after I had first set out on my morning jingle, we three were back at the cabin. That stands as the longest jingle of my career. Most wardens were not as fortunate as me. Some of their long-haul jingles outdistanced mine by far.

Wes Bradford experienced one of the longest jingles of his career in October 1982. He happened to be at Wolf Pass warden cabin as well, monitoring sheep and goat hunters along the boundary ridges during the autumn boundary patrol.

Wes had two horses with him, King and Marie. King had a reputation as a night traveller and Wes had heard of the difficulties of jingling in the area. After arriving, he led his horses up valley to the grazing site east of the cabin, hobbled and belled them, and returned to the cabin. But just as Harvey and Lucky had done with me, his horses came down past the cabin at night and headed towards the large meadows. Unlike my horses, however, his horses passed by the cabin around 10:00 p.m., *before* Wes turned in for the night. At 11:00 p.m., Wes grabbed a flashlight and walked out a few hundred metres to listen for a bell. Not hearing anything, he became suspicious. He picked up the horses' tracks and followed them for a couple of kilometres. The horses had bypassed the large meadow and mountain slope and were hoofing it towards Willow Creek. Still not hearing a bell, he knew the horses were well ahead of him.

Wes returned to the cabin and, expecting a long jingle, dressed warmly. He took a halter, a bridle, and a feedbag filled with oats from the tack shed and headed back down the trail. Sometime after 3:00 a.m. and 11 kilometres later, Wes caught up with the horses feeding in the moonlight in a small meadow next to the trail beside Willow Creek. He rode King bareback and led Marie by the halter shank on the long, slow journey back up to Wolf Pass. Dawn was breaking as they arrived at the cabin—a 22-kilometre jingle.

Park Warden Jane Emson had one of her own long jingles at Wolf Pass as well. In October 1984, I rode up from Willow Creek and spent two days at Wolf Pass. Jane came up from Moosehorn warden cabin with her horses a day later. I explained the history of jingling difficulties at Wolf Pass to her and recounted Wes Bradford's nightlong jingle down the valley towards Willow Creek. The next morning we found our horses without difficulty a few hundred metres up the mountain slope from the large meadow below the cabin. I packed up and left to return to Willow Creek, leaving Jane to patrol the Wolf, Grindstone, and Laura Pass areas for a few days.

The next evening I talked to Jane on the SSB radio. She had found her horses that day in the same general area. She had no such luck the next morning, however, and spent a few hours going in circles following her horses' tracks on the mountain's lower slope before she noticed the tracks heading down valley towards Willow Creek. Jane backtracked to the trail and studied the horses' tracks, wondering whether they were made by her horses or by mine the previous day. Jane had been Blue Creek District warden the previous year and had become fairly good at tracking. She was confident that the tracks were from her horses and set out down the trail.

Many hours later and not far from Willow Creek warden cabin, Jane turned back without her horses—she had been following *my* horses' tracks. Early in the evening, back up at Wolf Pass, and totally exhausted, Jane found her horses just a few kilometres away from the cabin, "high, high, high on the slope above the meadow," as she noted in the cabin log book. Jane finally arrived back at the cabin with her horses, 12 hours after she had set out on her morning jingle. Jane had broken Wes' record for a Wolf Pass jingle by several kilometres and a couple of hours.

Brazeau District Warden Mike Dillon had a jingle similar to Jane's. He was planning to ride to Brazeau from Isaac Creek warden cabin, a day's journey on the South Boundary. Mike set out in the early morning to look for his ponies in a small meadow they frequented just a few hundred metres from the cabin. He had packed up before the 8:00 a.m. radio call, cleaned the cabin, and left the pack boxes, rifle, and the rest of the gear on the porch ready to go. He closed the screen door but left the cabin door open. Mike had been listening to an AM radio station and left it on. He had prepared for a short jingle.

As the horses were nowhere to be seen, Mike followed their tracks to Isaac Creek a short distance away. It looked as if they had crossed the creek, so he too waded across. On the other side of the creek he walked through the forest for a few minutes. When he reached the trail leading to Southesk warden cabin, he could clearly see the horse tracks headed in that direction. A few hours later, Mike was still following the tracks. He eventually arrived at Southesk warden cabin, 16 kilometres away from where he had left his gear back on the porch at Isaac Creek warden cabin.

Mike followed the horses' trail across the Southesk River that marked the boundary between the park and the province near the warden cabin. He picked up their tracks leading to an outfitter camp on the opposite shore. It was evident that a small horse party had left one of the camps that morning, travelling east away from the mountains and into the foothills. It dawned on Mike that this party had ridden their horses to Isaac Creek the day before and stopped at the creek before crossing to the cabin where he would otherwise have noticed them. The outfitters had then doubled back to their camp by the Southesk River the same day. The tracks he had been following weren't his horses but those of the outfitters.

Mike got back to Isaac warden cabin around 6:00 p.m., 10 hours and 32 kilometres later, famished and bone tired. And there he saw them—his trusty horses, waiting patiently for him in the meadow beside the cabin. Mike's gear was still on the porch and the sounds from the AM radio were still drifting over the otherwise quiet meadow, keeping the ponies company while they leisurely grazed. The horses, under cover of the forest, had probably seen Mike walk right by them earlier that morning, just before he waded across Isaac Creek. If Mike had only taken five minutes to see if his horses had indeed *not crossed* Isaac Creek, he likely would have found them under the trees near the meadow only minutes away from the cabin.

Having us locate their whereabouts, whether early in the morning, late in the evening, after dark, or at any other time, seemed at times to be a game the horses relished. It was a mystery as to where you might find them—a game of hide-and-seek. I enjoyed the challenge of sharpening my senses, ever watchful for the freshest horse track or the most recent manure pile that would tell me how far away the horses might be and in which direction they had travelled. Tracking could prove difficult on occasion—in the dark, or after a late spring or early autumn snowfall had covered the horses' tracks, or on hardened soil, or through dense undergrowth. When tracking was unreliable, the challenge became one of picking up the slightest ringing of a horse bell, perhaps somewhere in the cover of forest, in the morning mist, or in the black of night.

Jingling the horses in the early morning hours was to me the best start to the day that you could ask for. The dawn or pre-dawn awakening of life in the wilderness invariably gave me the energy I needed for the rest of the day. Nature was my caffeine. As I tracked the horses, my senses shifted from slumber to heightened awareness. As dawn changed to light, nocturnal rhythms gave way to diurnal life. Flowers opened their petals towards the eastern sky, birds performed their morning chorus, and the chatter of squirrels or perhaps a pine marten made clear that I was intruding on their territory. Seeing a cow moose and its young calf feeding on vegetation near a creek or the quick flash of a deer moving away through the woods was not an uncommon occurrence. Life was far from lonely in the backcountry.

It was also common to see fresh sign of bears or wolves, confirming that the trails we travelled as backcountry wardens were commonly shared pathways. When the tracks were fresh, it often indicated they had detected our presence only minutes before and diverted their direction to avoid us. Occasionally, however, we'd have the joy of observing one of these two iconic symbols of our mountain parks during our jingles. On very rare occasions, a backcountry warden came across both of these magnificent animals during the same jingle.

Almost a year to the day after Mike's long jingle to Southesk, he was back at Isaac Creek warden cabin looking for his horses. Walking down the trail through the forest he ran into a grizzly ambling towards him. The bear, seeing Mike, bolted into the forest at a right angle to the trail. It then turned and crashed through the undergrowth parallel to the trail and sprinted past Mike. The bear then came back onto the trail not far behind Mike and continued on its way. The grizzly had given way and allowed Mike the trail. Mike gasped a sigh of relief and continued his jingle.

Shortly afterwards, he heard the welcoming sound of a horse bell on the river flats where Isaac Creek meets the Brazeau River. Emerging from the forest, he spotted the horses. Mike watched a wolf as it crossed the open river flats between himself and the horses. The wolf strode by, within 10 to 12 metres of Mike. Other than a quick glance towards Mike and the horses, the wolf was fixated on its destination. Not a bad jingle—the horses were not far from the cabin and Mike had had a couple of exhilarating wildlife encounters.

Despite the many hours we spent looking for our horses in the backcountry, we could never have done the job without them. Our horses carried us and our gear and travelled more quickly than we could on foot. Horses have more stamina and can easily travel twice as far as we can in a day. They saved our knees and eased our backs. Sitting in the saddle for much of the day saved our energy to use for work en route, for chores around the cabins, or for an evening foot patrol. They are wonderful companions—even when they drag out the game of hide-and-seek.

◆ ◆ ◆

Harvey, Lucky, and I remained at Wolf Pass warden cabin for another day after my record long jingle on the high mountain slope above the meadow west of the cabin. I didn't have to repeat the lengthy jingle of our last morning; they were only a few minutes away in a small meadow upstream from the cabin. We returned to Moosehorn warden cabin via The Notch.

The next morning, I took the horses up Laura Creek to Laura Pass. Laura Creek flows through a deep canyon cut between two peaks in the Bosche Range eight kilometres south of The Notch. Much like the canyon through The Notch, the trail is rough and strewn with hundreds of boulders brought down by gravity over the millennia from the lofty peaks above. Partway through the canyon, we found the going tough. I dismounted Harvey as we proceeded through an especially troublesome boulder field; he was having difficulty making it through without an occasional stumble. I led him by his halter shank as Lucky followed behind. Lucky was travelling well, finding his footing with no problem. Freed of my weight off his back and slowed down by my careful foot placement in front of him, Harvey improved his walk.

We went on for about 15 minutes. All was going well until Harvey's left front foot suddenly slipped as he attempted to navigate around two large boulders. His leg dropped down a space between the two boulders and was tightly wedged from the knee joint down. He tried to pull his leg out of the hole but it was jammed. Before I could do anything to help, he fell backwards in his struggle. Suddenly, I was looking down at my saddle horse with great apprehension. Harvey's left front leg was extended out in front of him, wedged from the knee downwards in the hole. His other legs were partially spread out on his left side and partially tucked under his belly. The space between the two boulders was only as wide as his hoof. There was no way I could move the heavy and mostly buried stone. My heart was pounding. Harvey was in an extremely serious predicament and the outcome looked very grim. He was struggling mightily. I was sure he had injured his leg.

I threw my full weight on top of Harvey's left shoulder in a desperate attempt to keep him pinned to the ground. He was absolutely frantic and I had to keep him from struggling any further; I thought he might pull his leg out of its shoulder socket or pull his knee apart. We had to go about this calmly, but how could I hold down a horse that was seven or eight times my weight? Somehow I did. Harvey was snorting, puffing, and sweating profusely. I could feel sweat beading down my forehead as well. My heart was still pounding. I talked softly to Harvey, attempting to calm him with my voice. I loosened my grip on his shoulders so he wouldn't feel I was overly restraining him. He stopped struggling and remained almost motionless. I could feel his muscles relaxing. His breathing remained deep and rapid. With my full weight still on top of his shoulder, I reached forward with one arm, and unbuckled his bridle and slipped it off. I didn't want his feet to get caught up in the reins.

After I removed Harvey's bridal, he calmed down more. His breathing became less laboured. I remained on top of him for a while longer, thinking of how we could proceed. I then recall saying something like, "Okay buddy, Harvey...we can do this...we can do this buddy." I loosened my grip on him, grabbed the top of his front leg with my left hand, put my right shoulder under his left shoulder and pushed. My meagre strength did little to lift his weight. But Harvey understood that we were working together.

He followed my motion by placing his back legs under his belly and he pushed up on his right front leg to follow my leverage on his left front leg. He then heaved upwards on his back legs in one quick motion and was on his feet.

But Harvey's hoof was still deep in the hole. His legs began to shake in shock. I was afraid he would begin to struggle again, putting both of us back on the ground. If he fell on top of me, it could have been the end for both of us. I wasn't ready to meet my death in this boulder field, nor did I want to be responsible for Harvey's. I knelt under his left shoulder, reached forward and pulled his trapped leg up from between the rocks. I got as far as the widening at the bottom of his hoof, just above his metal horseshoe, but I couldn't pull any further. My heart sank.

I quickly forced his ankle as far sideways as I could, placing the hoof at a slight angle to the opening. No go. I pulled again and again from slightly different angles. Harvey continued to shake uncontrollably. I tried again. Harvey's hoof finally slipped out. We stood together, both dazed, shocked, and soaked with sweat. I stroked his neck and patted him on the shoulder. Our eyes met. He nuzzled me. I put my arms around his neck and gave him a hug. Harvey did a body shake—think of a dog shaking after a swim. It instantly relieved his stress and stopped his uncontrollable shakes.

It took me a lot longer to calm myself. The horses' safety and welfare were my responsibility; the incident wasn't something I could shrug off. Some 30-odd years later, I still think of Harvey's close call.

I checked Harvey for injuries. All I could find was a small gash on one of his back legs from the sharp edge of a boulder. His left front leg appeared uninjured except for a few small scrapes that had taken away some hair but barely penetrated his hide. I had Harvey stand in Laura Creek for several minutes so that the cold mountain water would reduce any potential swelling.

Harvey, Lucky, and I made it through the canyon without further incident and followed Laura Creek up the valley slopes to its headwaters at the high alpine summit of Laura Pass. Rather than return to the cabin via Laura Creek with its treacherous canyon, I opted for the route down through The Notch. I switched my saddle over to Lucky and rode him for the remainder of the day, checking on Harvey's leg often; his gait was normal and there was no sign of injury or swelling. I had a good look at his leg the following morning, relieved that he showed no ill effects from his stumble the previous day.

Having to deal with a seriously injured horse is among a backcountry warden's worst fears. Our horses are family. We often take greater care of them than ourselves. I always knew that if something happened to me there was a good chance I would need my horses to get me out of a dangerous situation. Harvey and I were fortunate. Losing a horse in the backcountry rarely occurs but it has happened. Warden Darro Stinson experienced what was likely the toughest day of his career when one of his horses had a mishap.

In 1983, Darro took a welcome break from his hectic frontcountry duties to take a two-day horse trip into Middle Forks warden cabin along the Athabasca Pass trail. The Trail Office staff in town had requested an update on the trail's condition for the benefit of hikers trekking the historic fur trade route discovered by David Thompson and Thomas, his Iroquois guide, in 1811. Darro was also looking for a break in his schedule to get Patrolman Rick Blackwood out on a training session. Rick, new to the Warden Service, had not yet been on a horse trip and was eager for the experience.

Darro and Rick started their trip at Tie Camp, situated at the end of Moab Lake Road at the Athabasca Pass trailhead. They saddled the riding horses and loaded their pack horse Nitchie with a few sacks of dry concrete mix to repair the cabin's foundation at Middle Forks. The trip into the cabin was uneventful. As they made their way, Darro and Rick cleared the trail of downed timber. Rick was thrilled to be riding and Nitchie accepted her packing duties without incident.

Rick was soon to learn, however, that perils in the wilderness can present themselves at the next bend in the trail. On their return to Tie Camp the following day, all went well except that Nitchie, now carrying a light load, seemed "antsy," as Darro put it. At one point, the trail follows closely along a bank of the Whirlpool River that drops off five metres to the river channel below. As the horses passed by the bank, Nitchie, bringing up the rear, spooked.

Darro recalled: "She jumped forward and began bucking, exploding as she came alongside me, crashing into my horse with her legs flailing in all directions. As she spun around in a few circles, one of her lightning-quick kicks came right for my horse and me. Her hoof grazed my right leg and slammed into my saddle. My horse was taken off balance but remained on his feet. As Nitchie passed by me, she glanced back out of the corner of one eye...it was a dark, malicious expression...very unusual...the memory of that look disturbs me to this day.

"Nitchie continued to buck as she passed Rick, not letting up as she ran down a small hill off the side of the trail. She jumped over a log, landing awkwardly. Her right front leg snapped. I winced at the sound and the sight...it was sickening to hear and to see. I could immediately tell that she had a compound fracture of the tibia-fibula."

Darro, always a calm warden in an emergency, told me the remainder of the story with much emotion in his voice. Though many years had passed, he was still shaken, not only by Nitchie's unfortunate accident but also by the bizarre outcome. Darro went on to say, "Nitchie just stood there in shock, on her three good legs. It seemed everything went quiet for a while, but then I heard the other horses snorting in an anxious sort of way. They knew Nitchie was in trouble, that something was amiss. I got my thoughts together. There was no way Rick and I could walk her out, and we wouldn't be able to do anything with her anyway. I would have to shoot her. I looked towards the river to see if we could walk her down to the flats; we'd have to fly the body out." The Warden Service makes an effort to fly all dead animals away from trails to keep bears, especially grizzlies, from finding and feeding on the carcasses. Hiking along a trail anywhere near the vicinity of a bear protecting a carcass can quickly become a volatile situation.

Rick and Darro walked over to Nitchie and tried to get her to move. Still shaking in shock, she wouldn't budge. Darro was faced with having to shoot her on the spot. He pulled his .308

lever action rifle out of its scabbard on his horse's saddle. He pushed down on the lever to load the chamber. It wouldn't move. Nitchie had bent the lever mechanism when she had kicked at Darro and his horse.

Rick had not yet been issued a rifle. Darro had two choices: use either his Swiss army knife or his axe. He chose the axe. The axe would do the job, but the rifle would have given Darro more distance. Distance makes putting down a horse less personal, making it easier to deal with.

Darro doesn't recall much detail after he pulled the axe from its scabbard. Time stood still, he said, although later he thought it took about 45 minutes before he could find the nerve to do the deed. He was afraid Nitchie might shy when he dropped his axe towards her head, resulting in a miss. He does recall looking back at Rick for a moment while he was contemplating his swing, thinking what a terrible thing for a young guy to go through on his first horse trip. Darro finally found the right moment. His swing hit Nitchie square between the eyes. She went out like a light.

The next day, Backcountry Trail Coordinator Jim Suttill flew in by helicopter with a few other park employees to deal with Nitchie's body. They cleared enough trees so pilot Gary Foreman could drop a long-line. The crew tied the rope around the body and Gary flew it up to the headwaters of the Middle Whirlpool River, far from hiking trails.

CHAPTER SEVENTEEN

On Poachers' Trails

On the sixth morning of my 1981 boundary patrol in the Moosehorn Valley, Park Warden Norm Woody called me from the Park Warden Office on the SSB radio. Norm had learned that a hunting party guided by an outfitter known to Jasper wardens was suspected of poaching two or three bighorn rams somewhere inside the park, close to the boundary that runs along a series of high ridges of the Boule Range on the east side of the Moosehorn Valley. Norm's call was timely, as I had already planned to ride up to the ridges that day. Eager for some action on a poacher's trail, I rushed through breakfast and quickly prepared the horses—fortunately I had found them close to the cabin before the 8:00 a.m. radio call.

I rode north up the Moosehorn Valley for a couple of kilometres and found the faint blaze on a tree indicating the route upwards along Norman Creek to the boundary ridges. The creek had been named after Norm Woody years before. Norm had spent a lot of time in the area over the course of his long career and had made many contacts with hunters, guides, and outfitters. Hence the tip about a potential poacher.

The Boule Range is the last Rocky Mountain range along Jasper's northeast boundary. I dismounted Harvey just before we reached the top of the ridge and then led him by his halter shank with Lucky following closely behind. I kept a low profile as I came over the high alpine ridge crest and scanned the magnificent 360° view with my binoculars. We usually prefer to observe hunting parties before they notice us, but as far as I could tell, I was alone.

From my position beside the small park boundary marker where Norman Creek intercepts the ridge crest, the Moosehorn

Valley lay far below me to the west. Solomon Basin, a lush subalpine cirque on the province side of the boundary, spread out below the ridge in front of me to the east. Further east, the mountain range gave way to foothills that stretched to the town of Hinton 35 kilometres away. To my left, the park boundary followed the ridge north for three kilometres before dropping down to Moosehorn Lake, then crossed over into the Bosche Range in the Wolf Pass area. To my right, the park boundary followed the ridge for another kilometre to Sheep Lookout. This is a favourite spot from which hunters watch for sheep movements on nearby alpine terrain and across Solomon Basin up to the slopes of Mount Kephala. There were no hunters at the lookout.

Leaving Jasper National Park behind, I descended into Solomon Basin to check a camp used by hunters for many decades. I found that the camp had been abandoned within the last day or two. I suspected that the guide and his hunting clients that Norm Woody had been alerted about had been the last ones there. Their horses' tracks indicated they had headed back into the foothills down Solomon Creek. This left me wondering whether some sheep had been poached inside the park before they had broken camp.

I tied Harvey and Lucky to a tree and spent a few hours traversing the subalpine slopes of Mount Kephala above Solomon Basin. When I reached a boundary marker on the open rocky slopes of Mount Kephala east of the hunter's camp, I looked back towards Solomon Basin. From there I could see my horses about 200 vertical metres below me. Following the slope up from the horses, I had a clear view back to Sheep Lookout (another 100 metres above me) along the same boundary ridge where we had stood when we came up from Norman Creek. I focused my binoculars on the top of the ridge and thought I saw some movement near the lookout. I adjusted my binoculars and looked again—nothing.

I turned my gaze to the south and spotted four majestic bighorn rams on the Jasper side of the boundary. One ram had large, fully curled horns: the size trophy hunters set their sights on. I watched the rams for several minutes, aware that if they came just 70 metres towards me they'd cross over to the province side of the boundary where they'd be fair game for a bullet. I glanced back at Sheep Lookout far above on the ridge. Now I understood why that vantage point was a popular spot for hunters; anyone at the lookout would have an incredible view across Solomon Basin and the slopes of Mount Kephala where I was standing. I checked the lookout again through my binoculars. I saw nothing but I felt uneasy and exposed. I sensed that I was being watched. I was used to being the observer, not the observed.

I watched the rams for a while longer before descending Mount Kephala back to the horses. I untied Harvey and Lucky and let them graze while I ate a late lunch. We then slowly made our way back up to the ridge above Norman Creek. When we reached the Jasper boundary marker on the crest of the ridge, I saw three sets of horse tracks. The first set was of Harvey and Lucky, made when we crested the ridge coming up from Norman Creek earlier in the day. The second set (made by two horses) crossed over top of Harvey and Lucky's shoe prints. These tracks led towards Sheep Lookout. A third set, made by the same two horses, was imprinted on top of the second set, heading *back* from the lookout. Two hunters, with their horses, had been to the lookout while I was in Solomon Basin and on the slopes of Mount Kephala. They had since returned, likely not much ahead of me, back north along the ridge and towards their camp in the Moosehorn Valley.

I rode to Sheep Lookout. From the matted vegetation I could see where the two hunters had crouched to observe the sheep, *and me*, on the slopes of Mount Kephala. I had come almost full circle, now gazing across to the basin where I had been watched. This explained the movement I saw, and the unease I felt, when I was looking up at Sheep Lookout from the slopes of Mount Kaphala earlier in the day. The four bighorn rams were still in sight but now much farther into the park. They had not crossed the boundary into the province. I spent the rest of the afternoon along the ridge looking for other sheep and hunting parties. It seemed we were now alone.

I set out again for the Boule Range from Moosehorn warden cabin with the horses the following morning. When we reached the cairn on the ridge crest, I spotted two hunters and their horses a kilometre away on Sheep Lookout. Through my binoculars, I could see that the two men were sitting with their backs to me, looking out across Soloman Basin towards Mount Kephala. I was eager to find out who they were. As Lucky, Harvey, and I approached, one of the men's horses whinnied. The men turned to see us approaching and got up to greet me. I recognized one as a horse outfitter that I had met on the North Boundary a year before. The other was his client, an American hunter. They said their camp was at Moosehorn Lake and that they were the two who had watched the sheep (and me) from the lookout the day before. The American hunter commented that he had followed my movements through his rifle scope while I was traversing the slopes of Mount Kephala. He had me *in his sights*. A simple pull on the trigger of his gun might have dropped me in my tracks!

I was stunned at what he had said and paused a few seconds to let his comment sink in. I felt the muscles tense on the back of my neck. I asked him if the safety was engaged on his rifle to prevent accidental firing as he followed my movements. He paused for a second and then said it had been. I wasn't so sure. It is an offence under the Criminal Code of Canada for a person to point a firearm at another person, with a penalty of imprisonment for up to five years. The offence, however, does not clearly define whether a person viewing another person through a scope on a firearm meets the definition of assault. I didn't have a clear case to charge the hunter unless there was intent to harm. On the other hand, the hunter's actions were clearly against a firearm user's code of ethics.

I sternly admonished the hunter for his actions. He was taken aback by my remarks but understood the significance of his mistake. I then took the outfitter aside and reproached him for allowing his client to break a code of ethics and possibly face a charge of assault. He knew that he had made a mistake. There was always the chance the hunter might never return to Canada, or at least to hunt in the Rockies. The outfitter, however, had a long career ahead of him in guiding clients in the area and bore some responsibility for his client's actions. His retribution lay ahead—his movements along the boundaries were followed closely in the years to come.

We talked for an hour or so while scanning the slopes below for sheep. Interestingly, the same four rams I had observed the previous day were still feeding on a grassy slope a few hundred metres inside the park boundary on Mount Kephala. Frustrated that the sheep were not moving out of the park and across the boundary into provincial territory where they could be legally shot, the two men packed up and headed back across the ridge towards Moosehorn Lake. It was evident they were also uncomfortable with my continued presence. I patrolled along the ridges for the remainder of the day.

The next day I took the horses up to the same area. The outfitter and his client had not returned. All was quiet except for an impressive blond grizzly the horses and I encountered as we rounded a corner of the trail on our way up Norman Creek. The grizzly stood up on its hind legs, sniffed the air to catch our scent, then dropped to all fours and bolted uphill into the timber and out of sight.

And what of the possible poaching activity somewhere in the Boule Range that Norm Woody had alerted me to? Alberta Fish and Wildlife officers later confirmed that two trophy bighorn rams had been legally shot along Solomon Creek well outside the Jasper boundary by clients of the outfitter Norm was concerned about. I was relieved to hear that the sheep were killed outside the park on provincial land and that there hadn't been any poaching under my watch.

Wes Bradford was another warden who experienced an interesting couple of days on one of his boundary patrols along the ridges above Norman Creek. Wes tied his horses to a tree below the crest of the ridge at the head of Norman Creek. Keeping a low profile, he walked the remainder of the trail towards the top of the ridge. There he spotted a guide and his client with their horses coming across the ridge from the north. They were heading in the direction of Sheep Lookout on the south side of the ridge, above and to the right of Wes. Wes crouched down and watched the men as they passed by approximately a hundred metres above him. They travelled at a slow pace, all the while looking around with their binoculars in search of sheep. As they passed to the right of him, Wes knew they would be heading to the lookout.

Wes hurried back down to check on his horses. He then traversed the slope on foot, towards but well below the lookout, paralleling the hunters' line of travel a hundred metres below. Wes found a small grouping of krummholz and crouched behind it. Five bighorn rams alternately grazed and rested several hundred metres inside the park in roughly the same area where I had observed the rams on my patrol. Wes sat for four hours watching the hunters walk back and forth on the ridge above. At times they'd disappear from view for a few minutes, only to reappear again. They raised their rifles at the sheep several times to look through their scopes, hoping the rams would cross over the boundary and into the province, but the rams remained inside the park. Finally, late in the afternoon, the hunters moved out.

The next day Wes headed up Norman Creek once again. The same scenario repeated itself, except this time there were two guides and two hunters. The five rams were still in the area, having barely moved. When the hunters began packing it in for the day, Wes scurried back to his horses and rode up to the ridge so they would cross paths. He intercepted the four men as they approached the boundary marker on the ridge crest above the Norman Creek drainage.

The group was surprised to see Wes. One of the guides remarked, "Well it's about time a park warden showed up in the area. Where have you been hanging out?" Having waited for the opportunity to say so, Wes responded, "Well, I've been watching you guys for the last two days." Wes went on to describe how he had followed their every movement: when they had passed by him each morning; when they had eaten lunch; their movements in observing the rams; how many rams they had watched; and even the length of curl each ram proudly displayed. Both guides fixed their gaze on Wes, disconcerted that he had been watching their every move the past couple of days. Their clients' jaws dropped. Clearly they were taken aback by Wes' actions and yet impressed that a park warden would go to such lengths to protect park wildlife. They respected

Wes for doing his job and Wes respected them, as it was clear they had abided by the rules of the game, even when under the impression that a park warden was nowhere around.

A year later, Ric West was assigned to the Moosehorn-Wolf Pass area for most of the autumn hunting season. One day while roaming the ridges above Norman Creek, Ric spotted five big rams in Solomon Basin. Looking back across the Moosehorn Valley towards the Wolf Pass area with his binoculars, he spotted two hunters and their horses on the mountain slopes above The Notch six kilometres away. Ric, aware that there hadn't been any recent movement of sheep in that area, anticipated the hunters might venture up towards Solomon Basin the next day.

Back at Moosehorn warden cabin the next morning, Ric jingled his three horses in the dark to get an early start. He had a feeling the day would be eventful. He headed straight up valley to Norman Creek with one horse, leaving the other two in the pasture near the cabin. Part way up the creek, his horse lifted its head to the right and upslope towards an old fire burn. Ric followed the line of his gaze and spotted a grizzly sow with two yearling cubs feeding in a blueberry patch 75 metres away. His horse, as was often the case with our horses, picked up on the grizzlies before its rider, this time by sight as an upslope breeze carried their scent towards the grizzlies. Moments later the familiar smell of man and horse reached the sow's sensitive nostrils. She whirled around from her feeding and gave Ric and his horse a long look. She then swayed her head back and forth several times to confirm that the intrusive smell carried by the breeze was coming from them. Satisfied by what her senses told her, she detected no harm from Ric and his horse. Ric watched the family for a few minutes before they leisurely continued across the slope to raid another blueberry patch.

Ric continued up the Norman Creek trail and stopped short of the ridge crest. He tied his horse to a stand of krummholz in the same area Wes had and cut across the slope towards Sheep Lookout. As he neared the crest, he spotted two horses above him. They were tied up below a boundary cairn, inside the park boundary. Ric guessed the two hunters were below their horses somewhere *inside* the park, roughly parallel to him but further along the same slope. Ric skirted uphill to avoid detection. He then topped the ridge and walked up to the horses. He was now directly above the two hunters—he could not see them but heard them talking not far below. Unknown to Ric at the time, the five rams he saw in Solomon Basin the day before had traversed several slopes, crossed over the boundary, and were now well inside the park about 700 metres cross slope and slightly below the hunters.

Ric stayed out of sight and close to the horses instead of looking for the hunters, knowing they'd eventually return. He didn't know whether they were traversing across the slope below him or staying in one spot. Ric checked the horses and the immediate surroundings. He noted the absence of the hunters' rifles. They had carried their weapons with them into the park. Realizing the seriousness of the situation, Ric considered his options: intervene and locate the hunters; stay with their horses until they returned; or look for another vantage point from where he might be able to spot them.

As Ric was considering his next move, he heard a resounding crack coming from the direction of the hunters, shattering the stillness along the high mountain slopes. An explosion of gunpowder inside a brass shell propelled a bullet out of the barrel of a high calibre rifle at 800 metres per second, twice the speed of sound. The bullet ripped through the flesh of a magnificent bighorn ram.

An American hunter had bagged a bighorn with its impressive full curl horns, a trophy he could proudly show his mates back home. The ram had been shot illegally, several hundred metres inside the park boundary. It was only wounded, however, and had slipped out of sight after being hit. The hunter and his guide hastened upslope towards Ric to get their horses and go looking for the ram.

As they came into view of the boundary marker at Ric's feet, he stood up as if materializing out of nowhere. Both guide and hunter reeled back in shock, dumbfounded. Ric walked over to them and asked if they had a permit to hunt wildlife in a national park. Of course they didn't. Ric arrested both of them and seized the hunter's rifle and hunting license. After all three searched unsuccessfully for the ram, Ric retrieved his horse near the Norman Creek trail and led the hunters and their horses back to Moosehorn warden cabin a couple of hours away. At the cabin, Ric issued the hunter a court appearance notice, charging him with hunting in a national park. He was later convicted, fined, and lost his rifle, which was forfeited to the Crown. The guide was subsequently relieved of his duties by the outfitter who had hired him.

And what became of the grand mountain monarch with the massive curled horns—the ram that within a month's time, in the prime of his life, would have competed against rivals to breed during the rut? Ric was certain it had died from its bullet wound shortly after it was shot. He tried to locate the injured ram on foot and then from a helicopter the following day, but he was unable to find him. The ram had likely lain down in a secluded spot to take its last breath not far from where the bullet had sealed its fate, its massive curled horns left to slowly bleach in the sun.

I wouldn't be surprised if the grizzly sow and two yearling cubs that Ric had seen earlier found the carcass. It would have provided them with much energy to store in their bodies for the upcoming winter hibernation.

CHAPTER EIGHTEEN

Hit and Run

The end of autumn boundary patrol in late October each year signalled the annual shift of job responsibilities—from six months of intensive fieldwork to six months of work split between field related duties and deskwork. A fair amount of time was spent summarizing and evaluating summer activities so we could effectively plan for the coming year. We also undertook as much training as possible in the late autumn, winter, and early spring to allow more time for field responsibilities during the warmer months of the year.

During the winter of 1981-82, much of my work was with Jasper's Conservation Planning Processes. On the heels of the success in reducing bear-human conflicts through the implementation of the Bear Management Plan, we tackled our next management plan. In late autumn, Rod Wallace, Tom Davidson, and I began work on the Backcountry Management Guidelines for Jasper National Park. We completed the first draft in the spring of 1982.

The goal of the guidelines was to protect the backcountry environment from overuse and misuse while allowing the best possible experience for wilderness adventurers. We established a quota system for hiking and horse parties to prevent overcrowding at campsites. Horse quotas were necessary to ensure that meadows could sustain grazing over the summer without impairing the ability of various grass species to reproduce the following year. Registration and permit systems for all overnight users of the backcountry and visitors engaging in single day hazardous activities, such as mountain climbing, were reviewed and updated. We outlined procedures for enforcement and inter-agency co-operation. This included the establishment of formal processes whereby national park wardens and provincial conservation officers could work together to enforce national and provincial wildlife and hunting regulations. As with all guideline documents, we reviewed and updated the Backcountry Management Guidelines on an annual basis.

Much of my time the following winter (1982-83) was spent preparing and implementing a Wildlife Monitoring Plan for the park with fellow wardens Rod Wallace and Ivan Phillips. The purpose of the plan was to expand and update our resource inventory program. The Biophysical Inventory had provided Parks Canada with baseline information on the abundance, distribution, and habitat requirements of wildlife species in Jasper National Park. But environmental systems are dynamic. Accordingly, the Wildlife Monitoring Plan was developed to track natural and man-induced changes in Jasper's wildlife populations. This monitoring provided data to assist us in identifying wildlife species and habitat that required long-term protection to prevent or alleviate disruption or damage caused by human activities or park infrastructure.

Determining which species to monitor and how much area to cover within the constraints of the yearly budget was a challenge. The plan had limitations due to the large size of the park—we couldn't cover it all. In the end, we decided to monitor ungulate species by air survey. We concentrated on ungulates—deer, elk, moose, caribou, sheep, and goat—because they have the greatest impact on range conditions, which ultimately determines the abundance and distribution of other wildlife species as well as plant species.

Most of our ungulate air surveys were done by helicopter during the winter months. As well, daily warden observations of other large species such as bears and wolves were recorded and compiled. All observations were plotted on maps to determine distribution, movement patterns, and special-use areas such as mineral licks, critical wintering habitat, migration routes, and calving areas. We could then identify areas where human disturbances, activities, infrastructure, and settlement had detrimental impacts on natural habitat and wildlife populations.

We surveyed ungulate herds that roamed in and out of the park boundary areas and wildlife that frequented the montane habitat in the lower valley areas of the park—the same areas congested with human presence. Many of the park's ungulates that move daily or seasonally into provincially managed lands are subjected to various pressures and stresses not experienced inside the park, such as hunting, trapping, and disturbances and loss of habitat associated with resource development. Wildlife in the park along transportation corridors and areas of human settlement are strongly influenced by human activities. The greatest impact comes from the high number of railway and highway fatalities. Other than the loss of prime wildlife habitat from park infrastructure, transportation corridor related wildlife mortalities have been, and remain, the leading cause of decline in many wildlife species.

◆ ◆ ◆

Although park wardens began compiling transportation corridor wildlife mortalities in the 1950s, it wasn't until 1980 that more accurate statistics were kept. Jasper Warden Service data on the number of ungulate mortalities in the five-year period from 1980-84 is distressing. A total of 76 elk, sheep, mule deer, whitetail deer, and moose were confirmed railway mortalities. A total of 262 of these species were killed on highways in the same time period. Although highway related mortalities were approximately four times greater than those on the railway, there was not a mandatory system in place for railway workers to report collisions until 1999.

The number of animals killed in more recent years has increased dramatically. Data for a 10-year period from 2003 to 2012 shows that a total of 288 elk, sheep, deer, and moose were killed on the railway, and 1067 mortalities occurred along the highway corridor. Even when rounded off to a five-year average to compare with the five-year statistics from the 1980s, the railway mortalities of these ungulate species have increased nearly two-fold. Part of the increase can be attributed to the enhanced reporting system initiated by the CNR in 1999. Highway mortalities had increased slightly more than two-fold compared to the period from 1980-84.

Thirteen caribou were killed on Jasper highways between 1980 and 2003. As this species is now scarce, no caribou have been killed on transportation corridors in Jasper since 2003. Mountain goat mortalities along the corridors are relatively rare because they seldom descend to lower elevations. Eighteen goats were killed on the highways between 1980 and 2012.

From 2003 to 2012, 55 black bears and 47 wolves were killed on the rails and roads. Fortunately, there were no reported grizzly transportation related mortalities. Excluded from the lists are all mammal species smaller than and including coyotes, and all bird species. Also excluded are young animals that fail to survive on their own after their mothers are hit and killed by a vehicle or train. A further omission from these statistics is injured animals that are able to walk away from vehicles or train collisions only to die sometime later—undetected and therefore not confirmed as transportation related mortalities.

Furthermore, highway and railway wildlife collision statistics do not include those animals that are not reported and confirmed as mortalities. The Warden Service in Jasper estimates that only half of commercial truck collisions with wildlife are reported. Confirmed passenger vehicle-wildlife collisions are much higher at approximately 80 percent. Although buses comprise a small percentage of traffic on park highways, all commercial bus collisions with wildlife are reported. Since the CNR introduced the mandatory system for reporting train-wildlife strikes in 1999, very few wildlife mortalities along the tracks go unreported.

◆ ◆ ◆

Over the course of his career as an engineer with the CNR in Jasper, my dad was most troubled knowing he had little control over the fate of animals spotted on the tracks. An average sized train of 85 freight cars loaded with grain barrelling down the rails at 80 kilometres an hour travels approximately a kilometre and a half before it can stop. If animals moved off the tracks immediately after they heard or saw a train, there'd be very little mortality. The problem is, many animals take their time moving. Some will not move off the tracks at all; others do not see or hear the train until it is too late.

Many railway-wildlife related collisions occur when animals

travel down the tracks in the same direction as an oncoming train and simply do not hear the locomotive bearing down on them until it is too late. Most wildlife species have an acute sense of hearing. At times though, when their ears and other senses are focused on what is in front of them, they may not hear a train approaching from behind. Locomotive engines can be surprisingly quiet if the train is approaching directly behind one's back. Moreover, winds that create significant turbulence at ground level can dampen sound. It amazes me how these huge and very powerful engines can be so quiet under certain atmospheric conditions.

Turning off a train's headlights at night momentarily when an animal is spotted in the middle of the tracks staring down the locomotive will break the mesmerizing spell of the bright beams. The animal won't, however, always leave the tracks. Sounding the train's horn doesn't always work either. Dad actually found that these tactics often confused animals, stalling their decision to move off the tracks.

The first railway-wildlife collision I responded to remains vivid in my memory. I received a call from Jasper Dispatch at around 4:00 a.m. in late autumn. A CNR train had run through a small herd of bighorn sheep at Windy Point, which is located at the end of a ridge that drops over a steep rock face to meet the rail right-of-way at the south end of Jasper Lake.

I drove along Celestine Lake Road to a rock face above the railway and then scrambled down to the location of the collision just as dawn was breaking. I walked along the tracks for a few minutes until I came upon the carnage. I found a young ram lying beside the tracks; it was in one piece but had died instantly from multiple injuries. A few metres away I found parts of a ewe, and then a few more parts scattered here and there, both on and to the sides of the tracks. I stood for a few moments, appalled, thinking how the train had come around the curve without much warning, slamming into the herd. Fortunately, most of the sheep had escaped.

As I walked further along the tracks I spotted another sheep, lying on its side. It appeared to be dead, but then I heard it bleat. The sound wasn't the high-pitched tone of a lamb, but neither was it like the more guttural 'baa!' that a ewe makes when calling for her lamb. When I reached the animal, I saw that it was a ewe with several serious injuries. She was barely alive. I was surprised she had not died instantly from her horrible wounds. Her eyes expressed extreme shock and distress. As I raised my rifle to end her pain, she bleated again. It was a distress call. I pulled the trigger. Approximately 15 metres away from the ewe I found what I expected: her lamb. The lamb's battered body lay on one side of the tracks; its severed head several metres away on the other side—the ewe's calls to her lamb had been in vain. I moved all the bodies and body parts well away from the tracks so scavengers would not, in turn, be hit by a train while feeding on the carcasses.

Over the years, my dad took great pleasure in viewing the mountain scenery and wildlife from the elevated cab of the large diesel locomotives he operated. Unfortunately, he experienced many wildlife collisions first hand in his 33 years as a railroader.

One of Dad's most disturbing incidents involved a grizzly that had moved onto the tracks several hundred metres in front of the locomotive. Dad hoped the bear would move off the tracks after it turned its head and looked down the rails at the train quickly gaining ground. The grizzly had about 20 seconds to react. It didn't. The bear stood its ground until the last few seconds before making a move to leap out of the train's path—but it was too late. Dad's heart skipped a beat as the locomotive plowed into the big animal, killing it instantly. On impact, the bear, rather than being tossed to one side of the train that is the usual case in collisions with a large animal, rolled under the front wheels. Dad said he felt something he had never experienced before: the bear's body jammed under the locomotive for a few seconds, long enough to lift it slightly off its wheels, before falling back into place. (A large heavy steel front grill or bumper called a 'cowcatcher' usually pushes an animal off the tracks). Dad had never heard of an animal derailing a locomotive, but if there was ever a close call, perhaps that was it.

Although a train crew can be expected to see elk or deer on almost every run, a grizzly sighting is a relatively rare occurrence. Dad mentioned that the grizzly he hit was one of the largest and most impressive bears he had ever seen. He felt so terrible about the incident that he didn't talk about it until many years later when he was near retirement.

Dad told me of an equally disturbing collision during a heavy snow winter in the early 1970s when he encountered a large bull moose on the tracks a half hour west of town near the banks of the Miette River. Over a several week period of prolonged snowfall, the railway snow plow had created a snow bank several metres high alongside the tracks. Animals occasionally walk along the cleared railway right-of-way during the winter to avoid deep snow. To get onto the tracks, they must navigate through the deeper snow along the sides that has been deposited by the plows. Once on the tracks, they are reluctant to move off until they reach their destination.

Coming around a corner, Dad spotted the moose from his high perch in the locomotive. The moose was a half-kilometre away. The bull, walking between the rails towards the train, stopped for several seconds and fixed his eyes on the massive 7,000-tonne iron beast that was moving towards him. It was clearly challenging him for the right-of-way. Deciding not to confront his adversary, the bull turned on his heels and ran down the centre of the tracks, taking great strides with his long powerful legs. Before he got too far, however, he looked over his shoulder and could see that he was unable to outrun the train that was now quickly gaining ground. The moose stopped, spun around, put his ears back and faced the train. And then he charged. In relating the outcome of the story to me, Dad shook his head and with emotion in his eyes said, "It was like a fly hitting a windshield."

Wildlife mortalities along the railway are not restricted to mammals. Dad occasionally observed golden eagles feeding on the carcasses of railway-killed animals that CNR employees or wardens had not yet had the chance to move away from the tracks. One day, he came upon two eagles feeding on what he thought was a deer carcass in the middle of the tracks. The eagles immediately turned tail, but with their bellies full of meat they had trouble lifting off. Like a heavily-loaded cargo plane, they required a long runway. The train hit them before they were able to get more than a couple of metres off the ground.

Apart from the unfortunate head-on collisions with animals, Dad took delight in the thousands of wildlife sightings he saw from the train over the course of his career. He even had one very cheerful experience involving a family of geese caught in the middle of the tracks. Dad was travelling west alongside a marshy area across from Snaring Warden Station one beautiful spring day when he observed a family of Canada geese crossing the rails 150 metres ahead. They had approximately 10 seconds to get off the tracks. One parent was in the middle of the rails with three or four goslings. The second parent was on the outside of a rail coaxing another group of goslings to climb over. With only seconds remaining, the parent had the other goslings over the rail. Now, both parents and all the goslings were in the middle of the tracks. It was too late—the train roared over the entire family. Dad couldn't see over the nose of the locomotive but he imagined the parents having their necks torn from their bodies and the goslings rolling uncontrollably along the rail bed to their deaths from air turbulence under the train. But, perhaps not.

Dad hunted geese in his younger years and he knew about an interesting aspect of their behaviour. One behavioural trait the adults have when avoiding a predator is to lie flat and stretch their very long necks down in front of their bodies. The goslings dive under their parents' wings—something they learn when they are very young to keep warm. Dad hoped for the best, but feared the worse. He immediately called back to the brakeman in the caboose and asked him to rush out to the back deck and look for the geese. Dad waited. About a minute and a half went by before his radio crackled above the noise inside the locomotive. The excited voice of the brakeman was on the other end, telling Dad that he couldn't believe his eyes. After the caboose rolled over the geese, the whole family straightened up and scurried away from the tracks. They were likely a bit dazed and dirty but none the worse for wear. Dad was overjoyed. We heard this story as soon as he arrived home.

As with many aspects of a park warden's job, even the seemingly safe task of responding to an animal killed on the tracks can be fraught with danger. The most notorious location for sheep kills along the CNR through Jasper is around the western end of Brule Tunnel.

FOUR CONTIGUOUS ROCKY MOUNTAIN NATIONAL PARKS: JASPER, BANFF, YOHO, KOOTENAY

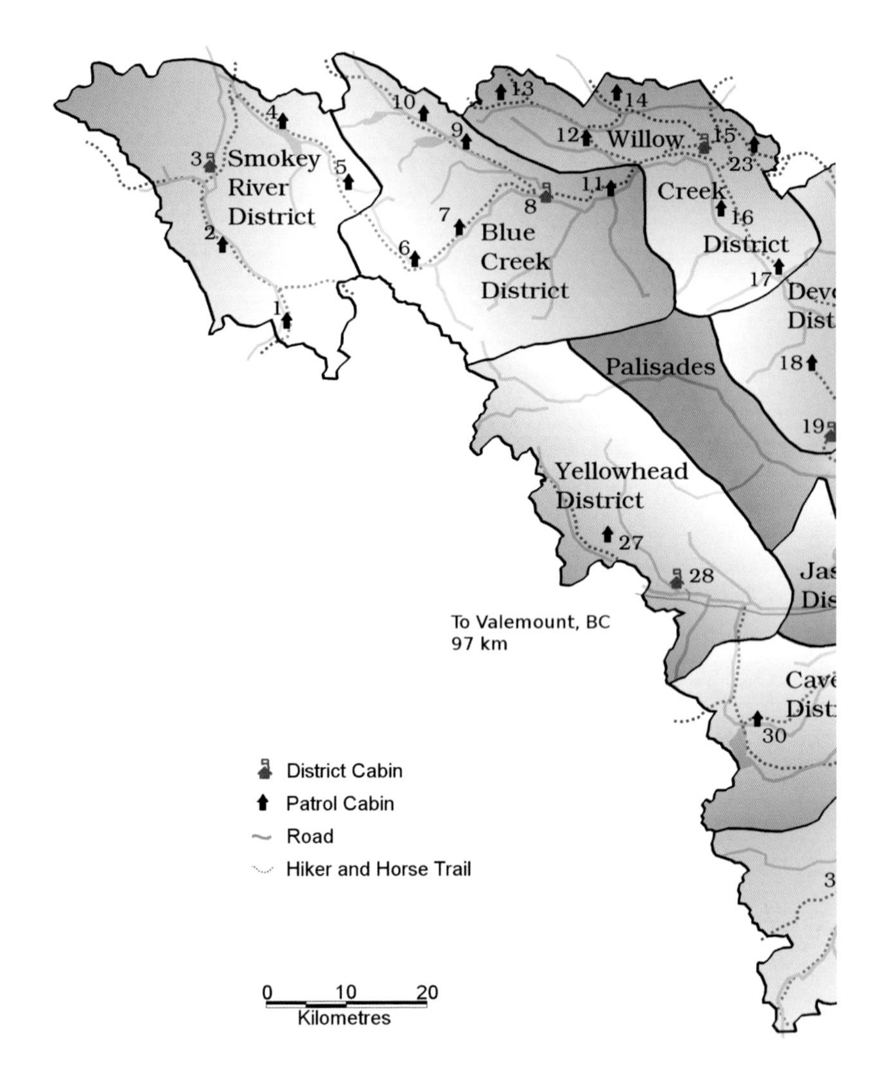

JASPER NATIONAL PARK WARDEN DISTRICTS AND CABINS

(circa late 1960s)

Refer to page 184 for listing of warden cabins.

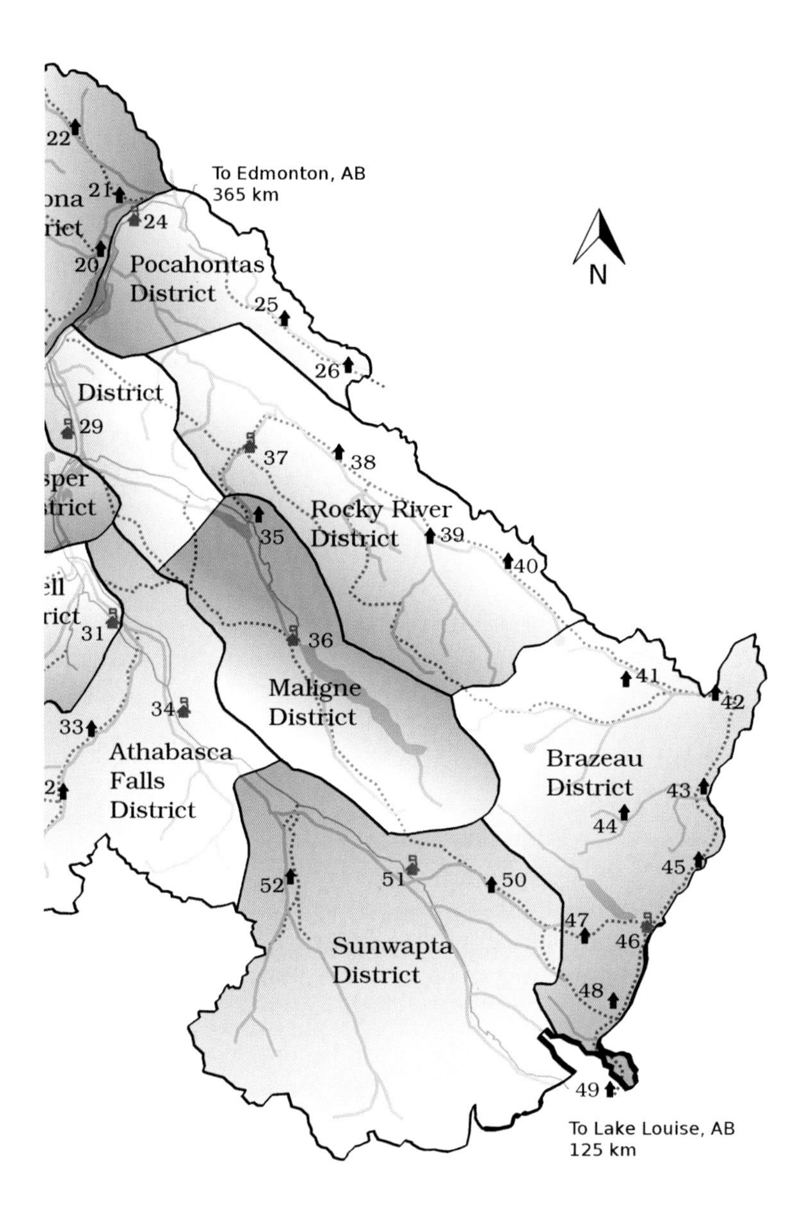

Nicole Eckert-Lyngstad (from an original topographical map courtesy of Parks Canada)

Smoky River District
1. Adolphus
2. Wolverine
3. *Smoky River*
4. Twintree
5. Byng

Blue Creek District
6. Hoodoo
7. Three Slides
8. *Blue Creek*
9. Topaz
10. Caribou Inn*
11. Welbourne

Willow Creek District
12. Little Heaven
13. Vega*
14. Starlight*
15. *Willow Creek*
16. Seldom Inn**
17. Shalebanks

Devona District
18. Vine Creek
19. *Snaring*
20. Devona**
21. Miette
22. Moosehorn
23. Wolf Pass*

Pocahontas District
24. *Pocahontas*
25. Fiddle
26. Whitehorse*

Yellowhead District
27. Rink**
28. *Decoigne*

Palisades District
29. *Palisades*

Jasper District
(Warden Office)

Cavell District
30. Tonquin
31. *Cavell*

Athabasca Falls District
32. Middle Forks
33. Tie Camp**
34. *Athabasca Falls*

Maligne District
35. Beaver
36. *Maligne Lake*

Rocky River District
37. *Jacques Lake*
38. Grizzly**
39. Rocky Forks
40. Medicine Tent

Brazeau District
41. Cairn
42. Southesk**
43. Isaac Creek
44. Sawtooth*
45. Arête
46. *Brazeau*
47. Poboktan
48. Four Point
49. Camp Parker

Sunwapta District
50. Waterfalls
51. *Sunwapta*
52. Chaba**

* Cabins built since the late 1960s.

** Cabins decommissioned since the late 1960s (Grizzly and Southesk cabins were rebuilt after being destroyed by forest fires).

*** Oldhorn cabin was removed from the Cavell District in the mid-1980s and moved to Sunwapta District. It was renamed Chaba.

NOTES:

The Jasper National Park Districts map and list of warden cabins on the preceding pages show the Jasper National Park District System as it existed in the late 1960s. District headquarters are listed in italics.

Beginning in the late 1960s, eight of the 13 districts were slowly phased out as a result of centralization. Wardens were no longer assigned to a specific district but were required to work throughout the park. The three backcountry districts on the North Boundary (Smoky, Blue Creek, and Willow Creek) and the two backcountry districts on the South Boundary (Rocky River and Brazeau), remained operational until 2013.

In 2004, regular backcountry patrol was reduced from five wardens to two—one warden for each of the Boundary (North and South) districts. As of 2013, wardens are no longer assigned backcountry postings. Very few now have the skill set and training to manage the park's expansive backcountry areas. Many warden cabins in Jasper and the other Canadian Rocky Mountain national parks are now in a state of disrepair and slowly fading into the past, much like the traditional role of the backcountry warden.

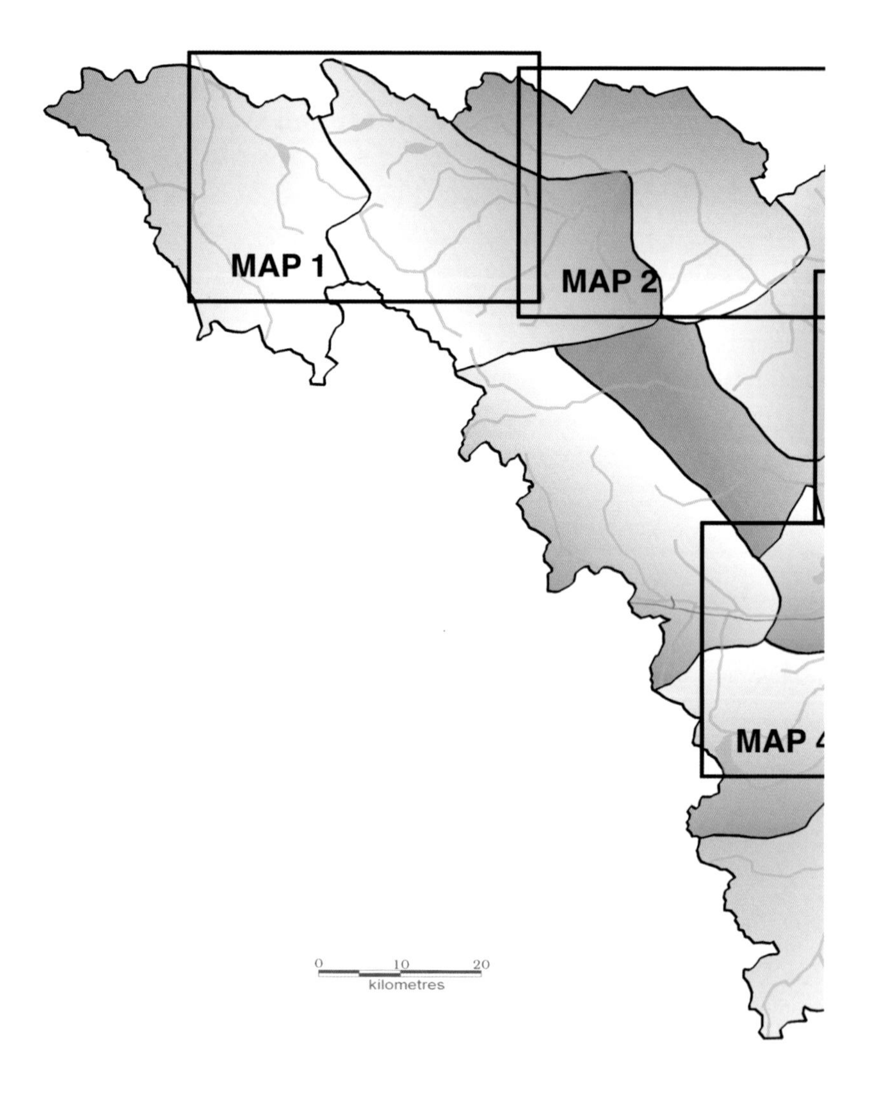

JASPER NATIONAL PARK – TOPOGRAPHIC AREA MAPS

(See Maps 1 to 6 on following pages)

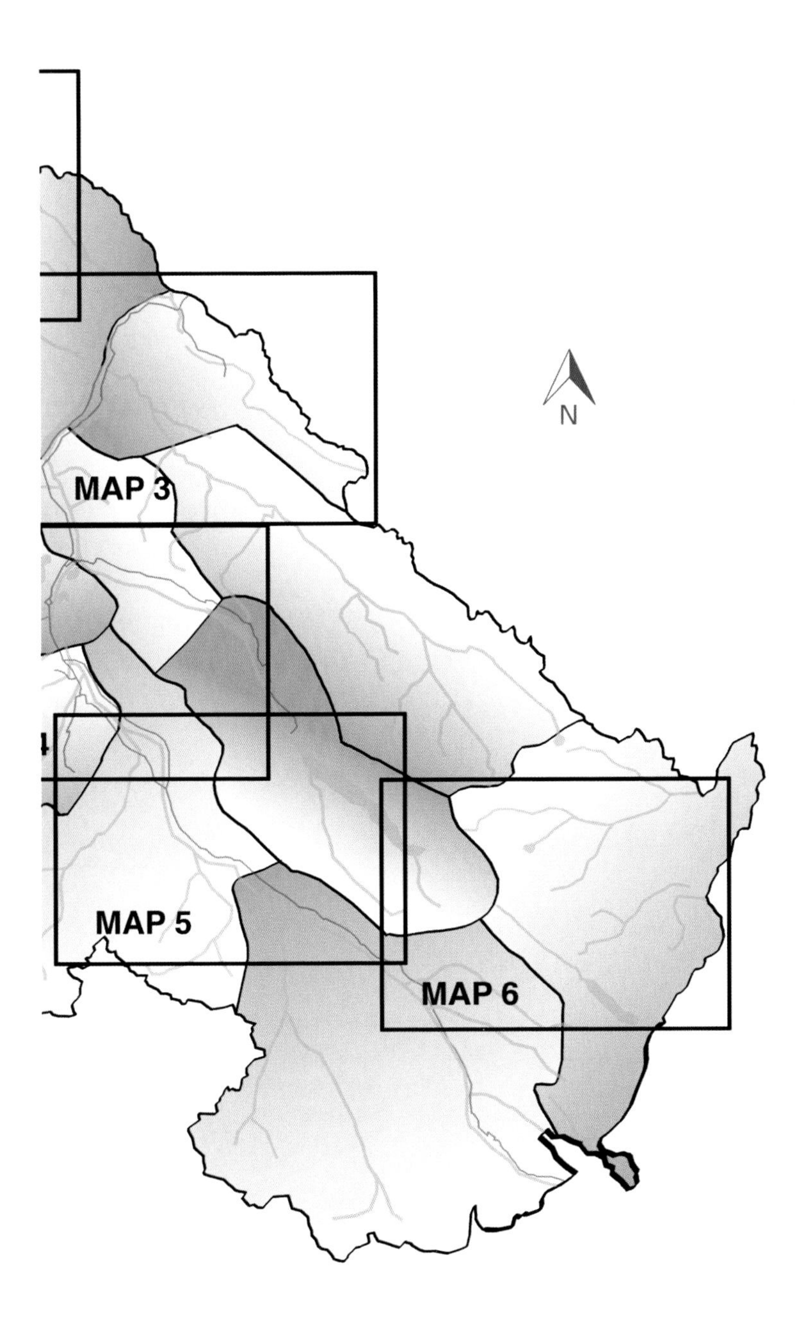

Nicole Eckert-Lyngstad (from an original topographical map courtesy of Parks Canada)

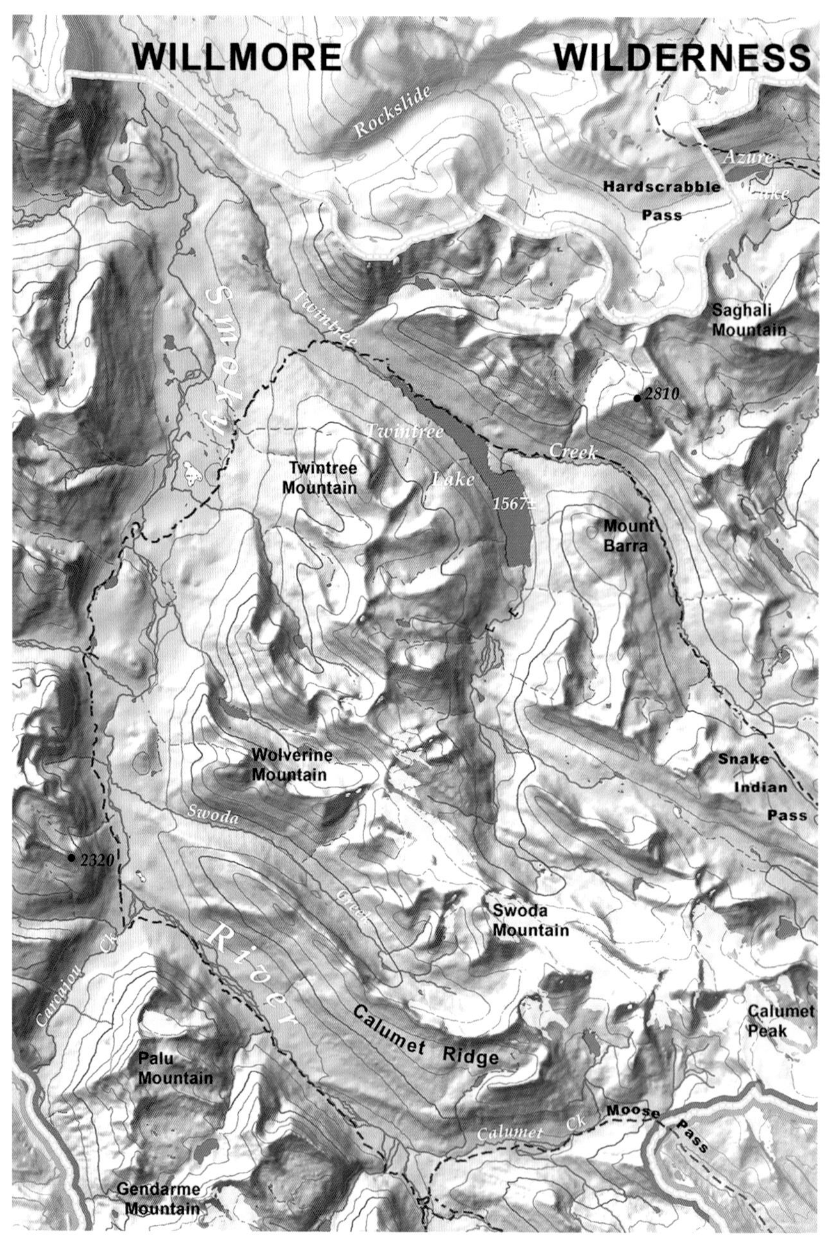

TOPOGRAPHIC MAP 1. North Boundary – West

Willmore Wilderness Park (bordering the north of Jasper National Park) Smoky River Valley, Snake Indian Valley, Blue Creek.

Map Scale: 3 centimetres = approximately 5 kilometres. Contour Interval = 200 metres

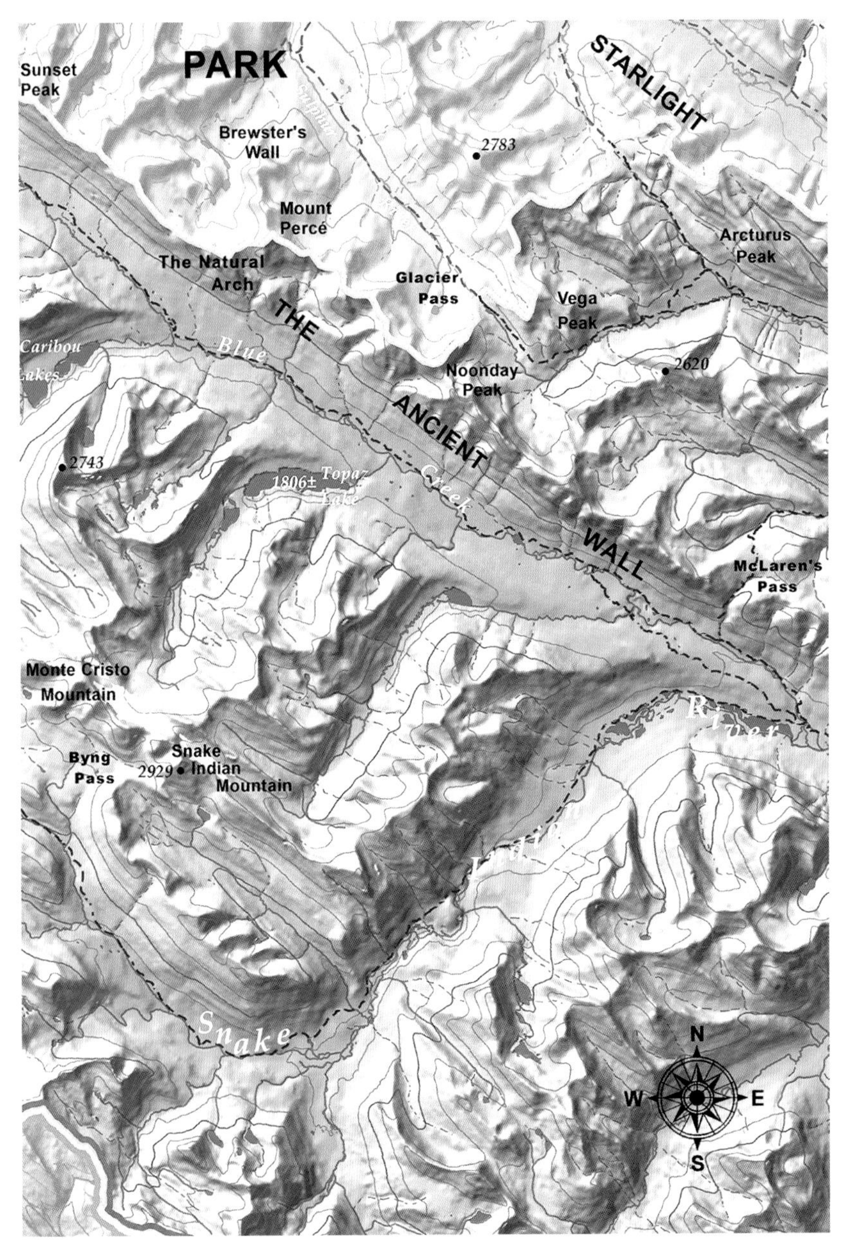

Base map ©2016 MM Cartographics.
Additional text added by the author.

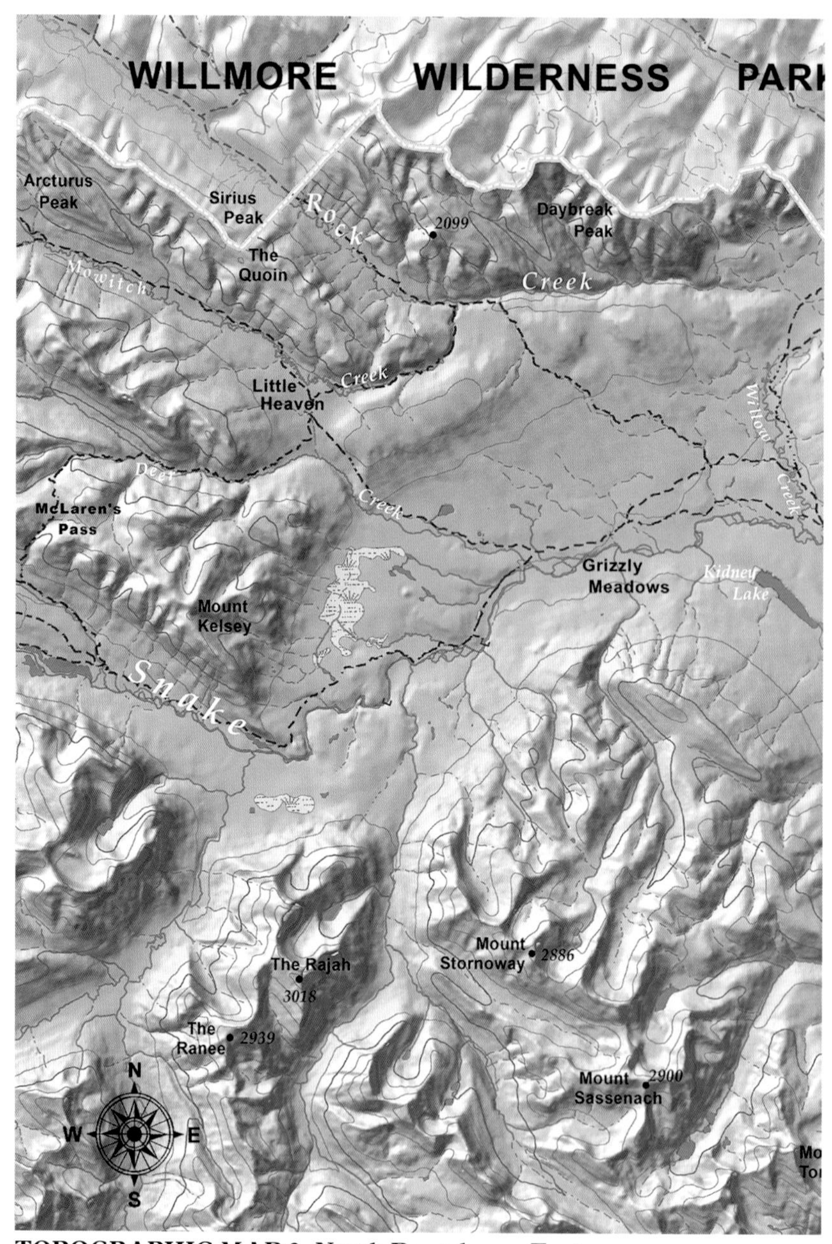

TOPOGRAPHIC MAP 2. North Boundary – East

Snake Indian and Moosehorn Valleys, Deer, Mowitch, and Willow Creeks, Willmore Wilderness and Rock Lake – Soloman Creek Wildland Parks.

Map Scale: 3 centimetres = approximately 5 kilometres. Contour Interval = 200 metres

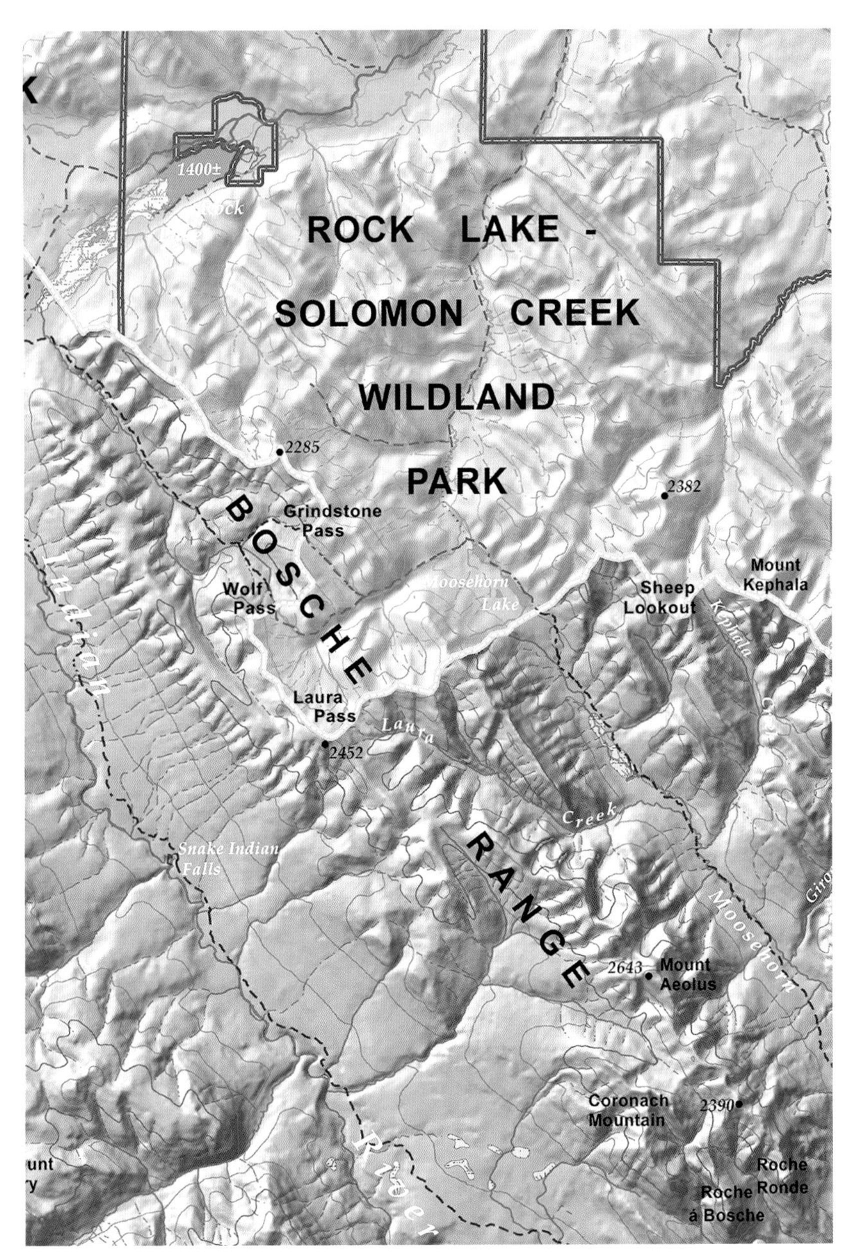
1400±
ROCK LAKE -
SOLOMON CREEK
WILDLAND
PARK
2285
Grindstone Pass
BOSCHE
Wolf Pass
Moosehorn Lake
2382
Sheep Lookout
Mount Kephala
Kephala
Indian
Laura Pass
Laura
2452
Creek
RANGE
Snake Indian Falls
Moosehorn
2643
Mount Aeolus
Coronach Mountain
2390
Roche Ronde
Roche á Bosche
River

TOPOGRAPHIC MAP 3. Athabasca River Valley – East

Athabasca River Valley, Jasper Lake, Devona, Snake Indian Valley, Moosehorn Valley, Rocky River Valley, Pocahontas, Fiddle River Valley.

Map Scale: 3 centimetres = approximately 5 kilometres. Contour Interval = 200 metres

Base map ©2016 MM Cartographics. All rights reserved.
Additional text added by the author.

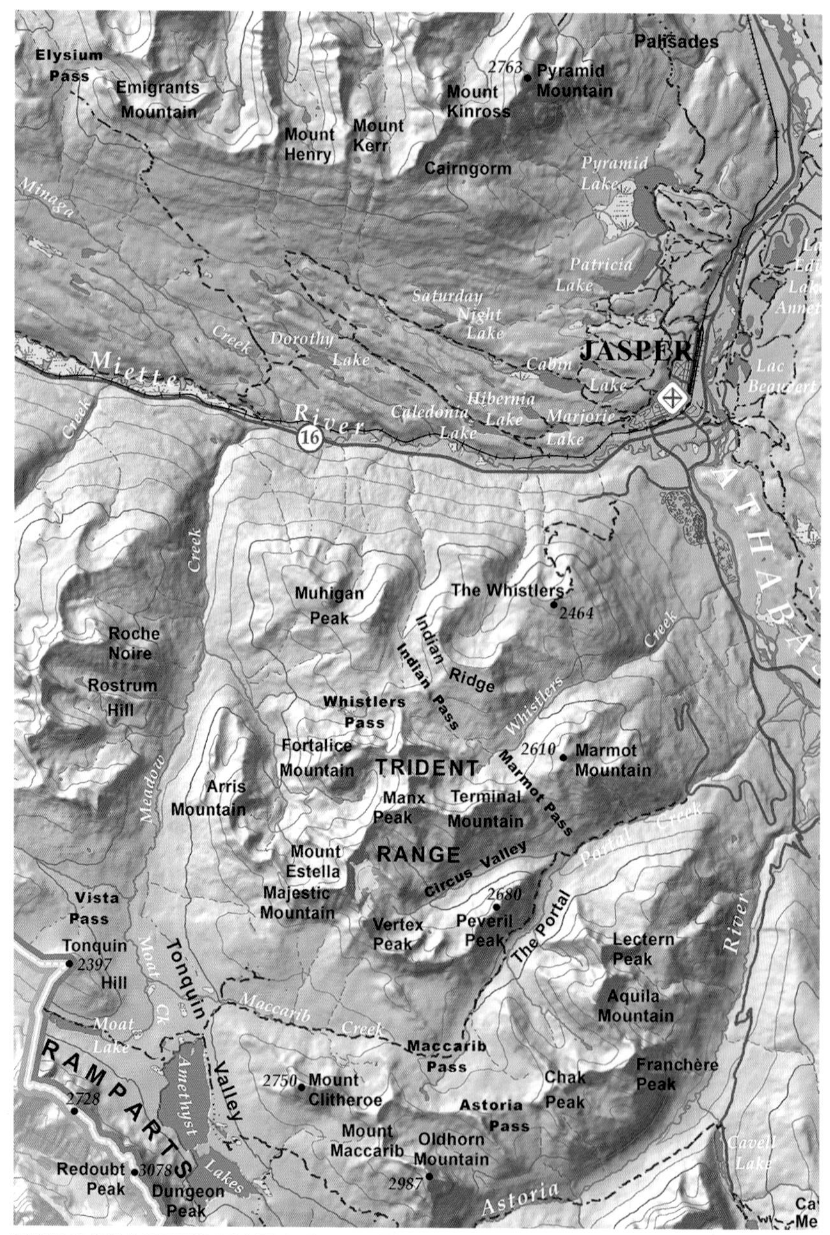

TOPOGRAPHIC MAP 4. Jasper Townsite and Three-Valley Confluence

Jasper Townsite, Confluence of Miette, Athabasca, and Maligne Rivers, Tonquin Valley, Medicine Lake.

Map Scale: 3 centimetres = approximately 5 kilometres. Contour Interval = 200 metres

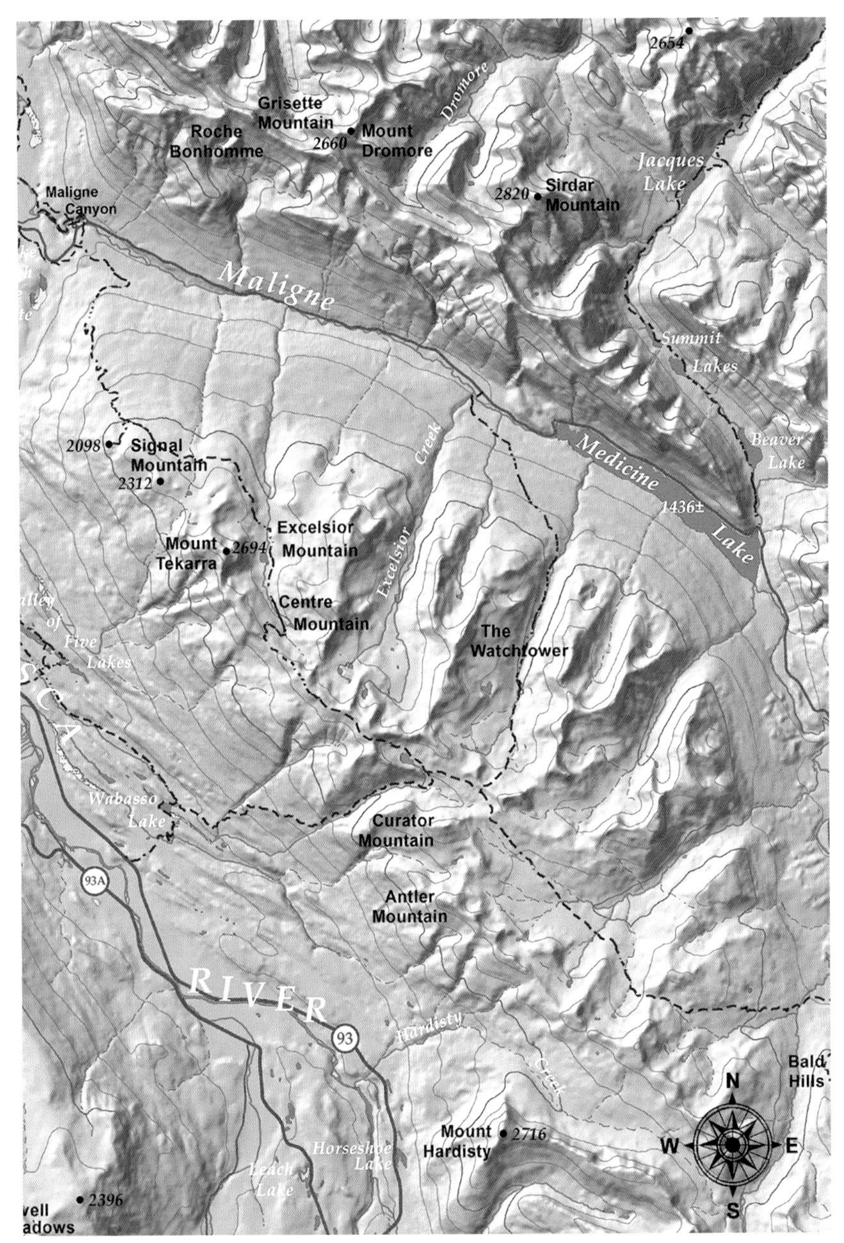

Base map ©2016 MM Cartographics. All rights reserved.
Additional text added by the author.

TOPOGRAPHIC MAP 5. Maligne Lake and Athabasca River Valley – South

Whirlpool River Valley, Athabasca River Valley, Sunwapta River Valley, Maligne Lake.

Map Scale: 3 centimetres = approximately 5 kilometres. Contour Interval = 200 metres

Additional text added by the author.

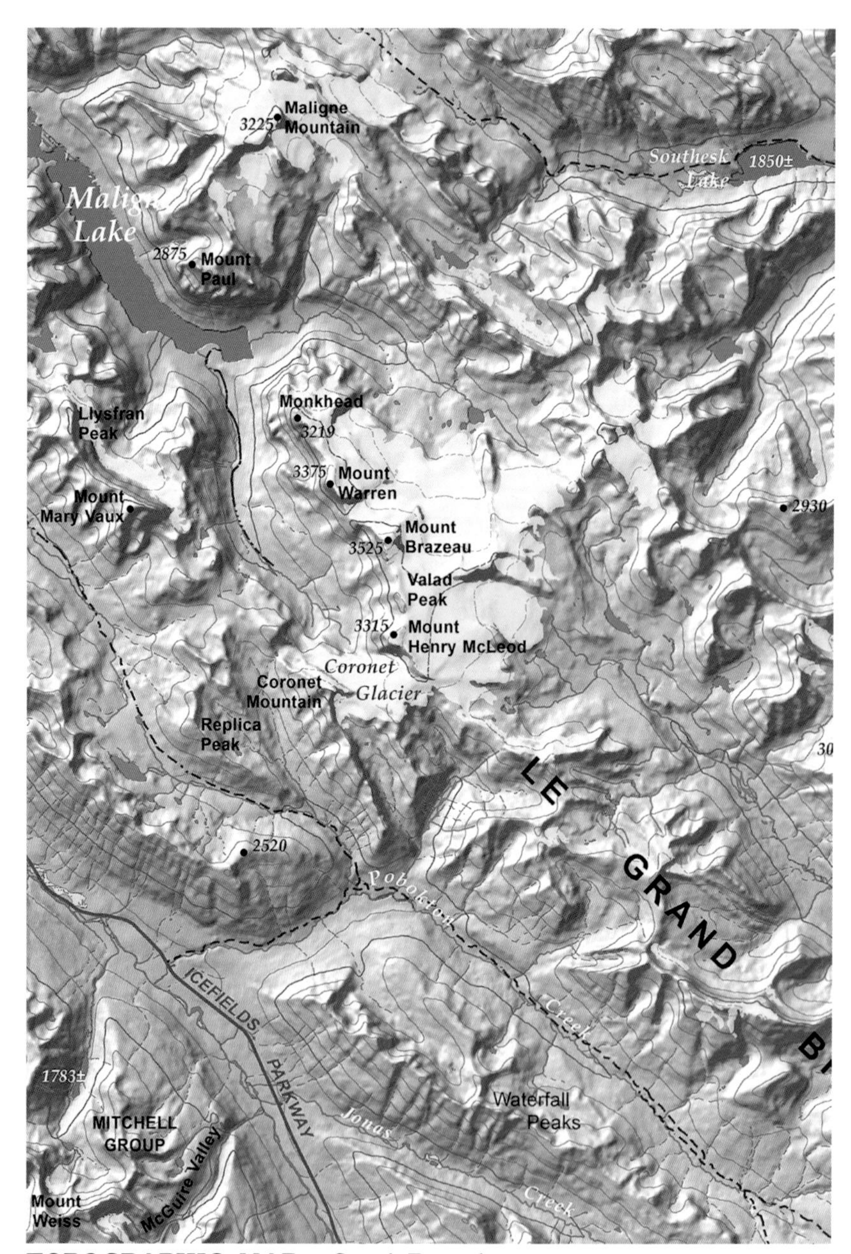

TOPOGRAPHIC MAP 6. South Boundary

Brazeau Lake, Brazeau River Valley, Isaac Creek, Southesk River Valley.

Map Scale: 3 centimetres = approximately 5 kilometres. Contour Interval = 200 metres

Base map ©2016 MM Cartographics. All rights reserved.
Additional text added by the author.

Jasper House. A Hudson's Bay Company trading post situated near the confluence of the Snake Indian and Athabasca rivers, 1872.

JASPER WARDEN SERVICE ARCHIVES, CHARLES HORETZKY.

Forest rangers (also known as game guardians before they were given the title park wardens) leaving Fitzhugh (renamed Jasper in 1913), 1911.

C.H. MORSE. DOMINION FORESTRY BRANCH, ALBERTA FOREST PROTECTION COLLECTION.

Feeding bears was a popular, but dangerous pastime in Jasper during the early years of park establishment, ca. 1920.

JASPER YELLOWHEAD MUSEUM and ARCHIVES (PA 18-144), GEORGE CAMP

A young black bear makes a hasty exit from a house in the town of Jasper, ca. 1920.

JASPER YELLOWHEAD MUSEUM and ARCHIVES (PA 18-103).

Park Warden Ed McDonald is carried out of the backcountry on a stretcher between two horses after sustaining a broken pelvis when his horse, spooked by a grizzly, bucked him off, 1937.

JASPER YELLOWHEAD MUSEUM and ARCHIVES (994.56.1606).

Park Warden Toni Klettl on the North Boundary with his daughter, Linda, and dog, Storm (pulling Linda in the home-made sled) in winter, late 1950s.

JASPER YELLOWHEAD MUSEUM and ARCHIVES (990.05.04), SHIRLEY KLETTL.

The lower Athabasca River Valley near Devona on the banks of the Snake Indian River. Archaeological studies in the area have unearthed 9000 year-old Aboriginal camps.

ROB KAYE COLLECTION.

The Jasper Rodeo at Marmot Meadows on the southern end of present day Whistlers Campground, 1950s.

ROD WALLACE COLLECTION.

Marilyn Monroe in a contemplative mood at Devona with one of the horses used during the filming of River of No Return, 1953.

JASPER PHOTOGRAPHY MM-3, RAY O'NEILL.

Ski jumping competition at Whistlers Ski Hill. The town of Jasper is in the valley below, 1961.

JASPER YELLOWHEAD MUSEUM and ARCHIVES (994.45.135.2), HARRY ROWED/KEITH ALLEN EXPOSURES.

Park Warden Rick Ralf at Blue Creek warden cabin on Jasper's North Boundary. A district headquarters cabin, it is roughly twice the size of the smaller patrol cabins in the backcountry districts.

ROB KAYE COLLECTION.

The interior of Brazeau warden cabin, the district headquarters cabin of the Brazeau District. Note both the cook stove and the heater stove behind it.

NICOLE ECKERT-LYNGSTAD COLLECTION.

Helicopters are used extensively to transport trail crews and their supplies into the backcountry.

JASPER WARDEN SERVICE ARCHIVES.

The Ancient Wall backdrops Topaz warden cabin. Topaz is the typical size of the smaller warden patrol cabins in the backcountry districts.

ROB KAYE COLLECTION.

Catching fish for dinner (cutthroat trout from Mowitch Creek here) provided fresh meals to supplement dwindling food supplies on my prolonged backcountry trips.

ROB KAYE COLLECTION.

A pair of hobbles, a bell, and an oat bag hang on tacks outside a warden cabin.

ROB KAYE COLLECTION.

Julia Paterson with horses (from left to right) Indian, Help, and Ernie in the upper Blue Creek Valley. The lower slopes and craggy peaks along the spectacular Ancient Wall mountain range provide optimum range for bighorn sheep and mountain goats.

ROB KAYE COLLECTION.

Bighorn sheep habitually rest where they can view the surrounding terrain for potential predators. The autumn rut, which features dramatic head clashes amongst the rams, is an impressive sight.

ROB KAYE COLLECTION.

Mountain goats usually remain on high rocky crags and sparsely vegetated mountain slopes. They can occasionally be observed from close range each spring at mineral licks along Jasper's roadways.

ROB KAYE COLLECTION.

Park Warden Patti Walker skids firewood at Little Heaven warden cabin with her horse, Oyster. Skidding wood with a horse and harness, much like many tasks performed by backcountry wardens, evokes simpler times and age-old traditions.

AL MCKEEMAN COLLECTION.

Evelyn, Gander, and Hawk enjoy a relaxing, non-travel day at Willow Creek. Daybreak Peak is in the distance.

ROB KAYE COLLECTION.

Speed and inattentiveness on park roadways can kill. A truck driver barrelled into these elk near the Palisades Training Centre, eight kilometres east of the town of Jasper.

WES BRADFORD COLLECTION.

Elk are frequently observed in the high visitor use areas of the Rocky Mountain national parks. A bull's piercing bugle attracts cows and sends a challenge to other bulls. The bulls' battle for dominance adds to the spectacle of the autumn rut.

WWW.DONALDMJONES.COM.

Bull elk should be given a wide berth—especially during the autumn rut. This photo was taken at the east end of the town of Jasper.

JAMIE BRUHA COLLECTION.

Bull elk that demonstrate overt aggressiveness towards people during the autumn rut are often tranquilized and relocated away from human activity. From left to right, unidentified park employee, and Park Wardens Norm Woody, Rod Wallace and Gord Antoniuk.

JASPER WARDEN SERVICE ARCHIVES.

Toni Klettl and Denny Welsh trigger controlled avalanches on the slopes above Marmot Basin Ski Area with a 105 mm recoilless rifle. The concussive force of the backblast, a powerful discharge of hot air and gases, is visible at the rear of the rifle.

JASPER WARDEN SERVICE ARCHIVES.

It is not uncommon for skiers venturing into closed areas or on slopes off the beaten path to trigger avalanches. Here, park wardens and volunteers search for a skier buried by an avalanche by probing with metal rods.

PARK WARDEN SERVICE ARCHIVES.

Maligne Lake from the summit of Leah Peak. Samson Peak (upper left) and the twin glaciated peaks of Mount Charlton and Mount Unwin (upper right) rise above the middle of the lake.

ROB KAYE COLLECTION.

Park Warden Terry Damm descending from our successful climb of Mount Charlton and Mount Unwin. Our earlier ascent route followed the steep ice slope between the two larger rock outcrops in the lower-right side of the photograph.

ROB KAYE COLLECTION.

A section of the boundary between Jasper National Park and Willmore Wilderness Park (in the far background) follows along the ridgeline between the mid-ground peak (left) and the highest peak (right). This is typical terrain wardens patrol during the provincial hunting season.

ROB KAYE COLLECTION.

Beavers, known as "nature's engineers", take raw materials (stones, logs, sticks, and mud) and convert them into complex lodges, canals, and dams that create diverse wetland ecosystems. The beaver's winter cache (food supply) is to the left of the family lodge.

ROB KAYE COLLECTION.

Osprey and a myriad of bird species, along with moose and beaver, depend on pristine wetland habitat in the lower montane valleys of the Rocky Mountains to sustain healthy population levels.

ROB KAYE COLLECTION.

Moose populations have declined significantly in the last half-century in the Rocky Mountain national parks due to the loss of montane habitat. Many are also killed on park railways and roadways.

JASPER WARDEN SERVICE ARCHIVES.

Wolves, a keystone species vital to a healthy ecosystem, are still culled indiscriminately throughout western Canada. Only in the national parks do they enjoy a relatively safe haven.

WWW.DONALDMJONES.COM.

Woodland caribou populations in the Rocky Mountain national parks are in a state of precarious decline. They are listed as endangered by the Committee on the Status of Endangered Wildlife in Canada.

WWW.DONALDMJONES.COM.

Black Bears habituate readily to the presence of humans and are commonly observed in the Rocky Mountain national parks.

WWW.DONALDMJONES.COM.

Black bears and other wildlife frequent highway corridors as travel routes and to feed alongside them. When "bear jams" occur, park visitors are advised to remain in their vehicles and proceed slowly.

WES BRADFORD COLLECTION.

Park Warden Rod Wallace demonstrates the workings of a bear trap to a Scouting group.

JASPER WARDEN SERVICE ARCHIVES.

Park Interpreter Adrienne Mason introduces my riding horse, Anita, and me to the audience at a campfire presentation at Pocahontas Campground before my talk about the role of a park warden.

ROB KAYE COLLECTION.

Grizzly numbers in Jasper National Park remain fairly stable. In recent years, however, their populations have declined in Banff and other Rocky Mountain national parks.

WWW.DONALDMJONES.COM.

A grizzly sow we captured behind a bungalow camp in Jasper. We tranquilized the sow and her yearling cub (not seen in the photo) before placing them in a cargo net and slinging them under a helicopter for relocation to the backcountry.

ROB KAYE COLLECTION.

The Fiddle River Valley meanders below the frontal ranges of the Rockies in Jasper. The foothills of west-central Alberta lie beyond the Jasper National Park boundary that traverses across Table Mountain (distant left) and Slide Mountain (distant right).

ROB KAYE COLLECTION.

With Gar at Grindstone Pass. We could always expect a snowstorm or two during the autumn boundary patrol season.

ROB KAYE COLLECTION.

An early evening nap with the horses after a long day in the backcountry.

ROB KAYE COLLECTION.

An October snowfall at the Fiddle River trailhead near Miette Hotsprings. Sara, my canine companion, stands beside the warden truck and horse trailer.

ROB KAYE COLLECTION.

I made one of my last trips into Willow Creek District shortly before my retirement with Park Warden Brad Romaniuk. Brad with our horses (from left to right) Duncan, Hootchie, and Wrangler in the Mowitch Creek Valley.

ROB KAYE COLLECTION.

Chrystyne (left) with Dr. John Di Toppa and his wife Paola, in the Fiddle River Valley.

ROB KAYE COLLECTION.

The tunnel cuts through 200 metres of rock through Benson Ridge along the eastern boundary of Jasper National Park just above the Athabasca River. Sheep spend much of their time in the area because there is excellent graze on nearby mountain slopes and rock outcrops around the tunnel provide them with escape terrain from predators. They also feed on grain that spills from trains in and around the tunnel. Sheep enter the tunnel, especially during the summer months, to get away from flies and heat.

The railway follows a tight curve through the tunnel. Its western end is in the park while its eastern end is on the province side of the boundary. I never had my back to the tunnel and never walked on the track. With a stiff wind blowing from the west, which is often the case, a train is almost soundless as it rounds the curve in the tunnel at its western entrance. It can appear from out of the tunnel's mouth with no warning—hence all the sheep deaths that have occurred over the years.

I was called out several times to respond to train/sheep collisions around the tunnel's western entrance. This required taking a canoe across the Athabasca River five kilometres downstream from Pocahontas Warden Station and climbing up a steep embankment of boulders. Our policy was to always check the tunnel itself for sheep that could be dragged inside after a collision. Because of its curve and darkened walls from years of diesel exhaust, the tunnel has no direct light and no reflected light at its centre. Walking through the black zone in anticipation of a train barrelling around the curve is a powerful adrenalin rush. The distance between the tracks and the blackened tunnel walls leaves very little room for someone to squeeze up against the wall if caught by a train. I scoped out the uneven cuts in the walls with a flashlight every time I walked through the tunnel, keeping in mind the spots where slight crevasses in the rock cuts gave a little extra squeezing room.

I was checking out a report of a sheep hit at the eastern tunnel entrance in the autumn of 1985. I walked the tunnel's length looking for it. I found the carcass right at the edge of the eastern entrance and dragged it off into nearby bushes. I listened for a train but could hear nothing, so I headed back through the tunnel. As I rounded the curve within sight of the west entrance, I heard a train behind me. Running like hell, I popped out the entrance seconds before the train whistled by.

A year later, Rod Wallace and Wes Bradford had a similar experience but with a different outcome. They were faced with the grim task of pulling out three dead sheep hit by a train at the tunnel's west entrance. One had been dragged into the middle of the tunnel, a long way from the welcoming light at either end. They got two of the carcasses out and then went back for the third deep inside. On their way out, they noticed a slight glow on the soot-plastered walls ahead of them. Almost instantly, they faced a blinding light accompanied by a deafening roar. They jumped for a crevasse in the wall face and were engulfed by smoke, noise, and extreme wind turbulence from the passing train, less than an arm's length away. After a few cars roared by, they realized they had tucked close enough against the wall to avoid being ripped apart. But freight cars come in different widths and it is not unusual for a car or two to be dragging a loose tie-down or strap. Any contact with one of those whipping by at fast speed could have sliced them in two. Fortunately, the train passed by without incident.

Today, before wardens enter the dark and dangerous interior of the tunnel, they must call in to CNR rail traffic control to check when trains are due to pass through the tunnel. Well, that just takes away from some of the excitement of the job! Ahh... the good old days.

A fencing structure at both Brule Tunnel entrances had been proposed for many years; it was finally constructed by the CNR in 2001. The fence, made from wire mesh, extends 50 metres from the tunnel's west entrance and 20 metres from the east entrance. The ends of the fences flare in close to the rails where they meet sections of Teflon board that are loosely bolted and unstable. Sheep, because of their hardened sharp hooves, find the Teflon difficult to walk on, so this fence has been very effective in reducing sheep collisions around the tunnel. If not maintained properly, however, the Teflon board becomes coated with dirt and grit; this has allowed a few enterprising sheep to gain enough traction to breach the barrier. Some of them have subsequently been trapped between the wing fences and have been unable to get out fast enough to avoid the trains, resulting in a few deaths.

Railway-wildlife collisions are a major cause of human related animal mortalities to this day. Why, after a century since the first iron horse steamed into the Athabasca River Valley, are significant numbers of wildlife still struck by trains in the park? One reason is that animals are constantly on the move. Herding animals such as sheep and elk are especially prone to collisions. Many sheep and elk collisions with trains and vehicles occur when traffic splits a herd; these animals are hard-wired to follow and don't like to be separated from their group. Stragglers in a herd, in their attempts to catch up to others that cross a road or railway just ahead of them, are especially vulnerable to being hit.

Grain is a common denominator in many railway-wildlife collisions. Grizzly and black bears, mule and white-tailed deer, elk, sheep, and smaller wildlife feed on grain spilled by trains. The problem begins at the loading terminals. Careless loading of cars causes grain to fall and collect on flat surfaces, including the tops and decks. This grain subsequently falls to the ground as cars are jostled when the train moves. Also, faulty, old, and improperly closed grain discharge gates at the bottom of hopper cars spill large amounts of grain along the tracks. Some trains have actually pulled into unloading terminals with cars emptied of grain.

The railways and government agencies respond promptly to derailments and large grain spills. Specially designed vacuum trucks are very effective in cleaning larger spills but are nearly useless in sucking up small grain leakage. To be fair, the railway companies have taken up the challenge to eliminate grain spillages, but compliance remains inconsistent. Much more must be done to address the problem.

CHAPTER NINETEEN

In the Fast Lane

I responded to my first highway wildlife collision in late spring of 1981. A commercial transport truck had blasted through a herd of elk on the Yellowhead Highway near the Palisades Training Centre. I arrived at the scene to find a young calf lying motionless on its side in the ditch beside the road. As I approached, I could see that the calf was moving its eyes in a normal manner. I ruled out a head injury. Its legs appeared unbroken and there were no visible injuries. I thought the truck might have just grazed the calf as it was running in front of it and then the calf had been thrown into the ditch from the impact. Perhaps it was in shock with only minor injuries. My heart told me it might be okay, but my head told me otherwise.

The calf's mother was standing 15 metres away, deterred from approaching her calf any closer because of the vehicles rushing by. The rest of the herd of 15 to 20 elk were milling about further from the road. I took a good look at the herd to make sure there were no walking wounded to deal with, then returned my attention to the calf. As I walked over to check the calf, its mother rushed me, stopping short of an all-out attack. I immediately backed off. I had to make a decision and I went with my head. I waited until a break in traffic before pulling my rifle from the truck.

I stepped close to the calf to ensure an accurate hit. It looked at me with big soulful eyes as I lifted the rifle to my shoulder. Its mother looked on from close by. I pulled the trigger. The noise of the rifle blast caused the mother to retreat further away, giving me the time and distance I needed to retrieve her calf. I picked up the calf and placed it in the back of the truck. It had massive rib and internal injuries on one side of its body. I drove away as its mother looked on. Over the course of my career I responded to countless accidents involving animals large and small, old and young, injured and dead.

More than twice as many animals are killed on the roadways than on the railway in Jasper National Park. Whereas many animals are hit along the railways while feeding on spilled grain, salt deposited on the highways in winter is the irresistible attractant that lures numerous animals to their death. All ungulate species are attracted to road salt, but sheep more so than the rest. Sheep access salt throughout the park where steep rock bluffs meet the roadside along the Icefields Parkway and the Yellowhead Highway from the East Park Gate to Jasper townsite. They are reluctant to move off the roads when confronted by traffic.

Caribou too, relish highway salt. The highways bisect critical winter ranges of both the Brazeau and Maligne caribou herds. The Brazeau herd is often observed along Beauty Creek Flats on the Icefields Parkway, and the Maligne herd spends much of the winter close to Medicine Lake on the Maligne Lake Road. Caribou at both locations use available winter habitat close to the roads where they have easy access to salt.

The Brazeau herd, in 2012, comprised 12 to 15 animals. With so few caribou left in Jasper, just one or two highway deaths severely dent the herd's population. Fortunately, no death has been reported in the Brazeau herd from a vehicle collision along the Icefields Parkway since 2003. But then, there are not many animals left to hit. Reduced speed limits (from 90 to 70 kilometres per hour) and roadside signage alerting drivers to caribou crossing areas have helped to reduce highway-related mortalities.

Elk are susceptible to both highway and railway collisions throughout the year but especially during autumn, winter, and spring when they feed on prime montane grassland habitat in the lower Athabasca River Valley. In the summer season, they spend much of their time at higher elevations.

Highway vehicles collide with more birds than one might expect. Vehicle collisions contribute to decreasing population numbers of uncommon or rare bird species already facing serious decline from loss of habitat and other human disturbance. Unfortunately, it is difficult to reduce the number of bird-vehicle collisions as they are much harder to avoid. Hawks and owls are particularly prone to vehicle collisions when they feed on small mammals and birds found along highway corridors.

Trades staff and park wardens in the Rocky Mountain national parks have experimented with numerous devices and methods to deter wildlife from roadways. These include both static and digital display road signage, alternatives to road salt, the placing of artificial mineral licks away from highways to deter ungulates from eating road salt, and various methods of fencing.

Predator scents were experimented with as a repellent during the reclamation stages of the twinning of the CNR railway tracks in Jasper in 1983. The aim was to keep ungulates off recently re-vegetated slopes where they were susceptible to being hit by trains. These scents worked for about a week. Sheep, deer and elk became used to the repellent, snubbed their noses at it, resumed feeding, and, as if in defiance, defecated on some of the scented areas.

In 1986 we experimented with small devices mounted on warden trucks that produced a high-pitched sound meant to deter wildlife from bolting across a roadway in front of vehicles. Our test results showed that wildlife had very little, if any, reaction to these devices.

Wardens also use cracker and screamer shells fired from pistols to move wildlife off highways, but this is only a short term deterrent. The animals scatter for a few minutes, but more often than not, reappear when the offending park warden drives away—much to the amusement and delight of motorists who stick around long enough to view the scenario.

Infrared, laser, and radar detection systems that sense when an animal approaches a highway have been tried. When an animal (or group of animals) is detected, the system activates signs that warn drivers of wildlife collision hazards. However, wind, temperature, and humidity influence the reliability of these systems.

Wildlife underpasses and overpasses, on the other hand, have proven quite effective in reducing highway-wildlife collisions along the TransCanada Highway through Banff National Park and Highway 93 through Kootenay National Park.

Unfortunately, experiments with other methods to reduce highway and railway wildlife collisions throughout the mountain national parks are continually being curtailed due to a lack of funding, staff shortages, and other park priorities.

CHAPTER TWENTY

Avalanche

My winter responsibilities in the 1980s encompassed more than just developing management plans. I conducted wildlife surveys, worked on other resource conservation projects, and performed many public safety, law enforcement, and administrative duties. Wardens were beginning to specialize in their chosen function, but we still wore our generalist hats.

A large part of our winter operations included preventative public safety work, primarily avalanche forecasting and control at Marmot Basin Ski Area. In the 1980s, two public safety wardens usually worked full time at Marmot assisted by one or two other wardens on a rotating basis. Assistant Chief Park Warden Toni Klettl, a leading Canadian pioneer in the development of standards for public safety operations in mountainous environments, oversaw the program at the hill.

Park wardens began working as ski patrollers at ski hills in the mountain parks in the 1950s. Toni began his career with the Warden Service in Jasper as a ski patroller at Whistlers Ski Hill in the winter of 1955-56. With the eventual closure of Whistlers, he transferred over to Marmot Basin in 1964. He established the public safety program at Marmot and trained wardens and ski hill staff in ski patrol and avalanche control duties. At that time, avalanche work was limited to blasting cornices off the peaks above the runs and packing snow on ski slopes after heavy snowfalls. The avalanche program at Marmot evolved throughout the 1960s and '70s. Toni brought in an Avalauncher and a 105mm recoilless rifle to trigger controlled avalanches from fixed positions on the hill.

The Avalauncher is a gun that uses bottled, pressurized nitrogen to propel a projectile with one kilogram of explosives to avalanche starting zones up to a few hundred metres away. The 105mm is a high-powered anti-tank recoilless weapon developed in the early 1950s and used in the Korean War. These guns allowed the Warden Service to trigger controlled avalanches from a much greater distance.

The purpose of triggering controlled avalanches is to prevent large self-releasing avalanches from sending massive life threatening accumulations of snow down onto the ski runs below the steep upper slopes of the mountain. We usually triggered avalanches very early in the morning after periods of heavy snow and before opening the ski hill.

We removed cornices by planting explosive charges on the cornice roof along the saddle ridge between the twin summits of Marmot Mountain, high above the ski area. This entailed strapping our skis to our packsacks (full of explosives) after reaching the top of the highest chairlift at the ski area, and then climbing several hundred metres up the steep east ridge of the mountain. We routinely began our climb a half-hour before dawn.

Some cornices never release; they just melt away in the spring. Others release naturally and can be a threat to skiers; these are the ones on which we set charges. Cornice removal involved placing hand-sized cast primer explosives into holes dug every few metres apart; snow was then packed back into the holes on top of the primers. Each cast primer was connected with a length of detonating cord to a longer truck line of the same cord running along the roof of the cornice. The detonating cord and primers exploded instantaneously on the ignition of a fuse at one end of the cord.

One of the largest avalanche releases I was involved with occurred after a few days of heavy snowfall. We blasted a long cornice on the high saddle between the twin summits of Marmot Mountain. The weight of the cornice falling on the deep layer of steep snow directly underneath triggered a huge slab avalanche that ran down to the mid portion of Basin Run in the upper ski area. This particular avalanche could have wiped out many skiers if we hadn't closed the basin beforehand.

Ski runs are cleared of avalanched snow by Marmot Basin staff before they open the runs to skiers. As for us, after we released the cornices, we chose less avalanche prone slopes to ski down from the top of the mountain.

A fascinating aspect of our work at Marmot Basin was the art and science of avalanche hazard evaluation, also called avalanche forecasting. We completed a daily avalanche hazard forecast by combining weather data with snowpack conditions. Snowpack conditions are dependent on when the last snowfall occurred, the amount of snowfall, wind speed and direction, cloud cover, temperature, humidity, and also the surrounding area—the degree of slope, slope aspect, amount and type of vegetation, and underlying terrain. Every snowfall creates a distinct layer of snow. Snow crystals and the various layers of snow within the snowpack undergo an endless process of metamorphism—a process whereby the continuous change in the temperature and pressure of the various layers within the snowpack alter the shape and density of snow grains.

An evaluation of snowpack conditions is necessary to assess when an avalanche might naturally release, or when the weight of a skier or group of skiers is likely to initiate a fracture in a weak layer of snow that could result in an avalanche. This analysis is of utmost importance for evaluating backcountry avalanche hazard. In a ski area like Marmot Basin, this analysis is used to determine the avalanche hazard of slopes above the ski area as well as those on steeper ski runs, in particular those that have not yet been controlled after heavy snowstorms. Hazard evaluations allowed us to determine when to use explosives for controlled avalanches.

Snow profiling is the technique we used to evaluate conditions within the snowpack. This involved shovelling out a pit of snow to ground level with smooth sided walls. The walls reveal the snowpack's layers as they have accumulated throughout the season. The snow crystals that make up those layers provided us with information about how well those layers were bonded to one another. In general, the better the bond, the less chance of an avalanche.

We carried out several different tests in the snowpack to determine bonding and weak layers of snow. These included determining the hardness, depth, density, and temperature of each layer, the size and shape of snow crystals (which we referred to as grains) and the bonding between each. What impressed me most about the snow pit evaluations, beyond the serious business of avalanche forecasting, was the amazing array of crystal formations within the snowpack. We used terms like *graupel*, *needles*, *columns*, *plates*, *stellar*, *rounded*, *faceted*, *decomposed*, *pellets*, *ice layer*, *surface hoar*, and *depth hoar* to describe the various forms of grains we viewed through our magnifying glasses.

Avalanche hazard evaluation is complex. Predicting how, when, and where the snowpack on a benign-appearing slope may unleash its potential destructive fury involves objective, analytical thinking, but it is often referred to as an art because it also requires intuition. The more experienced a forecaster becomes in evaluating snowpack conditions, the more intuitive the process. The advanced level forecaster gets a *feel* for what has happened and what is happening in the snowpack.

Although it takes the trained eye of an avalanche forecaster to correctly evaluate some weak layers of the snowpack, other potentially unstable layers immediately stand out even to the untrained eye. One such layer might be a thin crust of ice formed from either a very wet snowfall or a melted top layer of snow, which, after subsequent snowfalls, ends up in the middle of a snowpack. Depending on the bonding strength of the layer of snow above and below the crusted layer, the icy crust makes an ideal platform for the propagation of a slab avalanche.

A few years after I had taken avalanche forecast training, I was backcountry skiing in late December with a group of friends who were accomplished skiers but had little knowledge of avalanche safety. I dug a snow pit on a gently sloped hill away from avalanche terrain to demonstrate some basic avalanche forecasting procedures. Once the pit was completed, I did a shovel-shear test to identify potentially weak layers in the snowpack. This test involves cutting an approximate 30 cm by 30 cm column on the uphill wall of the pit with a ski or snow saw. The sides of the column are cut to the floor of the pit. The back of the column is cut as deep as a shovel blade is long. After completing the cuts, I placed the blade of my small collapsible backcountry shovel 20 cm down into the back cut and gently pulled forward. I was unable to shear a block of snow away from the column. I then placed my shovel another 20 cm down into the next layer and repeated the procedure. After only a very slight pull on the shovel, a near perfect block of snow easily sheared away and slid over a weak bond on the top of another layer of snow beneath it. I had just propagated a mini-slab avalanche that deposited itself at my feet.

I like demonstrating the shear test as it is visually powerful. My friends were impressed and somewhat humbled by the ease at which the slab was released from the snowpack. The shear test cannot quantify snow stability in itself without further snowpack evaluation, but it demonstrates that the potential of a snow avalanche always exists.

One section of the snow pit that always drew my interest was the bottom layer. We dug snow pits in varying outside air temperatures of between a few degrees above freezing to lower than -30°C. No matter what the surface temperature reading, the temperature within the snowpack at the base of the pit was always close to 0°C. Snow is a very effective insulator, and coupled with the earth's warmth, produces a temperature gradient in the snowpack. In the Rocky Mountain snowpacks, depending on daily heating and cooling cycles, the temperature of the snow generally warms through each layer, going from top to bottom.

The temperature gradient creates a layer of weakly bonded crystals at the bottom of the snowpack called "depth hoar." These snow crystals begin to break down, forming water vapour. Since warm air can hold more water vapour than cold air, a higher overall water-vapour pressure exists in the pores of the snow at the bottom of the snowpack. This starts a process whereby the water vapour is forced to move upwards. When the vapour reaches slightly cooler snowflakes, it recrystallizes and the reformed snow crystals become larger and change to a fragile facet shape. These crystals are weakly bonded. In the Canadian Rockies, depth hoar can form early in the winter and persist for months. It can be a very weak layer of the snowpack and is responsible for major slab avalanches and many backcountry fatalities.

Many winter wilderness travellers at one time or another have trekked across snow and felt the snowpack suddenly settle beneath them with a resounding "whumpf." The sound is the compression of air during the collapse of the snowpack. This is caused by a traveller's weight creating a shear fracture, resulting in a collapse of the hoar frost layer at the base of the snowpack. It might also be the collapse of surface hoar. Surface hoar, a fancy term for frost, is formed in much the same way as depth hoar. Once buried by subsequent layers of snow, surface hoar can create the same conditions for catastrophic avalanches as depth hoar.

Triggering a hoar collapse on avalanche prone mountain slopes is a very serious matter. It can signal *very* high instability within the snowpack—in which case by the time the "whumpf" sound is heard an avalanche may have already begun its quick and deadly descent. Large avalanches on steep slopes can reach speeds of up to 280 kilometres per hour.

Backcountry travellers should be aware that it is not uncommon to trigger depth or surface hoar avalanches on seemingly safe terrain far from steep slopes. These avalanches can even be set off from flat terrain below, above, or to the side of avalanche prone slopes. Many avalanche victims have been killed in this way.

I won't go into further avalanche hazard evaluation in this book. I recommend that all backcountry enthusiasts planning on venturing into untracked snow slopes should take at least a basic level 1 avalanche skills training course, and that at least one member of their group should have level 2 training. In Canada, professional avalanche safety educators that follow curriculum standards set by the Canadian Avalanche Association teach these courses. There are also excellent avalanche safety books and guides available. Backcountry enthusiasts must recognize that no matter how much training and experience they receive, avalanche hazard prediction will never be an exact science. Snow avalanches are always a serious risk in backcountry areas and in closed-off areas within or adjacent to ski resort boundaries. One must travel with great caution in the backcountry and never in closed-off areas.

◆ ◆ ◆

Predicting snowpack stability and preventing the natural release of avalanches through controlled release measures were only part of our responsibilities at Marmot Basin. We also patrolled the ski area to ensure skier safety, including roping off and posting area closures on slopes with potential avalanche risk. We closed many of these areas on a temporary basis until we had time to control the slopes and evaluate the hazard. All avalanche-prone slopes located on the other side of mountain ridges beyond the Marmot Basin Ski Area boundaries were permanently closed.

With assistance from ski patrollers and other staff employed by Marmot Basin, we kept constant vigilance for skiers dying (pun intended) to test virgin snow in closed areas. And they tested our abilities to spot them when they crossed into closed-off areas, knowing full well they were closed and the reason why. Fortunately, we caught most of those heedless of the risk before they actually ventured far enough onto the dangerous terrain.

On one occasion, Rick Ralf and I caught two young men crossing into a particularly hazardous closed area along the boundaries of the ski area. Although we usually issue a warning notice to first time offenders, we felt the conditions in the closed area were dangerous enough to warrant a court appearance notice. We also revoked their ski passes. The two men were lucky. A few weeks later, on February 22, 1982, a group of five skiers chose to cross the ski area boundary into the same closed area. One failed to make it out alive.

The five men skied into the closed area along the east ridge of Cornice Peak. They decided to enter a gully outside the ski area boundary that led down to Portal Creek on the other side of the mountain. One of the skiers set out downslope of the others to take pictures of his friends as they carved turns in the untracked snow above him. As the other four skiers were about to proceed, a 300-metre wide fracture line opened up along the ridge above them. They heard the familiar "whumpf" sound as a weak layer of snow within the snowpack collapsed.

Gravity took over. Thousands of tonnes of snow, which only a second before were resting on a weak layer of depth hoar, hurtled downhill. Three of the skiers were close to some trees alongside the avalanche path. They hung on to the trees as the brunt of the avalanche roared by them. The fourth skier had fallen and was swiftly engulfed by the avalanche, as was the photographer. The avalanche travelled over one and a half kilometres, taking out a wide swath of trees and the two unfortunate skiers with it. They were both deposited near the toe of the avalanche. The skier that had fallen was very fortunate, suffering only a broken leg. A large party of wardens, a search and rescue dog, and Marmot ski patrol staff searched the lower avalanche area. The dog finally located the skier who had planned to take pictures of his buddies under a half metre of snow. He had died from suffocation and multiple injuries sustained when he was slammed against several trees as the avalanche carried him down its path.

Working with the avalanche forecasting and control program at Marmot Basin provided a training ground for park wardens to pick up essential mountaineering skills. These included getting a feel for avalanche terrain, managing risk, and working as a team—a vital part of public safety work. By the mid-1980s however, Parks Canada managers began to seriously question Warden Service involvement at the ski hills in Jasper and Banff. Ski resorts are private enterprises and park managers required justification for government agency involvement in an expensive control program. At the same time, ski resort managers were pushing for more control over the avalanche program. In 1987, after a full review, a policy change took Parks Canada out of the ski hill avalanche forecasting and control program. By this time the Warden Service was working with ski resort patrol staff, transferring the necessary knowledge and skills needed to take over the program. By 1992 the transfer was complete and the Warden Service ended 35 years of keeping the slopes safe for downhill skiers in Jasper and Banff national parks.

CHAPTER TWENTY-ONE

Fire and Ice

In the spring of 1983, I gladly put down my pen after a long winter of developing management plans, but reluctantly hung up my skis that marked the end of my work with avalanche forecasting and control at Marmot Basin. Toni Klettl requested that I work with him within the Public Safety Function for the summer. Maligne Lake Warden Station would be my home base. After working the two previous summers based at the townsite, I was looking forward to being posted at a warden station. I was reunited with Lawrence Baraniuk, whom I had worked with on the North Boundary three years previously. Bradley Bischoff was assigned to work with us as well. Bradley was going into his third year as a park patrolman. He had worked the previous year out of Sunwapta Warden Station and the year before that in the backcountry on the South Boundary. Our horses Hank, Holly, and Indian rounded out our crew.

Maligne Lake Warden Station sits on a hillside at the northern end of the lake. The views down the 22-kilometre lake are stunning, with the glaciated peaks of Mount Unwin, Mount Charlton, and Maligne Mountain dominating the skyline. Across the lake from our station we often saw mountain goats grazing on the slopes of Opal and Leah peaks. Moose and deer regularly browsed along the lakeshore beside the warden station. The 44-kilometre Skyline trail, one of Jasper's most popular backcountry hikes, begins behind the warden station and winds its way across vast areas of subalpine, alpine, and barren rocky ridges to its terminus near Maligne Canyon. A challenging 48-kilometre backcountry trail follows along the upper Maligne River to high alpine meadows at Maligne Pass and down to Sunwapta Warden Station along the Icefields Parkway. The district also includes many popular day hikes within the Maligne and Queen Elizabeth Ranges between Medicine Lake and the northern area around Maligne Lake.

Maligne Lake itself is the main attraction. Much of our time was spent interacting with park visitors on the trails around the shores of the north end of the lake or out on the lake itself with our patrol boat. Maligne is popular with anglers and is known as one of the best eastern brook and rainbow trout fishing lakes in the mountain national parks. Many anglers day fish on the lake's northern end, and others canoe or kayak down to the southern end where they camp overnight and fish. Maligne Lake Tours runs boat trips back and forth throughout the day to Spirit Island at the southern end of the lake. The island and the surrounding peaks are one of the most photographed spots in the Canadian Rockies.

Lawrence, Bradley, and I had an exceptional spring and summer working in the district. We often worked overlapping shifts. At least one of us was always on hand to carry out routine patrols and public relations duties and to respond to important occurrences or emergency situations. Each of us was also able to get out on day and overnight trips with the horses to Maligne Pass and along the Skyline trail. Other than our regular workload, I attended several training sessions including a one-week fire management and forest fire control exercise in Banff, followed a few weeks later by a three-day climbing and rescue course in the Lake Louise area. The 1980s marked a time of intensive public safety training for all Warden Service members in response to the ever-increasing numbers of mountaineering accidents. As part of our ongoing in-park public safety training, I joined my colleagues in climbs of Samson Peak and the twin peaks of Mount Unwin and Mount Charlton. All three tower above the glacier-fed turquoise waters of Maligne Lake.

Gerry Israelson, Marv Miller, and Terry Damm joined Lawrence and me on our climb of Unwin and Charlton. We boated down to Samson Narrows halfway down the lake and bivouacked on the edge of a glacial moraine part way up the twin peaks for the night. We then set out early the next morning and summited Mount Unwin by early afternoon, then crossed the saddle between the two peaks and summited Mount Charlton a few hours later. The climbing involved ascending snow and ice slopes of varying degrees with ice axes and crampons, all the while avoiding deep crevasses that could swallow a climber into the dark cold depths of the glacier. Crevasses have a life of their own, continually changing size and depth with the constant flow of glacier ice. The most dangerous crevasses are the ones hidden by a thin covering of snow not strong enough to hold the weight of a climber.

One form of crevasse, called a bergschrund, presents a menacing obstacle and danger to snow and ice climbers. A bergschrund forms when the downward flow of a portion of glacier breaks away from a stationary portion of the same ice sheet above. It can be several metres wide and over 100 metres deep. Whereas the chasm of a typical crevasse is usually on a nearly flat or moderate slope, the chasm created by a bergschrund usually opens up on a much steeper slope. A bergschrund can be difficult to see from above, especially if the uphill lip of the chasm is higher than the downhill lip.

We had to be very careful of bergschrunds when descending the twin peaks. Slipping and falling on a steep uphill slope above this form of crevasse is a serious risk for climbers. They must quickly self-arrest their slide by ramming an ice axe into hardened snow or ice and hang on for dear life. Given the steepness of the slope, it can be difficult for climbers attached to a rope above a fallen companion to arrest that person's fall or subsequently their own falls as the rope tightens between them.

We chose a slightly different descent route as we made our way down from Mount Charlton. Terry, Gerry, and I were roped together. Terry led the way down, I was in the middle of the climbing rope, and Gerry brought up the rear. Lawrence and Marv were tied together on another rope. Part way down, Terry slipped, fell, and then quickly slid over the uphill lip of a bergschrund before he could self-arrest. The slack on the rope between us tightened instantly. Terry's downward momentum pulled me off balance before I could arrest his fall—or mine. I also shot over the upper lip of the deep abyss.

Gerry, at the tail end of the rope, lost sight of us as we disappeared over the lip of the bergschrund. Having more time to react, he was able to jam the spike end of his ice axe into the snow and loop the climbing rope around it. The rope on his end tightened, bringing Terry and me to a halt. Concerned that we had plummeted into the depths of the bergschrund, Gerry called out to see if we were okay. Terry and I both stood up and poked our heads over the downhill slope of the bergschrund. We responded in the affirmative. Our downhill speed had carried us over the mouth of the crevasse and deposited us on the other side, rather than deep inside the ominous vertical cave of ice. We had been very fortunate and we made our way down the rest of the mountain without further incident.

◆ ◆ ◆

I also climbed Leah Peak during the summer of '83 with Julia on one of my days off. Unlike the more technical climbs of Samson, Unwin and Charlton, Leah Peak is a fairly easy scrabble. As with all the mountains surrounding Maligne Lake, the views from its summit are spectacular. We were blessed with a crystal clear day and had a commanding view of the great ice and snow-capped pyramid summit of Mount Robson, 120 kilometres to the northwest.

Julia and I took a break to rest from our descent of the summit on a grassy alpine knoll halfway down the mountain. As we quenched our thirst, we focused our attention on the lake, still far below. We watched two Maligne Lake Tours cruise boats, small objects on the large lake from our high vantage point, spreading sparkling silver V-shaped wakes across the turquoise waters behind their sterns.

As I was scanning the upper reaches of the Maligne Valley across the lake from us, I noticed a small column of smoke rising above the trees. The column was coming from an area near Schäffer backcountry campsite on the Maligne Pass trail, approximately eight kilometres up the valley from the lake. Within minutes the smoke column doubled in height and spread in size.

I knew that the smoke column was too large to be from a campfire. This was a wildfire in the making. My initial thought was that the valley needed a fire; we had suppressed naturally caused fires for far too long. But, I had a duty. Because of our vantage point on the mountain we were likely the only ones that had spotted the blaze. We were still a couple of hours hike away from my canoe and five kilometres across the lake from the warden station. When we reached the canoe, we paddled out into the centre of the lake and minutes later met a tour boat cruising back to base. I waved the driver down, informed him of the fire, and asked him to call the tour base radio operator to alert Lawrence and Bradley.

Within a few hours, Bradley and I, along with several members of a Saddle Lake Cree Nation trail crew and a few other wardens, flew into the fire by helicopter and were fully engaged in fighting the blaze. We spent two days keeping the fire from spreading by pumping water around the perimeter and extinguishing hot spots and flare-ups, thus keeping it to half a square kilometre in size. We determined that a smoldering fire left behind by careless backcountry campers had started the blaze. The culprits were never found.

◆ ◆ ◆

With heavy summer visitor use in the Maligne Valley, public relations duties occupied much of our time, as did enforcing park regulations, especially boating and fishing regulations on Maligne Lake. We also managed public safety concerns such as recreational injuries, lost hikers, mislaid children, and stranded boaters.

The beginning of September marked the end of the busy tourist season in the park. We were glad to have gotten through it without major incident on Maligne Lake or along the trails and areas that receive high visitor use in the Maligne Valley. September is still a popular time for hiking, however, and on the second weekend of the month, George Bradd received a report about a backpacker with a possible heart attack near the Third Summit Lake on the Jacques Lake trail. George had been working as a fisheries assistant with the Warden Service for the summer and was stationed at Beaver Lake warden cabin located close to the trailhead.

A party of six backpackers had left for a trek into Jacques Lake earlier in the day. When one of the group, a middle-aged man, fell ill, his friend alternately walked and ran seven kilometres back down to the trailhead to report the incident to George. George reached me by radio at Maligne Lake. I called the Park Warden Office requesting helicopter assistance and headed out for the trailhead 15 minutes down the Maligne Lake Road from the station. Julia, a recent nursing graduate, was eager to assist and she accompanied me.

George, Julia, and I drove down the trail's first four kilometres as it followed an old dirt road. From there, we ran three kilometres to Third Summit Lake carrying a backboard stretcher. We arrived to find the family in obvious distress and the victim with all the classic signs and symptoms of a serious heart attack leaning up against a fallen tree. He was pale, perspiring heavily, and had initial severe pain in his mid-sternum area that had radiated down his left arm and hand. He was still experiencing pain and a tightening in his chest and was nauseated and restless. What struck me most though, as I knelt beside him to introduce Julia and myself before beginning our assessment, was the look of shock and fear in his eyes. He knew that time was of the essence and he might die unless we could get him to the hospital quickly. Julia and I reassured him that we were going to get him to the hospital and a helicopter would be arriving soon.

There was a problem though. A suitable landing spot for the helicopter was nowhere to be seen. I had Julia stay with the victim to monitor his vital signs and keep him as comfortable as possible while George and I ran several hundred metres back down the trail and searched for an opening in the heavy timber. We located a small spruce bog that appeared just large enough to serve as a helicopter landing area. I called pilot Todd McCready on my radio and notified him of the pickup location. He expected to be en route from the Park Warden Office with Gerry Israelson and Ric West in 10 minutes with an estimated time of arrival within half an hour.

George and I returned to the group. With the help of Julia and the family friend, we took great care in getting the man onto the stretcher. We then set out for the bog. It was an excruciatingly long journey for him. As careful as we were, every few jarring steps we took along the rough trail intensified his level of pain and discomfort. Carrying the heavy set man on the stretcher the last 100 metres through heavy forest and uneven ground to the bog was difficult for us, but much worse for him. Soon, we heard the welcome sound of the 206 Jet Ranger blades slicing through the air. Todd expertly dropped the helicopter into the tight canopy opening. Gerry and Ric rushed out to assist us in loading the stretcher. The helicopter was back in the air within minutes, headed down valley towards Seton General Hospital in Jasper. The man survived his heart attack.

The use of helicopters for search and rescue purposes has become an almost daily occurrence in the Rocky Mountain national parks during the summer. Without helicopters, many of our rescues would not have ended on a happy note. When a fatality does occur, rescues become "recoveries." A week after the heart attack rescue, Lawrence and Brad faced one of those situations.

Late in the afternoon of September 16, three men in their mid-20s drove into the yard at the warden station as Julia and I were preparing for a 10-day boundary trip with the horses in the Fiddle River Valley. There had been snow flurries at Maligne throughout the day with several centimetres already on the ground. The three men had registered at the Park Trail Office in town to climb Mount Charlton. Park staff warned them that conditions were marginal and recommended that they speak to a park warden at Maligne Lake.

I had a lengthy discussion with the party at the warden station and strongly advised them not to follow through with their plans. More snow was forecast throughout the night and I expected the avalanche hazard on the mountain would be high to extreme by morning. I talked about the climb that the group of us five wardens had undertaken six weeks previously and the many hazards the mountain held for the unwary under even ideal weather conditions. But they had planned the climb for some time and were convinced they could carry it through. Despite my repeated cautions, they insisted they wanted to attempt the climb the following day. After they left, I turned to Julia, shrugged my shoulders, and said, “I can’t chain them to a tree.”

Julia and I loaded our horse gear and our horses, Hank, Holly, and Indian, into the park stock truck early in the morning and headed out. It was snowing, and several more centimetres had accumulated on the ground overnight. More was forecast. I thought that surely those three young men would abandon their climb.

Julia and I rode into Fiddle warden cabin under a miserable sky. It rained, sleeted, and snowed throughout the day. The next day we took the horses up to a boundary ridge to monitor hunting activity. All was quiet with 15 centimetres of freshly fallen snow. There was considerably more snow higher up on the peaks. The weather system had been entrenched over the park for the past three days.

Two days later found us further up-valley at Whitehorse warden cabin. The snow cover made it look very much like winter. It was cold and windy outside the comfortable confines of the warm log cabin. As we made our dinner over the wood stove, we listened to CBC AM radio out of Edmonton. The 6:00 p.m. news broadcast came on and the announcer began with the evening’s opening story—a climbing accident with one reported fatality on Mount Charlton in Jasper.

The three climbers had decided to climb the peak on September 17 despite my warnings and the inclement weather. They had hired a small boat to take them down Maligne Lake and then spent the remainder of the day travelling up onto the glacier, establishing base camp two-thirds of the way up the mountain. The next day they made their way up moderate snow and ice slopes to a prominent rock buttress. They scouted the area for possible routes but decided to abandon their climb. Approximately 30 centimetres of snow had accumulated on the slopes around them over the last three days. All three men, roped together, began their descent, with the leader taking a diagonal line across a steep snow slope. Before they got far, they triggered a slab avalanche that carried the party 100 metres downslope.

The lead climber vanished head first into a large bergschrund. The other two climbers came to rest a few metres above, one on the surface with an ankle injury and the other one partially buried. The partially buried climber, sore but without injury, was able to dig himself out. The injured climber then set up a belay for the second climber who followed the rope down into the bergschrund. He chopped through hard packed consolidated snow for two hours before he uncovered one of the lead climber's boots. Half an hour later, he reached the lead climber's head and applied CPR to no avail. The man had suffocated. The two surviving climbers raised their dead partner from the bergschrund and left him on the surface. They struggled back to base camp, reaching it just before dark.

The next morning the two surviving climbers left base camp early and arrived on the lakeshore at Samson Narrows late in the afternoon. They waved down the driver of a Maligne Lake Tours boat who immediately called his boat dispatcher on the radio to alert the warden station. Bradley received the call, notified the Park Warden Office in town, and started down the lake in a Maligne Lake Tours boat with one of their staff. Lawrence and Ivan Phillips followed shortly after with the warden boat. Bradley returned with the two surviving climbers while Lawrence and Ivan waited at Samson Narrows for the helicopter.

Wardens Gerry Israelson and Al McDonald brought the victim's body off the glacier in a Yellowhead Helicopter at 7:30 p.m. and passed it on to Lawrence and Ivan. As the two wardens ferried the body down the lake, Lawrence thought of our triumphant climb on the mountain only weeks earlier. What a shame that the lead climber died only minutes after deciding to turn back, having recognized that the conditions were too hazardous to continue.

CHAPTER TWENTY-TWO

Welcome to My Morning – Little Heaven

My work during the winter of 1983-84 was enjoyable as always. Each day brought new adventures and fulfilling experiences. I loved my job. That winter however, I was distraught because of a serious medical condition that had begun in my early childhood.

Back in July at Maligne Lake, I noticed a slight discharge from my right ear, evoking an immediate feeling of dread. In 1966, when I was entering Grade 7, it was mandatory for all children in Jasper to get a medical examination, which included a physical check of the inner ear and a hearing test. When the doctor looked into my right ear he said I had a serious ear infection and asked about my hearing. I told him that I could hear better with my left ear. That was *my* normal—I never thought much about it.

The hearing test established significant hearing loss in my right ear with some hearing loss in the other. The condition that caused the hearing loss was otitis media, commonly called a middle ear infection. Neither my parents nor I could recall a time when I had experienced pain or a discharge from the infected ear, which is very unusual. For this reason the otitis media went undetected, and indeed, worsened over time.

An appointment with an ear, nose, and throat specialist was immediately arranged in Edmonton. My parents were advised that my condition could be serious and I was operated on in November 1967. The surgeon opened my ear from behind the head to access the inner ear and clear away the infection. What should have been a couple of days stay in hospital extended into more than a week. Complications as a result of the surgery left me in a state of post-operative fatigue and dizziness. Although I recovered, I experienced some additional hearing loss. Over the years, periodic checkups, cleaning, and the occasional use of antibiotics kept further infection at bay.

◆ ◆ ◆

After noticing the renewed discharge from my ear in July of 1983, I immediately made an appointment with my doctor who confirmed that my condition had flared up again. Over the remainder of the summer and into the early autumn, I made several trips into Edmonton to see my ear, nose, and throat specialist, Dr. Backstrom. He examined and cleaned the infected ear and prescribed an antibiotic. Several different antibiotics prescribed over a period of two months proved unsuccessful. It was back to my family doctor and back to the specialist. Antibiotic treatment continued without success.

In early September, when Julia and I left for a ten-day boundary patrol in the Fiddle River Valley, my spirits were high. I was in my element, surrounded by nature and accompanied by the ponies. During the last two days of the trip, however, I began to feel a slight nausea; the discharge from my ear continued. On our last morning, as we were packing up for our ride out to the Miette Hot Springs from Fiddle warden cabin, Julia noticed that the right side of my face was slightly swollen. I sensed the severity of my situation. I was terrified. Julia was a nurse and she *knew* the severity of my situation—the infection had returned with a vengeance.

After several visits to the specialist and a new treatment of antibiotics, the swelling subsided. The infection was controlled but not stopped. In the meantime, surgery was scheduled for April (seven months away) in Edmonton. My intuition told me that the surgery was needed much earlier.

◆ ◆ ◆

By the time I was lying on my back on the operating room table, I was all too aware of the complexity of the operation. The infection may have advanced to a condition called malignant otitis externa—"malignant" in this case meaning a raging infection rather than a malignancy, or cancer. Malignant otitis externa can damage the bones of the ear canal and the tissues and bone structure at the base of the skull. This infection can spread and affect the cranial nerves, brain, and other parts of the body. *Why* had I had to wait so long before surgery?

Malignant otitis externa of the ear is an aggressive and acute infection. The organism responsible for my infection was likely Pseudomonas, a bacterium found in water. It is difficult to treat once it has invaded the depths of the ear canal and the bones of the skull. From there it can infect the brain, form an abscess, and develop into meningitis, an infection or inflammation of the protective membranes covering the brain. It can be life threatening. The operation consisted of scraping away all infected tissue and bone around the area of my inner ear and adjacent bone structure of the skull.

I don't remember regaining consciousness in the operating room, but I do recall a moment of wakefulness in the hospital hallway as I was wheeled to my room. The hall was spinning and I was extremely nauseous. Sometime later I became more aware as I lay on the hospital bed. Besides the dizziness and feeling ill, something was very wrong. I raised my hand up to the right side of my face. There was no feeling. During the operation, Dr. Backstrom, trying his best to scrape away the infected bone from the back of my ear and around my skull, accidently hit the right facial nerve. The infection was so massive inside my head that he was not able to properly see the nerve. These large nerves, on each side of the face, control all facial muscle control. I now had total paralysis on the right side of my face—the most severe form of facial palsy. Most frightening, the infection had progressed to the fibrous membrane lining the inner surface of my skull, the dura mater layer that protects the brain. The inside of my skull was now like a slice of Swiss cheese—full of holes.

The facial palsy caused my mouth to droop like a grossly animated one-sided frown. I couldn't talk properly, slurring speech as if very drunk. Chewing food was very difficult and drinking without having the liquid dribble down my chin was problematic. I was soon drinking with a straw. With complete facial paralysis, the eye remains open. I had to tape my right eye shut during sleep, and manually, with one finger, gently "blink" my eyelid every few minutes of the waking hours to keep it moist. On top of the paralysis, I was so dizzy I could not stand unaided. I was now totally deaf in my right ear, although at that moment this did not concern me in the least.

Dr. Backstrom explained that if the facial nerve had been severed, the paralysis would remain for life and I'd have to live with the complications I was now experiencing. Furthermore, with full paralysis, there was a chance that I would, in time, lose the vision in my right eye. This could come about from several possible issues affecting the proper functioning of the cornea. Although the dizziness and loss of balance that I was experiencing usually goes away within a few days after this type of surgery, my case was unusually severe. There was a possibility that I would not recover my balance.

A few days after the operation, Dr. Backstrom brought three other surgeons into my room. One of the surgeons, Dr. Di Toppa, another ear, nose, and throat specialist, was just beginning his career. He spoke in a confident and caring manner and engaged me in the conversation. I immediately liked the man and felt reassured by his presence. After examining me, the doctors told me that I needed another operation. Dr. Di Toppa was elected to lead this second surgery, called "facial nerve decompression." The procedure involved lifting the nerve away from any residual bone matter, swelling, or infection that remained in the area after the initial surgery.

A week after the initial operation, I was once again taken into the operating room. My heart was pounding as I wondered how—or even whether—I might come out of the surgery. When I was wheeled into the room, I knew that this surgery was altogether different from the last. I sensed that all members of the medical team were now treating my condition as a very critical and unusual case. Dr. Di Toppa spoke to me and introduced the nurses, helping me to relax. He continued to talk to me as the anaesthesiologist administered the sedative. Both doctors were very reassuring about the procedure as I succumbed to the effects of the anaesthesia.

When I recovered in the operating room, I felt everyone's presence around me. As my brain haze dispersed, they came to greet me. None of the doctors or nurses had left the room. I thanked them all. This was a very special day in my life. I had made it through.

Later, when I had fully recovered from the anaesthesia, Dr. Di Toppa went over some of the details of the operation with me. He explained that he had cleaned the area around the nerve as much as possible and removed some additional bone fragments. Carefully moving the nerve to keep from compromising it any further, Dr. Di Toppa saw that the myelin sheath covering the nerve had been damaged by the infection. He explained that apart from the bruising, the facial nerve had been shredded. Swelling around parts of the nerve prevented him from determining if the nerve had been completely severed. He couldn't promise that my nerve would regenerate even if it hadn't been severed. Nor could he promise that I would ever regain full balance—or that the infection would not return.

Despite the gloomy outlook, Dr. Di Toppa's professionalism and personal manner impressed me. I trusted that he had succeeded with the surgery even though he could not promise the desired outcome. I placed my faith in him, knowing that I was fortunate to have received the best care a doctor could provide. He had done his part. The rest of the healing process was up to me.

Two days after the second operation I experienced frightening rigor attacks (uncontrolled severe trembling accompanied by fever) which is often a marker for significant and serious infections; in my case a sign that my body was not well and my condition might be worsening. This scared the hell out of me. Fortunately, the medical staff was able to control the rigor and my condition improved.

Two weeks after I had walked into the hospital for what was to be a few days stay, I was still confined to bed, getting up only for bathroom breaks and short walks around the ward. Still very dizzy, I was unable to walk the entire length of the corridor without assistance. Dr. Di Toppa—now my primary care physician—the nurses, and other medical staff on the ward were overwhelmingly supportive, caring, and attentive. Although my condition had improved very little, there was not much more the medical staff could do for me. And I was ready to leave—I felt like a caged animal. I needed to be back in Jasper and close to nature.

◆ ◆ ◆

During the first week of May, two weeks after being released from hospital, I was still experiencing severe dizziness. I was only able to wobble about 100 metres before I needed to rest. I was worried that I might never regain my balance. There was no sign of my right facial nerve returning to its former glory and doing what it does best: allowing me to chew my food, smile, drink without spilling, speak clearly, blink thousands of times a day to keep my eye moist, and close my eyelid at night. My neurologist and Dr. Di Toppa both informed me that if my facial nerve was going to function again, I'd notice within two months. After that there was not much hope. In the meantime, I lifted my hand up to my face every few minutes, manually blinking my right eyelid and massaging my face to prevent muscle atrophy.

By the third week in May, my balance was improving. Every day was better than the one before. I terminated my leave and went back to work, beginning with light duties.

Several months previously, Chief Park Warden Don Dumpleton had assigned me to a backcountry posting in Willow Creek District to start in late May. I was more than thrilled at the thought of returning to the North Boundary with the horses.

Just after I returned to work, Don called me into his office. I knew what was coming. He was concerned that I was not yet fit for a backcountry posting that summer and wanted me to work close to the office. I sat in silence for a few moments. Even though I had expected this, I was stunned. He could see my great disappointment. I knew it was difficult for him to brief me of his decision as he focused on the right side of my head, seeing a sad man with a sad face. But it was essential for me to return to the wilderness and heal.

Over a period of a few days I pleaded with Don, and he finally relented. In the long term, I feared that I might not keep my job if my facial nerve did not heal and my balance did not fully return. And much more disturbing was the possibility that the severe infection that had threatened my life could return. I did not want to keep those dreadful thoughts in my mind, and focused on my pending return to the wilderness.

On June 4, I packed up my gear for Willow Creek. The significance of the date did not escape me. It was exactly two months to the day since my initial operation. This was when Dr. Di Toppa and my neurologist expected to see a hint of facial nerve recovery if the nerve was to regain function. There was no change.

Early the next day I met Bruce McInnis at the Maligne Horse Range. This was Bruce's first year as a warden in Jasper and he was assigned the Blue Creek District for the season. We picked up our saddles and assorted horse tack from Denny Welsh at the horse range. Denny had arranged for Rod Wallace to transport our horses up to the pasture at Seldom Inn a week earlier. Denny had assigned me three horses for the season that were well acquainted with the Willow Creek District: Gander, Hawk, and Evelyn. Bruce and I drove up to Celestine Lake and then up the old 23-kilometre dirt fire road to Seldom Inn warden cabin where we joined up with Al (B.J.) Bjorn and Rick Ralf. B.J. was assigned the Smoky River District and Rick was assigned to rove throughout the North Boundary assisting the three of us with our duties.

The four of us rode to Willow Creek and spent the next couple of days clearing trails from winter blowdown, making necessary repairs to the cabin, barn, and pasture fence, and building a bridge over the creek between the hiker and horse camps a few kilometres downstream from the cabin. We also felled and de-limbed several dead trees on the fringes of the pasture for firewood and left them to be skidded to the woodshed later. I had not regained my full strength and was grateful that my three North Boundary companions assisted me in getting my home base cabin and area in shape for the summer.

After a few days of hard physical work we were ready for adventure. We decided to ride over to Kidney Lake and document the new growth within the burn of a wildfire that had swept through the area in the early spring of 1980. Leaving our pack horses at the pasture, we rode to Willow Creek campsite, chatted with a pair of hikers from Switzerland, then continued west a kilometre to the banks of the Snake Indian River. We had to cross the river before riding an hour further on to the burn area at the southeast end of Kidney Lake.

As we expected, the river was in spring flood. Although the Snake Indian River was swollen from several weeks of winter snow melt cascading down its tributaries across 900 square kilometres of barren mountain slopes, alpine tundra, and high elevation forests, we all agreed to attempt a crossing. Thinking back, our decision was foolhardy, but all four of us thrived on adventure. As for me, although going on 30 years of age, I hadn't evolved one iota from the craziness of my youth. What was outrageously stupid about my own decision to cross the river was that I had to avoid getting any amount of water in my healing ear canal because of the risk of further infection. But my right brain's quest for adrenalin overpowered my left brain's signal for caution. We prepared to cross.

We scouted up and down the river on our horses and chose the widest (about 50 metres) section to cross. Although fast flowing, it wasn't as turbulent as the narrower sections of the river. We also hoped there'd be a reduced chance of hitting a deep hole; we couldn't see much more than a hand's length below the surface of the water due to the sediment brought down from the mountains with the spring flooding. We had to rely on our horses' footing to get us across.

Bruce, B.J., and I decided that Rick would be our fearless leader. He'd be the first to attempt the crossing while the three of us would watch from shore. Rick reined his horse Kiwi into the water and took a diagonal line against the current. The river was soon inching up towards Kiwi's chest. He powered his strong muscles into the river's flow, however, and kept his footing until three quarters of the way across. Suddenly he dropped past his upper chest and was swimming with urgency for the riverbank across from us. Rick was no longer in the saddle. He was swimming frantically next to Kiwi.

Within seconds they were swept towards a logjam between a gravel bar and the shore. Kiwi was swept under the logjam and disappeared. Rick was able to grab the branches of a fallen tree spanning the river (a "sweeper") and quickly hoisted himself onto it. He looked for Kiwi but couldn't see him, and thought, "Oh my god, I lost my horse!" An instant later Kiwi popped up on the other side of the logjam and made it to shore. Rick had to crawl across the narrow and slippery sweeper to reach terra firma.

Kiwi shook himself a few times, ridding his hide of most of the water, and looked none the worse for wear. Rick, on the other hand, weighed down by his waterlogged clothes, looked like a drowned rat. He walked over to Kiwi and checked him over.

We yelled across the rushing noise of the river to Rick, asking if all was okay. He yelled back saying yes but that he had lost his Stetson, along with its band and his badge. Although Rick was obviously annoyed at this, there was a more important matter to be concerned with; he was shaking from the dunking in the near freezing river. It was clear he was becoming hypothermic. Furthermore, the air temperature was only about 6°C and it was raining. We all agreed it was best that Rick cross back over so we could quickly get him back to the cabin. With the advantage of now being able to scout the river from both sides of the shoreline, we picked a route we thought was less hazardous.

The situation was serious. Bruce, B.J., and I felt helpless, as there was no point in us crossing over to Rick and risking the same fate. Rick was in a bind with only one way out, although another plunge into the freezing water would greatly increase his state of hypothermia. Even now, he was having difficulty readjusting the saddle on Kiwi with his stiff, shaking, and freezing hands as he prepared to re-cross the river. We read the concern on his face as he swung up into the saddle.

It was at this point that Bruce broke the tension. He called over to Rick and asked if he could have his camera if he failed to survive the crossing. This brought a slight smile to Rick's face and a negative answer. Bruce's comment relaxed our tension. I followed Bruce's example, shouting across the water to Rick, reassuring him that I'd look after his horses if worse came to worse. B.J. then broke in; “Hey Rick, you mind if I have your girlfriend?” All of us, including Rick, broke into laughter. Rick then shouted various profanities back at B.J. and told all three of us where to go. Our spirits were lifted and Kiwi carried him across without incident. B.J. told Rick he still wanted his girl. This brought more laughter as Rick emptied the water from his riding boots and re-mounted Kiwi. We trotted the horses back to the cabin and got the wood stove going, restoring Rick to a semblance of his self.

After lunch we thought about what to do for the remainder of the day. It was unanimous: we’d attempt the river crossing again. You’d think we would have learned from our first attempt. We were not so young but still foolish. Once again we rode towards the banks of the mighty Snake Indian River. We took the necessary precautions to find a safe line across the river and settled on the same spot where Rick had returned. We couldn’t follow his route exactly because we had to take the opposite diagonal to the flow of water. (For better balance and control, it is always best to navigate across flowing water by cutting slightly up current).

Rick took the lead again. There was no debate; it was clear that he wanted to prove to himself that this time he and Kiwi could find a safer route to the opposite shore. Rather than wait for him to cross we all plunged in together, one behind the other. Not quite halfway across, all was going well. The horses were up to their bellies and finding good purchase on the river bottom. I can’t recall who was riding ahead or behind Gander and me. The horse in front slowed somewhat and within seconds, Gander was on its tail. The horse behind us caught up to Gander’s rear, squeezing him in. Gander took a few steps sideways and suddenly dropped to his upper chest. His hooves were no longer touching bottom. We had hit a deep hole and he was swimming. I slid off Gander’s back and swam with him, keeping one hand on the saddle horn. The current and Gander’s horsepower steered us back toward the shore from where we had started.

So much for my day. I shouted across for the others to continue on and said I would make it back to the cabin myself. It had warmed to about 12°C and the sun edged out from behind the clouds now and again. I was cold but not nearly as bad as Rick had been with his earlier swim. I had even managed to keep the Stetson on my head. Most importantly, I had kept my ear dry.

Back at the cabin, I began preparing dinner. Sometime later Rick, B.J., and Bruce rode in. Busy over the stove, I waited until they had taken care of the horses and come over to the cabin before greeting them. They came bursting in, full of bravado and bliss. They had had a wonderful afternoon at Kidney Lake checking out the nearby burn.

Noticing that I had dinner on the stove, with much jesting they asked why I hadn't set the table yet. I told them I hadn't brought out the plates yet as I wasn't sure how many of them would make it back alive. They questioned my faith in their river-fording skills, called me a few names, and the banter flew back and forth. I concluded the ribbing by telling them they could make their own damn dinner. We all had a good laugh. I also seem to recall a bottle of rum landing on the table. It was great to be out in the backcountry again with my friends and colleagues. We made the best of it while we were together. For the next five months, all four of us would be on our own most of the time with only the occasional rendezvous in the wilderness. These were happy times. I almost forgot my facial palsy and my fears of reoccurring infection in the hollowed-out right side of my head.

A few days after our river adventure, Rick and Bruce packed up and headed for Blue Creek District. B.J. and I rode up to Mowitch Creek and Little Heaven warden cabin, clearing trail along the way. We worked together for three days in the Mowitch Creek Valley before I returned to Willow Creek. B.J. left for a several-day trip through Blue Creek District and on to his district in the upper Smoky Valley.

◆ ◆ ◆

Later in June, after a few days off in town, I returned to Willow Creek with my childhood friend Pat Paul and his partner Julie Bauer. It was Julie's first trip on the North Boundary and a nostalgic trip for Pat. Pat and I had both been caught up in our careers since our last backpacking trip together on the North Boundary 11 years earlier in 1973. Pat and Julie had both graduated from the NAIT Forestry Program in 1975. Since then, they had worked on various contracts with the Canadian Wildlife Service, Alberta Fish and Wildlife, and Alberta Forest Service.

Pat and Julie had taken an extended leave from their jobs to join me. They backpacked half their gear and the horses carried the rest. We spent several days in the Willow Creek area before heading up to Little Heaven. Pat and Julie split their time between exploring and helping me with my work.

I was slowly getting my health back except for my facial nerve, which remained unchanged. On the morning of June 25, coming up to three months post facial paralysis, I woke up in Little Heaven warden cabin as the dull light of dawn was filtering through the windows. I pulled back the tape closing my right eyelid and massaged my paralyzed facial muscles for a few minutes. I was tired of this daily routine. After removing the tape, I closed my right eyelid with my finger every few minutes throughout the day to keep the eye moist. I was almost past the point of expecting the nerve to regenerate. In my case, the recovery of facial nerve function had been poor. I tried not to think about it. I took solace in having almost completely regained my balance and strength. Most importantly, the severe infection that put me into hospital had not returned.

Pat and Julie were still asleep. Rather than getting up, I lay in bed and thought about the previous day. The three of us had completed much of the maintenance work required around the cabin and Little Heaven horse camp situated a few hundred metres up-valley. I had begun the day by cleaning out the new wood/horse-tack shed that had been built by the cabin crew. A red squirrel sitting on a lower branch of a pine tree outside the shed gave notice with its scolding chatter that it was upset by my presence. Assuming that the squirrel was a female, with perhaps a nest nearby, I looked into the trees and around the shed but saw nothing to explain its urgent calls. Moving back inside the shed, I took a canvas water bag off a peg on the wall. It seemed heavy. When I looked inside, I saw four young squirrels, only a few weeks old, huddled together in a nest. Hair was just beginning to grow on their otherwise wrinkled, naked bodies. Blind and deaf at birth, their eyes were now open. I wondered if they could hear yet, and wished them good hearing, so important to their survival in the wilderness.

Their cosy confines in the shed, however, were about to come to an end. I had to evict them. Squirrels and mice can make a mess of backcountry sheds once they find, or chew, a way inside. I took the water bag outside and gently placed it under the tree branch from which the mother was scolding me. She was now in a fit of rage.

I backed away and waited. She descended her perch, went straight to the water bag, and checked her young. Then, one by one, she lifted each by the scruff of its neck with her jaws and carried it 10 metres up the nearby tree. With the boundless energy squirrels are noted for, she had all four youngsters safely up the tree in a couple of minutes. Afterwards, I walked over to the tree and looked up. I could see that the young had been placed in a nest. I concluded that the mother, witnessing our arrival the day before, had wisely built a new nest with the intention of moving her young out of the shed. She must have known that the two-legged creatures with green uniforms were prone to cleaning out sheds and patching rodent holes in the floorboards.

I finished cleaning the shed, built a new workbench onto which I installed a vice, and put up a new tool rack. Pat, Julie, and I then took the rest of the morning to clean the cabin and reposition a countertop and cupboards. In the afternoon we put up a new hitching rail and built two saddle racks at the nearby horse camp, then felled three dead trees for firewood. We de-limbed the trees and left the main trunks to be skidded by horse to the wood shed later in the summer.

◆ ◆ ◆

A loud metallic "rat-a-tat-tat," followed by a few seconds of silence, and then repeated, abruptly took me away from my reflections on the previous day. A hairy woodpecker was drumming on the tall metal radio antenna behind the cabin to claim its territory and attract a mate. It had discovered that pounding on metal produced a sharp metallic pitch, outrivaling the traditional territorial drumming on tree trunks. The other hairy woodpeckers around Little Heaven didn't stand a chance.

Once we were all up, Pat and Julie started breakfast and I went out to get the horses. A few rays of sunshine pierced through the cloud over the De Smet Range across the Snake Indian Valley far below. When I reached the grassy knolls a few minutes from the cabin, I sat down and looked out across the idyllic scene in the meadows below. It was calm and peaceful; I could hear the horse bell on Hawk in the distance. I moved my head back and forth trying to detect with my left ear which direction the clang of the bell was coming from. This was very difficult. Since becoming completely deaf in my right ear, I have, out of interest, asked many people why they think we have two ears. I rarely get the answer I am looking for. The answer is so that we can hear in "surround sound". As I am monaural (I hear in mono), I have trouble detecting the direction, distance, and movement of sound.

Not seeing the horses, but knowing from the bell that they were close by, I spent a few minutes relaxing and taking everything in. Several songbirds were singing among the hummocks of grass nearby. I could also hear the distinctive tremolo "winnowing" of a Wilson's snipe, one of the few bird sounds I can easily detect. The male Wilson's snipe, a long-billed shorebird found in marshy habitat, produces the sound by flying high in the air and then making a dive towards the ground. The winnowing sound is made from the rush of air passing through feathers designed by nature to produce the tremolo notes. This is his courtship presentation, performed for the females somewhere below. A variety of flowers were beginning to bloom, their quest for rebirth in the spring. I remained entranced by the busyness of life around me for some time before getting up to find the horses. It was a wonderful day to be alive.

When I reached the meadow, I followed Mowitch Creek to a backwater where Julie had spotted a beaver the day before. The beavers had built a dam across one channel of the creek to create a wetland habitat for themselves, and in the process, a myriad of other life forms. I walked over the top of the dam to cross the creek and headed for the trees where I eventually picked up the horses' tracks. I followed their tracks into the woods and found them resting in the trees, their bellies full from the abundant grasses they had been feeding on in the meadow.

When I got back to the cabin with the horses, I fed them oats and then joined Pat and Julie inside. I splashed my face with fresh cold water that Pat had brought from the creek behind the cabin, took the small cabin mirror off the wall, and placed it on the table. I sat down and looked into the mirror—my right eyelid gave a very subtle twitch! This was nothing short of the most joyful moment in my life! As if waiting three months for the trauma inside my head to settle, my facial nerve had now decided to come to life.

Over the course of a few weeks, the nerve began slowly and wondrously regenerating. I could speak without slurring. I was able to chew food and drink properly without much of it dribbling down my chin, and my eyelid started to blink on its own. I slowly lost my one-sided frown as the facial muscles, responding to signals from the nerve, began to pull upwards once again.

◆ ◆ ◆

I had twice-yearly appointments with Dr. Di Toppa for 26 years after the operations. Each visit required an extensive cleaning of the ear canal and reassurance that all was well deep inside. In April of 2005, after one of my appointments, we sat down for a chat. He told me that after his more than 25 years as an ear, nose, and throat surgeon and thousands of patients, my case was the most serious he had ever dealt with. He went on to explain the details of the massive state of the infection in my head and how I was extremely lucky to have pulled through it all.

After my appointment in 2005, and knowing that Dr. Di Toppa loved the outdoors, I invited him on a backcountry trip. He was extremely grateful for the opportunity. Three months later we backpacked to one of my favourite warden cabins in Jasper. It was a very special time and an opportunity for me to give thanks to Dr. Di Toppa for his excellent care.

CHAPTER TWENTY-THREE

Grizzly Attack

In mid-September I rode down from Little Heaven to Willow Creek after spending ten days on autumn boundary patrol. I had brought Gord Anderson's dog Sara (a cross between an English Sheepdog and another breed or two) along to join my trio of horses and me for the autumn season. I decided to ride up to Ram Pass the following morning. The pass is located across the Snake Indian River from Willow Creek warden cabin and high in the alpine on the south facing slopes of Mount Stornoway, a 40-kilometre return trip. I had wanted to explore the area for several years and this was my first opportunity.

I was up at 05:30 in the dawning light to bring Gander, Hawk, and Evelyn in from the meadows and give them their morning oats. I saddled Gander, ate breakfast, and, led by Sara, hit the trail before the sun broke the horizon. When we reached the same location on the Snake Indian River that Rick, B.J., Bruce, and I had crossed in the spring, I took a careful look at the river. The autumn flow of water was less than half what we had experienced in the spring. The water was clear and about a metre at the deepest. I hoisted Sara up into the saddle with me; it was snug, but there was room for two. Gander took us across without a hitch.

From the south side of the Snake Indian River, we made our way west for an hour before arriving at a horse camp established by outfitters and wardens during the park's early years. The camp, now rarely used, is situated in Grizzly Meadows, a beautiful open shrub and grassland meadow where Grizzly Creek drains into the Snake Indian River. The creek flows from two narrow valleys that drain from the high elevations of Mount Stornoway. Ram Pass is at the head of one of these valleys.

Five gruelling hours after leaving Grizzly Meadows and travelling up a very rough trail alongside Grizzly Creek, we arrived at Ram Pass. I had alternately ridden and walked Gander on our ascent to the pass. Sara led when she could make out a discernible trail and stepped aside to let Gander and me pass when she couldn't. It was a gorgeous autumn day. I brought out lunches for Sara and myself and took Gander's bridle off so he could graze on alpine grasses. As I gazed across the valley, my thoughts wandered back 16 years to a terrifying sow grizzly attack on the slopes just below the pass.

◆ ◆ ◆

On June 3, 1968, local Jasper outfitter Leonard Jeck left Seldom Inn horse camp with two clients, Steve Rose from California and Dave Slutker from Alberta, for a two-week photography trip into the northern areas of the park. They headed up-valley towards Willow Creek with their three riding horses and three pack horses, crossed the Snake Indian River, and set up camp in Grizzly Meadows.

On the third day of their trip, they saddled their riding horses, left the pack horses in camp, and rode up Grizzly Creek toward Ram Pass. Several hours later, they reached a slope leading to a high alpine ridge above Ram Pass. They tied their horses to trees beside the trail at the base of the slope and set out on foot for the crest of the ridge a kilometre away to get a commanding view of the area. Dave chose to walk at a steep angle uphill to reach the ridge. Leonard and Steve took an easier route, following below Dave at a gentler angle upslope. Leonard had to walk and gain elevation slowly as he was still recovering from open heart surgery a year earlier. After climbing half a kilometre, Steve stopped to take pictures. The tree cover had thinned out as they reached the more open habitat in the subalpine, allowing them a better view of the surrounding terrain. Leonard said he would carry on slowly and let Steve catch up to him when he was finished taking his shots. Before they left each other, they scanned uphill and could see Dave making his way to the ridge a few hundred metres above them.

Not more than 10 minutes after leaving Steve, Leonard heard a commotion uphill. He looked upslope, horrified to see a grizzly barrelling downhill at him. He had a split second to react and shouted, "GRIZZLY!" hoping Steve would hear him. The bear slammed into Leonard, hitting him with the claws of her left paw. She took him with her, rolling and tumbling downhill. They came to a stop at the base of a small gnarled spruce tree.

The grizzly began biting, clawing, and rolling Leonard until he was lying on his left side with his head at the base of the tree. Leonard raised his right arm to shield his face. As he opened his eyes and looked through the bend of his arm, the grizzly took her attention away from biting his right thigh and looked up. Their eyes met. Leonard realized she was going to lunge for his face. He just got himself turned over onto his stomach when she bit into the back of his neck at the base of his skull. When her teeth penetrated the muscles, Leonard thought she had crushed his neck, giving him only a few moments more to live. Instead, she released her grip and left.

While Leonard was being mauled, Steve had climbed a small tree and started yelling. He hoped to distract the sow away from Leonard, thinking he was safe up the tree. Hearing Steve, the sow turned her attention to him. Steve's boots were only two or three metres off the ground and the grizzly had no difficulty reaching up and pulling him out of the tree. Steve received a severe mauling. Every time he tried to resist the bear, she ripped and tore at him.

Meanwhile, Leonard, shaken and weak from his mauling, tried to pick himself up from the ground. Dave, several hundred metres above his two companions at the time of the attack, had heard Steve hollering. Dave began running downslope to find out what was wrong, unaware that a grizzly had just mauled the other two. He yelled, trying to get their attention so he could locate them. The grizzly, hearing Dave shout, left Steve, and within seconds Dave was caught by surprise as the grizzly charged him, knocking him to the ground. She left him almost immediately and angled uphill, back towards Leonard. As she approached Leonard, she started woofing, her vocalizations getting louder as she closed ground on him once again. He lay prone, his face to the ground, not moving a muscle. The bear passed very close to Leonard, then angled uphill in the direction from where she had come. All was now silent.

After locating each other, the three men evaluated their injuries. Leonard's right thigh and arm were badly bitten and torn. Both sides of his left hand were ripped and a hole had been bitten through his palm just below his little finger. Leonard thought he might have pushed his left hand into the bear's mouth. He had deep claw marks and a large piece of muscle missing from his left buttocks and thigh when she had initially hit him, sending them both tumbling downhill. He also had a large section of skin peeled away from his chest and neck from the bear's last go at him before she left to attack Steve.

Steve's shoulders were in rough shape and bleeding badly. His right shoulder was broken. Leonard and Dave put Steve's right arm in a sling and bandaged him the best they could. He also had long tears on his lower left leg.

Dave recalls being bitten in the face, but Leonard and Steve judged from the appearance of the wounds that the sow had clawed at his head as she barrelled over him, tearing off half of his face and his entire nose. His cheekbone was also badly broken. Leonard noticed that Dave's right eyebrow was missing; he pushed aside the skin and blood to check if his eye was gone as well, but it was intact and not damaged.

The three of them were now faced with the daunting task of getting out of their predicament alive. Leonard was very weak from a combination of his injuries and his recent heart surgery. Furthermore, he could barely walk as a result of his leg wounds. Steve was experiencing more pain than the others and Dave was concerned about losing too much blood.

On top of everything else, Steve and Dave were concerned about developing tetanus. Leonard, injecting humour to ease their predicament, assured them they had nothing to worry about—the grizzly had first cleaned her teeth and claws on him. Leonard realized he had to keep the men focused and positive. They were his clients and it was his responsibility to take care of them.

Of the three men, Leonard had the most difficulty walking. When they finally made it back to their horses, Leonard, despite his condition, tightened the horses' cinches, checked his clients' wounds, and made sure the men were ready for travel. He was barely able to mount his own horse.

All three men suffered from horrendous bites and clawing, yet none experienced heavy blood loss.The wounds made by the grizzly's teeth and claws were blunt, creating a crushing effect. These jagged and blunt wounds generally swell and clot quicker than a clean-cut wound made by a knife that can cause profuse bleeding. And luckily for the men, the grizzly missed their major arteries.

Leonard kept upbeat throughout the long ride back to camp, constantly reassuring Steve and Dave by keeping a conversation going and singing as best he could. The grizzly attack occurred at 12:30 p.m. They arrived back at their camp in Grizzly Meadows at 6:00 p.m. Leonard tended to the horses, started a fire while the other two men ate some food, and helped both men into their sleeping bags. He set a kettle of water and a cup within their reach. Although worse off and weaker than Steve and Dave, Leonard focused on his clients' needs before setting out for help. Leonard showed his true character: a tough and dependable man of the mountains.

Leonard set off for Willow Creek warden cabin, concerned about crossing the Snake Indian River due to high spring water levels. Fortunately, his horse made it across without difficulty. He arrived at the cabin to find it unoccupied and locked. He'd have to break in and hope the old crank telephone was in working order. Leonard was so stiff and sore that he was barely able to pull himself out of the saddle.

Leonard thought about breaking a window but doubted he could lift himself over the sill and into the cabin. The lock was too heavy for him to break, but he thought he could pull the rasp far enough out to loosen the screws that held it to the door. He had a small jackknife in his pocket. With his body now seizing up, he found it very difficult to get the knife out of his pocket and open the blade. In time, however, he had the screws out and the door open. He called the forestry switchboard (the precursor to the Jasper Dispatch radio system) in Jasper. One can only imagine the immense relief Leonard felt when he heard the voice of the dispatcher, faint but audible across the antiquated single strand wire. She connected Leonard to Chief Park Warden Mickey McGuire, and Mickey set the wheels in motion to have the three men out before twilight.

An hour later, a helicopter sent out from Hinton with a doctor on board dropped out of the sky and landed in the meadow beside the warden cabin. After the doctor gave Leonard a quick examination, they flew to Grizzly Meadows. The doctor determined that Steve's injuries required immediate care. The pilot, leaving Steve in the doctor's care, flew Leonard and Dave to Seldom Inn warden cabin at the terminus of Celestine Lake Road. He immediately returned to Grizzly Meadows, picked up Steve and the doctor, and flew them to Hinton in the gathering darkness.

Mickey McGuire and Park Warden Bob Barker met Leonard and Dave at Seldom Inn. Mickey drove Leonard and Dave to Seton General Hospital in Jasper, arriving just after midnight, 12 hours after the attack. Bob and one of Leonard's hired hands rode to Grizzly Meadows and Willow Creek the following day to pick up the horses that Leonard and his two clients had left behind.

Dave was rushed into the operating room while Leonard waited in the care of the nurses. Dr. Betkowski and the operating room staff did a tremendous job of restructuring Dave's face. The only long-term impairment he experienced was a tear duct drainage issue in his right eye. Steve stayed in the Hinton hospital for a week before flying back to California where he spent considerable more time in hospital, followed by therapy. Over time, he recovered well from his injuries.

Leonard was not taken in for surgery until 5:30 a.m. It took over four hours to mend his extensive puncture wounds, lacerations, and the peeled skin from his chest. Dr. Betkowski considered skin grafting for his chest but it healed in time, leaving a massive scar. Leonard was kept in the hospital for three weeks. But you can't keep a determined man down for long; Leonard was back in the saddle, albeit with considerable pain and discomfort, soon after his release. Leonard spent the next four months on the mountain trails guiding outdoor enthusiasts and living in a tent. He pulled out only when early winter snows prevented further horse travel.

Why did the grizzly attack occur? Leonard had worked 42 years in grizzly country before the attack and he understood bear behaviour well. He believed the attack was likely unavoidable as the bear was a sow with cubs. Leonard thought that Dave, climbing ahead, came onto the grizzly family without seeing or hearing them. The bear was aware of Dave's presence and fled in an attempt to move away from him. The bear moved downhill with her cubs in tow. When she encountered Leonard, she signalled for her cubs to stay put. At this point the sow thought her family was in danger. With Dave behind her and Leonard in front, she was left with two choices: fight or flight. She had already fled once; faced with a second threat, she chose fight.

After mauling Leonard, she heard Steve yelling, searched him out, mauled him, then heard Dave yell and mauled him as well. When she was satisfied that all three men no longer posed a threat, she went back for her cubs, passing Leonard on the way. Leonard, with his understanding of bear communication, believed the woofing he heard as she went by him was her signal to the cubs that she was coming back for them.

Leonard documented the details of this grizzly attack and other bear stories over his 45-year career as a guide and outfitter in his book *Female Grizzly Rights: Grizzly Attack – A Seventeen-hour Ordeal*. Leonard's lifelong experience in the wilderness led him to the firm conviction that grizzlies have no more interest in attacking humans than humans have in being attacked, and that unless provoked, they generally avoid direct contact with people. He maintained, however, that these great bears require suitable habitat with enough space to live an unmolested life, free from fear of constant human encounters. Leonard felt no animosity towards the sow that attacked his party. In making it clear that grizzlies are an integral part of mountain life and should be appreciated and respected, he advocated for the protection of wilderness areas and recognized the importance of national parks in preserving pristine habitat for all wildlife species—bears included.

CHAPTER TWENTY-FOUR

Mountains In Peril

A week after my trip to Ram Pass, an early winter set in on the North Boundary. On September 24, the mid-to-high elevations in the mountains received up to a metre and a half of snow. The lower Snake Indian Valley between Blue Creek and Willow Creek received less snow, yet still looked like a winter wonderland. The weather chased all but a few hardy and determined hunters out of Willmore Wilderness Park.

I spent the last few days in the northern part of my district at Rock Creek horse camp, close to hunting camps just across the boundary. For many decades, wardens had pitched boundary camps along the creek during hunting season. During my stay, all was quiet. On October 3, I took down the big wall tent that I had erected five weeks earlier and packed it on the horses. Log cabin builder Mark Deagle and a crew of three were putting the finishing touches on a new cabin two kilometres downstream from the tent campsite to replace the wall tent. I assisted Mark and his crew for two days before we moved some gear and supplies into the cabin. I then rode down valley to Willow Creek the next morning and the cabin crew was flown out by helicopter.

Managers in Jasper had suggested naming our small log abode after the creek that meandered close by. I respectfully pointed out that we had enough "Rock" names on our maps and suggested "Starlight" after the mountain range that rises above the creek to the south and west of the cabin. Starlight warden cabin it became.

I rode up to Wolf Pass from Willow Creek after leaving Starlight and patrolled the boundary ridges above Wolf and Grindstone passes the next day. Ascending the transition zone where the stunted krummholz in the upper subalpine give way to the open meadows of the lower alpine slopes on the ridges, I observed a striking change since my initial patrols in the area five years earlier.

Photographs taken in the mountain national parks in the early 1900s compared to those of today show that the treeline has been extending upslope at an annual rate of between one and two vertical metres. The density of trees has increased, as has the density of woody shrubs. Until the late 1970s, the gradual encroachment of forest into alpine habitat in Jasper was barely noticeable. And frankly, I never thought much about it. By 1984, I was shocked by the dramatic change in the treeline throughout most of the subalpine-alpine transition zones. Lower elevation stands of denser and taller spruce and pine forest were also expanding upslope.

By 2013, 30 years since I first noticed the dramatic upward movement of subalpine forests into previous treeless alpine meadows, the rate of vertical expansion appeared to be increasing. When I compare the exponential increase in the vertical expansion of tree growth in Jasper over the past century to graphs that plot the rise of fossil fuel-related CO_2 emissions and the corresponding upward trend of global temperatures, the rates of increase are strikingly similar. Not surprisingly, human population growth follows the same upward trend as CO_2 emissions and global temperatures. Back in 1984, "global warming" and "climate change" were not yet in my vocabulary. I was, however, noticing marked changes in the park's environment.

What should we make of this phenomenon? Climate change is a reality and humans appear to be largely responsible. Studies suggest warming temperatures in the Rocky Mountains are affecting forest succession, specifically the loss of meadows to forested habitat. High elevation mountain habitat, defined by verdant alpine meadows and an abundance of grasses and wildflowers, is slowly disappearing.

The Rockies support an immense diversity of landforms, flora, and fauna; no other physiographic region of North America compares with its variety of wildlife. Much of this diversity is contained in the alpine and subalpine meadows, which support a multitude of species found only in alpine life zones. Numerous mountain birds depend on alpine meadows for their existence. The alpine is equally important to many mammals such as marmots, picas, mountain goats, bighorn sheep, woodland caribou, weasels, wolverines, and grizzlies. The grizzly, more of a vegetarian than a meat eater, absolutely depends on alpine habitat. Hedysarum (commonly called sweetvetch), a legume that thrives in alpine meadows, is one of the most important food items in the grizzly bear's diet in Jasper. The plant is a prime spring and autumn food source for grizzlies when its protein content is at its highest levels. I have seen areas the size of a football field mined by these bears digging for the legume's nutritious root.

Meadows are receding not only in the park's alpine areas but also in the montane zone. Coniferous trees and woody shrubs, largely unpalatable to ungulates, have invaded large tracts of the montane life zone, squeezing out meadows and reducing the size of aspen forest and grasslands important to many species of wildlife. It is not known to what degree climate change is affecting these lower elevation meadows.

Additionally, a century of fire suppression has resulted in the encroachment of more forested habitat. Fire, one of nature's most important renewal agents, has been snatched away from entire ecosystems by the controlling hands of humans, resulting in the creation of a near monoculture forest with little variety of flora or fauna. The Rockies are losing species diversity, so essential to a healthy ecosystem.

◆ ◆ ◆

After walking the ridges above Wolf and Grindstone passes, I returned to the cabin in the late afternoon to find Jane Emson and her horses. Jane had travelled up to Wolf Pass from the Moosehorn Valley. Although most of the snow that had fallen two weeks earlier had melted from all but the higher elevations above the treeline, she reported that only one hunting party remained in the area. The next morning I left Jane to patrol the area and returned to Willow Creek.

More snow and very cold temperatures moved into the mountains in mid-October. I joined Rick Ralf at Blue Creek on the 19th. We had planned one last trip up to Caribou Inn horse camp and over the boundary into the Willmore Wilderness at Hardscrabble Pass, but we were turned back by thick ice forming along the edges of Blue Creek, a considerable risk for horse travel. An overnight low of -14°C froze our water source, a small tributary creek beside the cabin.

On October 22, we returned to Willow Creek for a few days before closing down the cabin for the fast-approaching winter. Rick and I spoke of our regret at having to leave the sanctum we found in wilderness as we tied our diamond hitches on the pack horses and settled into our saddles. As we rode out of the horse pasture heading to Rock Lake, we heard a pack of wolves howling from somewhere along the creek behind us. We had come across the pack in a meadow near Kidney Lake the previous day. I sensed that they knew we were leaving their domain in the backcountry. The pack itself would be leaving the upper Snake Indian Valley soon to hunt the more plentiful game in the lower elevations of the Athabasca River Valley during the winter.

Riding out to Rock Lake, I contemplated the last six months of living and working in the park's northern wilds, much of it spent alone or with my horses. It had been a joy to have my canine companion, Sara, accompany me for the last two months of the season. She had proven to be an excellent companion for the horses and me. When travelling, Sara usually led the way, never leaving my view for more than a few seconds. Occasionally, demonstrating her herding nature, she'd turn around and dart back and forth between the horses, checking that all was well before she returned to lead. When we were bushwhacking, she'd follow immediately behind the heels of the second pack horse, eager to lead again once we reached a defined path.

Travelling with Sara and the horses was a unique opportunity to share a part of my life with them. All of us on our wilderness journeys together: human, horse, and dog—travelling as one, bridging the species barrier by communicating through touch, body language, and a few verbal expressions. Our actions and reactions were completely dependent on and in sync with the natural world around us. This was nirvana: my place of peace where I felt at one with nature.

Our ancestors lived like this for countless generations: being at one with the natural environment. It is only in relatively recent times that humanity has moved away from a direct engagement with nature. Most of us have lost the ability to be at one with our environment. We have become disconnected. Aboriginal cultures never imagined wilderness as separate from themselves. Modern cultures regard nature as something to exploit and conquer. With our natural world slipping away, we now have to protect the relatively small pockets of wilderness left and we must manage them. It's a strange concept—having to manage wilderness—but we must do this in order to achieve the delicate balance between human use and environmental protection.

Our national parks might look pristine to the average visitor watching the scenery go by while motoring down the roadway in the comfort of his or her vehicle. But the parks are far from the natural state they were in before the arrival of European settlers on this continent brought devastation to First Nations cultures and the natural environment. Our parks have not been spared the spoils of human use: loss of habitat, serious declines in both number and diversity of flora and fauna species, the introduction of invasive non-native species, commercial exploitation, and overuse (loving our parks to death).

Nor have our parks been immune to monumental change from well-intentioned but misguided resource management programs such as predator control, elk slaughters, lack of proper garbage management, and the prevention of naturally occurring forest fires. And we have little, if any, control of the threats that originate from beyond the parks' borders, notably global climate change and pollution. Additional threats await mammals and birds that don't recognize human boundaries, spending a part of their lives outside of protected areas where they are subject to additional habitat loss, pollutants, human disturbances, and for many, hunting and trapping.

Despite these factors, the vast wilderness areas in the largest national parks remain largely undisturbed, although not in the same state that they'd be in without human interference (e.g., forest fire prevention). This holds true for the wilderness beyond the areas of congested recreation use in provincial and territorial managed parks as well.

The numerous threats to the national parks' high visitor use areas are a different story. For over a century, we have been incrementally adding to the variety of recreational activities and encouraging ever-increasing use of our parks. Continued high visitor use in much of the Rocky Mountain national parks' most threatened habitat—the montane valleys—is destroying the ecological integrity of our parks. Our human footprint has had an immense impact on natural ecological processes and it continues to expand. Unless modern cultures come to terms with the natural world, we will lose much of the environment in our only remaining pristine areas—the tiny pockets of protected wilderness left on this small planet we all share.

Such were my thoughts as we left Willow Creek, leaving nature to take care of itself in the backcountry for the winter.

CHAPTER TWENTY-FIVE

Pocahontas

I spent the winter of 1984-85 working in town on several assignments, including the ongoing wildlife monitoring program, which entailed flying many hours conducting wildlife surveys with Yellowhead Helicopters pilots Todd McCready and Gary Foreman. Wardens Rod Wallace and Ivan Phillips also continued to be involved in the program, and a few other wardens joined us on a number of flights. As in previous winters, I worked on various resource conservation activities and worked several shifts with the avalanche control program at Marmot Basin.

In the spring of 1985 I received some great news: I was assigned to Pocahontas Warden Station at the east end of the park. I ended up staying for four years. The allure of Pocahontas was that it was still largely managed as a working district even after the switch to centralization. (Sunwapta and Maligne also still functioned as year-round working districts).

An exciting new aspect of my duties at Pocahontas was working with the federally administered Environmental Assessment Review Process—the precursor of today's Canadian Environmental Assessment Act. Before the 1970s there was little if any consideration given to the environmental impact of construction projects in our country. Our national parks still bear numerous scars from the days of careless construction of roads, railways, pipelines, and visitor infrastructure without consideration for the natural environment—scars like open pit dumpsites, large gravel pits, terrestrial habitat and waterways affected by pollutants, slopes devoid of vegetation, erosion of soils, and unrehabilitated roads. It wasn't until 1979 that the Environmental Assessment Review Process was formally recognized and integrated into Parks Canada Policy.

Rod Wallace moved out to Pocahontas in the spring of '86 and joined me in managing the district. We monitored the construction of the new Miette Hot Springs facility, its associated infrastructure, and a major upgrading project on the Miette Road to ensure environmental compliance. Jane Emson, working out of the townsite area, monitored all phases of the construction when Rod and I were unavailable. We worked with Parks Canada officials from various departments including Engineering and Public Works, Historical and Archaeological Research, Professional Services, Program Management, Natural History Research, and Interpretive Planners. These federal employees consulted with the numerous contractors involved with the projects and assisted Rod, Jane, and me in identifying construction activity that had the potential for adverse environmental effects and ensuring that measures to minimize or eliminate impacts were followed.

We learned a great deal as the projects proceeded through their various stages as many of the rehabilitation techniques used to protect or restore habitat were cutting edge. The new order of environmental impact assessment and the application of mitigating measures to reduce the effects of human development had arrived. Just as importantly, the impact assessment process gave us the tools (and legislation) to reject projects in the planning stage that did not meet environmental guidelines. If, after initial rejections, the proponent was unable to ensure that environmental standards could be met, the project could be cancelled. Regrettably, in the years that followed, we learned how politics occasionally overruled the results of impact assessments that clearly indicated certain projects should not be approved. Allowing these projects that failed to meet environmental compliance to proceed made a travesty of the intended process.

◆ ◆ ◆

In the mid-1980s, the frontcountry area of Pocahontas was extremely busy during the summer, with Pocahontas Campground and two bungalow camps in the area booked to capacity. Jasper National Park was experiencing close to two million visitors annually. Miette Hot Springs received over 100,000 visitors each summer. With all the vehicle traffic on the highway and on Miette Road, we responded to numerous highway accidents.

Park wardens, as public safety specialists, are expected to provide first aid to victims of wilderness accidents and incidents. We also had a long-standing responsibility to attend to medical emergencies in the high visitor use areas, including highways and national park townsites. Paramedics were not stationed in Jasper until the mid-1980s. Up until then, park wardens and a handful of other Jasper residents (mostly ambulance attendants) were the only responders to accidents and medical emergencies with advanced levels of first aid training.

Even after paramedics began working in Jasper, wardens were often the first responders to motor vehicle accidents. With eight warden stations scattered around the park and at least a few wardens out on patrol at any given time, we were usually the closest to accident scenes. In recent decades, this has changed somewhat as all but a few warden stations have been phased out.

Our first duty at an accident was to secure the scene, which meant taking measures to ensure that no further accidents took place. This entailed directing traffic around an accident site blocking normal traffic flow. It was always a great relief to us when the RCMP appeared at the scene of an accident, as they would take over traffic control and accident investigation procedures. This allowed us to devote all of our attention to first aid responsibilities.

Interaction with park visitors throughout the Pocahontas area comprised a large part of our daily work schedule. Most of our dealings with the public were of a positive nature, however, we occasionally had to enforce park regulations to ensure visitor safety or the protection of the environment.

One of the more satisfying experiences I had interacting with the public during my four years at Pocahontas was giving campground presentations, or "campfire talks." Pocahontas Campground has a small and intimate setting, complete with a campfire ring. Typical evening presentations at Pocahontas began with a park interpreter presenting topics on the natural environment of the park and the activities available for visitors to experience nature. Meanwhile, I would saddle one of our three horses at the warden station and ride up a two-kilometre trail to the campground, planning my entry just as the interpreter was finishing his or her program. While the campers were thrilled to have a park warden appear out of the forest, I must admit my equine friend was the big draw.

My talks were about a park warden's working life. The audiences were especially captivated by stories about wildlife and our work in the backcountry. I had a lot of fun with those presentations, as it was an ideal opportunity for the horse and me to connect with the visitors. We often stayed until after sunset, when my trusty companion, having much better night vision than me, carried me safely back home in the darkness.

CHAPTER TWENTY-SIX

Grizzly Country

The backcountry area we patrolled most often in the Pocahontas District comprised over 200 square kilometres of wilderness along the upper Fiddle River Valley, south of the northern terminus of the Miette Hot Springs Road. The headwaters of the Fiddle River originate from several alpine basins near Whitehorse Pass. Two warden cabins are situated at strategic locations in the valley to allow effective monitoring of the environment, backcountry users, and hunters along the boundary areas during the autumn season.

I took my first horse trip of the year into the Fiddle River Valley a few weeks after my move to Pocahontas in May. My last visit into the area was in September 1983 on a 10-day autumn boundary patrol. Now that the valley was part of my district, I looked forward to spending much more time exploring its winding river channels, deep canyons, quiet forests, numerous creek tributaries, high elevation side basins, verdant alpine meadows, and windswept mountain ridges. The valley's more remote terrain has long been known for its plentiful wildlife and especially for its abundance of bears.

A few hours after leaving the trailhead at Miette Hot Springs, I descended a long hill from Fiddle Pass with my riding horse Anita and pack horse Jock. The relative silence of the forest was broken as the click-clack of the horses' steel shoes met the rocky banks of the Fiddle River. Moments later, Anita splashed chest deep into the rushing torrent and carried me across with Jock bringing up the rear. We were heading to Fiddle warden cabin. Just beyond the cabin, Slide Mountain, with its near vertical south face, stood sentinel-like, guarding the wild upper reaches of the Fiddle River Valley. I loosened my grip on Anita's reins and gave her the lead. She took us back and forth across the swift river current several more times. After each crossing, she deftly followed an undefined route to the next safest ford. The horses had been in the Pocahontas District for several years and knew every metre of trail and every river ford along the way.

After leaving the river channels we ascended a small hill to the cabin. As we approached the hitching rail beside the tack shed, both Anita and Jock startled. Something was amiss. As was usually the case, the horses had sensed something before I did. Thinking it might be a bear, I followed their gaze down the hill. A 45-gallon drum containing the horses' oats had been taken from the open shed and tossed 30 metres below. Recent rains had washed away all evidence of tracks on the hardened ground beside the shed, but trampled vegetation around the drum indicated a bear as the obvious culprit. As I suspected, a check of the edges along the steel locking ring on the top of the drum revealed a few brown hairs left behind by a grizzly in its failed attempt to pry off the lid. I spent a good part of the afternoon transferring numerous buckets of oats into another barrel in the shed before rolling the empty one back up the hill.

This early introduction to bear sign in the valley lifted my hopes that I would have sightings throughout the next several months. Five months later, in early October, I boarded up Fiddle warden cabin for the winter. I hadn't seen a bear in the valley all season and it wouldn't be long before they headed to their hibernation dens. It had snowed 45 centimetres overnight and snow was still falling heavily when we left the cabin. Anita, Jock, and I plowed through 80 centimetres of snow over Fiddle Pass on our way out to the trailhead.

◆ ◆ ◆

Rod Wallace and I had a busy summer in the high visitor use areas of the Athabasca River Valley in 1986, which limited our time in the backcountry. I got away for a 10-day boundary trip at the end of August to coincide with the opening of hunting season in the high elevation basins and along the mountain ridges bordering Jasper's boundary in the Fiddle River area. Alberta Fish and Wildlife Officers Bill Carruthers and Ron Martel joined me at Whitehorse warden cabin, and we spent a few hectic days monitoring sheep movement and hunting parties looking for trophy rams. Because of the disturbances caused by hunters in the area, many of the sheep had moved into Poachers Basin within the park near our cabin. Four big rams, however, were shot just outside the park boundary during the first few days of hunting season. Shortly afterwards I moved down to Fiddle warden cabin and Rod rode up to join Bill and Ron at Whitehorse to continue monitoring the area there.

There was very little hunting along the boundary ridges between Mystery Lake and High and Low passes above Fiddle warden cabin the four days I spent patrolling there. I did, however, finally run into a few bears—what the Fiddle River Valley is noted for. Riding back from checking for hunting activity around the Mystery Lake area, I spotted a black bear with two yearling cubs feeding on vegetation on an open ridge a kilometre and a half from the cabin. I noticed a large adult boar grizzly, also feeding on vegetation on the same slope and at the same elevation, approximately 700 metres away from the black bears. This was interesting, as the grizzly and the black bear family appeared to be aware of each other's presence on the slope. Grizzlies are usually not tolerant of black bears within their range and will occasionally kill and eat those they see as intruders. Obviously this big male was content with its herbivorous diet for the time being.

At 7:30 the next morning, I was preparing breakfast in the cabin after bringing the horses in from the meadows when I caught the movement of something big and black near the woodshed. Seconds later a sow black bear appeared from behind the shed no more than 15 metres away from the horses. Three exuberant cubs bounded up the hill behind her. The sow took a quick sideways glance at the horses and ignored the cabin. The cubs showed some curiosity in the horses and their surroundings but were more focused on playing. The horses followed the movement of the bears through the yard with interest but little concern.

When the bears moved out of sight behind the cabin, I opened the door and stepped around the corner. Seeing me, the sow stood on her hind legs and gave me a quick, inquisitive look. She dropped to all fours, spun around, and fled with her cubs into the surrounding forest.

During the last week of October, I watched a sow grizzly and her two yearling cubs digging for sweetvetch roots for half an hour in the alpine meadows on the boundary ridges between High and Low passes four kilometres above Fiddle warden cabin. The family, approximately 150 metres away, was in full view of the horses and me but, other than the occasional glance, showed no concern. I continued along the ridge with the horses in the opposite direction.

In the summer of the following year (1987), Rod and I made regular observations of grizzly tracks throughout the subalpine and alpine slopes above Fiddle warden cabin. The tracks indicated a sow with at least two young-of-year cubs. They were keeping us company but at a distance, avoiding us as much as they could. From the amount of diggings for sweetvetch roots and other signs, it was evident the bears had been spending a lot of time in the area. However, up until midsummer, neither of us had run into a single bear. This was about to change.

On July 30, I left my horses at the cabin early in the morning and set out on a 20-kilometre trek to Mystery Lake and back to check out a basin for signs of recent hunting camps. The area had not been patrolled for a few years, and Rod and I had concerns hunters may have been using camps in the basin from which to access areas within the park to poach wildlife.

My route began with a climb up the steep slopes towards High Pass. From the pass I traversed rocky alpine terrain in a northeast direction along the park boundary and climbed to the summit of Table Mountain. I gained another 200 metres to the summit of Mount Drinnan and then dropped to approximately the same elevation on the other side before once again gaining elevation, this time to the summit of an unnamed peak two kilometres north of Mount Drinnan. I had observed abundant signs of a sow grizzly with at least two young cubs along the route.

I descended the steep scree slopes of the unnamed peak and entered into the basin. Within a few hundred metres I entered a thicket of dense, high shrubs reaching over my head. I had not seen any fresh sign of the bears for over an hour and assumed they were somewhere behind be. However, I felt uneasy as I made my way through the dense undergrowth—I sensed that I wasn't alone. I had grizzly on my mind. Other than exercising appropriate caution when in close proximity to bears, I have never feared them, except when I've inadvertently invaded their space and found myself much too close to them for their, and my, comfort.

As I was moving slowly through the thicket beside a small creek that drains the basin, the hair on the back of my neck stood up. I stopped dead in my tracks, my heart pounding. I smelled the unmistakable rankness of bear and heard a faint huffing. Then came the rustling of bushes so close I thought I could reach out and touch grizzled hair. But I couldn't see beyond 10 metres into the dense foliage and the trickling of the creek interfered with my ability to hear clearly. Equally disconcerting, because I hear in mono due to total deafness in one ear, it is extremely difficult for me to locate the direction of sound. I had no idea from where to expect the bear, its comfort zone violated, to attack. And not knowing which way to turn to avoid contact was very troubling.

I turned my head back and forth in an arc, trying to pinpoint the direction of the rustling bushes, but to no avail. And then I was able to detect something—different sounds seemed to be coming from different directions. This was very alarming—there was more than one bear. It was a sow with cubs. I called out, "Hey bear, hey bear," to ward off a bluff charge or an all-out attack by letting the sow know exactly where I was so she could gather her cubs and flee in the opposite direction. However, with excellent hearing and one of the most sensitive noses in the world, she no doubt was well aware of my location. And of course, rather than flee, she might choose to attack in defence of her young if she perceived a threat.

The rustling stopped. Instinctively, I ducked to the ground to see if I could detect the bears' whereabouts under less dense foliage and at the same time prepare myself to flatten out in case of attack. The smell of bear still filled the air, but I saw and heard nothing. With adrenaline pumping, my senses were on high alert. Time slowed; seconds seemed like minutes. I had expected a quicker reaction from the sow. Was she making a decision? Suddenly, I heard the rustling of bushes. I feared the worst and anticipated several hundred kilograms of raging fury hitting me at blinding speed. The rustling, however, rapidly moved away from me. The bears were fleeing.

I rose to my feet, nerves shaken. Despite a huge sense of relief, the tension of the encounter was not over. I couldn't tell in which direction the bears had fled. I debated whether to turn back or continue forward. I continued on through thick undergrowth to Mystery Lake.

I reached the shores of the lake an hour later. Not seeing any fresh signs of bear along the way, I relaxed, regained my composure, and headed back to Fiddle warden cabin via a valley below the ridges that I had been on earlier in the day. When I arrived at the cabin in the early evening hours, I came to a decision about the suitability of the basin for hunters: the lack of a defined trail and dense undergrowth made it a poor travel route to the boundary ridges and unsuitable as a camping area. The bears could have it.

Mid-October found me walking up to High Pass once again to check for boundary activity before the snows set in for the winter. And once again, I left my horses back in the pasture near the cabin. I had no plans, however, to check out the basin south of Mystery Lake. When I reached the subalpine below the pass, I ran across fresh grizzly tracks, both large and small. Thinking of my experience with the grizzly family six weeks earlier, I continued on cautiously. I was only minutes away from breaking out into the open rolling alpine habitat where I would have a clear view of what lay ahead.

As I was ascending a bend in the trail around the last group of fir krummholz that gave way to alpine, I came to a startled halt. About 20 metres away, a sow grizzly was sitting on her haunches on the side of the slope, her body motionless and her eyes fixed on me. Three young-of-year cubs stood directly behind her, their eyes on me as well. The facial expressions and body movements of the cubs showed intense curiosity mixed with caution. The sow appeared perfectly calm, as if she had been expecting me. She had. She had sensed me long before I came up over the last stretch of hill and around the grouping of small trees and she'd had plenty of time to signal her cubs to get behind her and stay put.

I did two or three double takes. Was I really observing a sow grizzly and three small cubs at such close range? I was standing well within what would normally be a mother grizzly's fight or flight zone and she showed absolutely no sign of doing either. I would have expected her to react well before I appeared. But the sow remained motionless and continued her steadfast gaze. Her narrowly spaced, dark brown eyes penetrated mine. She was reading my intentions. I knew she would react to my body language.

It was crucial that I reduce any perceived threat. I looked away from her and cautiously moved my stance to an angle so as not to directly face her and the cubs. To avoid confrontation I had to remain calm and back away. But I was afraid to move. As the seconds ticked by my thoughts were on rapid fire, trying to grasp why she was not reacting. I became acutely aware of the strong rush of adrenalin pumping into my system, signalling my own fight or flight response. I wasn't about to do either.

Incredibly, I began to relax a little. It was clear that the sow had no intention of confronting me, that she trusted me as long as I kept my distance. But I also felt she expected me to back off; I couldn't violate her comfort zone for much longer. She was waiting for me to make the first move. Then a really stupid thought crossed my mind. I had my old 35 mm camera in the top pocket of my daypack. I considered taking off my pack, pulling out the camera and taking a picture, maybe my last.

I decided to make a slow retreat. I turned around and took a few hesitant steps down the trail before looking back at the bears. I expected some response; perhaps a bluff charge to send me on my way and to give me the clear message I was in *her* territory, or a full out attack. Neither she nor her cubs budged. I took a few more steps back down the trail, then a few more. I turned to see if she might be on my heels. She wasn't. I picked up my stride, not believing the sow had let me off without so much as a bluff charge or a disapproving huff.

As I continued downward, out of sight and facing away from the bears, I became nauseous and shaky. Suddenly, both my knees gave out and I dropped to the ground. It took me a few seconds to realize that my body was reacting to shock. My muscles, in a state of adrenaline-induced tension from the encounter, had become weak and tired. By freezing and suppressing the fight or flight response, the blood sugar that had risen so rapidly in my body had fallen just as fast. Combined with the unused adrenaline in my system, the onset of muscle weakness was very rapid. My knee joints gave way.

On the ground and in a kneeling position, I lowered my body further to raise the blood pressure in my head. My dizziness subsided and I felt the muscles in my limbs strengthen enough so that I could pull myself off the ground. I started walking again, but with a very wobbly, drunken-like gait. It took five or ten minutes before my muscle tone felt somewhat normal. Although I understood how my response to the adrenalin rush had affected me, I was surprised by the severity of my symptoms.

I wondered afterwards if the sow and cubs were the same family I had run into before. She had shown tremendous restraint regarding my intrusions into her territory.

A few days later and with winter approaching, I left the alpine slopes and ridges to the coming snow squalls and the bears.

◆ ◆ ◆

Our fear of grizzlies is largely unjustified. Bears are extremely tolerant of humans and want to avoid confrontation as much as we do. Thousands of relatively close encounters between humans and bears occur each year in North America—thankfully not as close as mine with the sow grizzly and her cubs. Few people who live in rural areas or who participate in outdoor recreational pursuits in bear country have not run into a bear at some time; for some, hundreds of times. Despite this, only a few bear attacks are reported each year in North America. Of course, we must respect bears and take appropriate precautions in bear country. If we do so, we can live with these animals without fear.

Of the miniscule number of grizzly attacks on humans, most are in self-defence to a perceived threat, and many could have been prevented. Grizzlies do not see humans as prey. There are only a *very few* isolated cases within the last century of a grizzly bear killing and eating a human. Despite its reputation as a vicious predator, the grizzly is largely herbivorous. Results of a grizzly study undertaken in the park between 1975 and 1978 revealed that 95 percent of the bears' diet in the mountains consists of plant species such as sweetvetch roots, grasses, sedges, horsetails, forbs, and berries. Approximately 5 percent of their diet consists of small mammals, like marmots and Columbian ground squirrels, and an occasional large animal (often in the form of carrion). More recent studies of interior British Columbia grizzly bear populations have shown similar results.

Over the past century, hundreds of park wardens have spent a good portion of their careers capturing, handling (with the aid of tranquilizers), tracking, and monitoring this great monarch of the mountains. We often completed the fieldwork alone, further subjecting us to potential bear confrontations. Despite the hazards of working with bears and travelling in grizzly country, Percy Goodair has the tragic distinction of being the only park warden killed by a grizzly. Remarkably, apart from Goodair, there is not a single incident on record of a warden sustaining an injury from an encounter with a grizzly.

◆ ◆ ◆

Another of my close encounters with a grizzly while on foot happened on the subalpine slopes of The Ancient Wall above Caribou Inn horse camp in the upper Blue Creek Valley in 1980. Julia had joined me during this particular trip. We were climbing towards 44-40 Pass (named for an empty shell casing from a poacher's rifle found there many years before) when we spotted the largest grizzly I have ever run into. The enormous boar had an unusually dark brown to almost black coat with shades of silver-grey across the shoulders and back.

The grizzly was about 100 metres away, not an alarming distance, but it was headed at a cross slope angle straight towards us at a brisk walk. We first noticed the bear from behind a grouping of krummholz only two or three metres high. The bear hadn't spotted us. We decided to step out into full view to alert him of our presence and avoid a face-to-face encounter. Before we reacted, the bear reached a slight rise in the terrain 50 metres from us. It caught our scent, stopped in its tracks, reared up on its hind legs, and looked towards us. Without further hesitation, the big boar spun around 90° and continued its quick pace downslope towards our camp below The Natural Arch. It wanted nothing to do with us.

We spent two more days in the area. During that time we saw the bear's huge tracks and diggings near our camp. On our last morning in camp I was up early to jingle the horses before moving down valley to Blue Creek warden cabin. I found them resting after their morning feed two kilometres downstream from the camp. Very close to the horses were the fresh tracks of the big bear. The tracks showed that he had been feeding near the horses before crossing the valley into another drainage basin. I guess he figured if we were leaving the valley it was time he did the same. He and the horses had kept company long enough.

Four years later, in July of 1984, while jingling for the horses at Willow Creek, I walked up onto a low ridge overlooking a marsh beside the creek. I was startled to see a huge black grizzly feeding on vegetation in the marsh a stone's throw away and directly below me. The bear looked up at me and without any sign of unease, resumed feeding. I backed off a short distance and watched the bear for a few minutes before it moved away from me and into a thicket of willows. From its size and distinct blackish coat it appeared to be the same bear Julia and I had run into below 44-40 Pass.

A few months after I sighted the bear at Willow Creek, B.J. rode over from the Smoky River District to assist me during the autumn boundary patrol. On one of his trips up the Mowitch Creek Valley in mid-September, he stopped at Little Heaven for the night. Early the following morning, blurry eyed and half asleep, his coffee still brewing on the stove, he set out to jingle his horses in the meadows below the cabin. Twenty minutes later, with dawn barely breaking and halter in hand, he spotted the dark form of what he thought was one of the horses at the edge of the treed slope beside the meadow. He jumped across Mowitch Creek and navigated around a few hummocks before he reached the edge of the forest. Moments later, he almost ran smack into the largest grizzly he had ever seen. The bear remained steadfast: cool, unflinching, and with a stance and stare that warned B.J. not to take another step forward. B.J., hands shaking and heart racing, slowly backed away. The bear carried on with its business. B.J. found his ponies nearby, packed up, and still rattled by his experience, left for Rock Creek horse camp.

The following day, as he was riding back from checking hunters along the boundary a few kilometres upstream from the tent camp, B.J.'s horses began snorting and prancing about. They had sensed a bear but felt uncomfortable not being able to pin-point its location. Half a minute later and a little further down the trail, he spotted the animal on a slope not far above them. As B.J. was attempting to bring the restless horses to a standstill, the grizzly stood up on its hind legs, shook his head, scanned the air to get a scent of the man in green and his companions, popped his jaws a few times, and took off at a run up the hill, disappearing into the timber within seconds. It was the same huge black grizzly B.J. had run into at Little Heaven.

When B.J. rode back into camp, he noticed the tracks of the grizzly. The big bear had checked the campsite over while B.J. was out for the day and circled the large canvas wall tent but left it intact. His interest had clearly been directed towards the oat barrel that contained the horse's treats. Fortunately the bear was unable to pry the bin open. Not surprisingly, B.J. had a few restless nights of sleep in the wall tent before moving on. When we later compared our descriptions of the dark-coloured bear we both agreed it was likely the same bear that I had run into first in 1980 and then again along Willow Creek.

Encountering a grizzly at close range when alone and on foot is unnerving to say the least. We generally felt much safer when we were with our horses. There are only a few incidents on record in North America of an all-out grizzly attack on horse riders. What is very dangerous, however, is being thrown from a horse that has panicked from a surprise encounter with a bear at close range. Horses are generally comfortable around bears and occasionally graze in close proximity to one another. It's when they suddenly and without warning enter one another's fight-or-flight zone that a situation can go haywire.

A year after B.J.'s encounters with the grizzly at Little Heaven and Rock Creek, he was in the middle of a 10-day boundary patrol in the Moosehorn Valley with Tom MaCaskell, an RCMP friend. They were returning to Moosehorn warden cabin after spending the day along boundary ridges checking out hunting parties. The weather had turned nasty with snow blowing sideways and low visibility. B.J. was riding in front and leading his pack horse. Tom, on his riding horse and with the second pack horse bringing up the rear, trailed several metres behind. All four horses and the two riders had their heads down shielding their eyes from the driving snow.

Relating the incident to me later, B.J. said, "I saw something big and dark coming out of the trees toward us about 20 metres away. At first I thought it was a bull moose but it was a bear. The events that unfolded happened in a matter of seconds but it seemed like it all happened in slow motion. When the bear came running at an angle toward us, my riding horse and pack horse took off running. I turned back in the saddle and yelled at Tom. The grizzly reached the trail just behind my horses and just in front of Tom's horses. Tom's pack horse took off sideways through the willows and Tom's saddle horse swapped ends (did a complete 180°) and headed back the other way."

The grizzly had been travelling or feeding beside the trail when the horse party suddenly appeared out of the blowing snow. It made a quick decision to high tail it but for whatever reason came out of the woods and crossed the trail between B.J. and Tom's horses when doing so. Just as alarmed as the men and horses, the bear fled into the woods on the other side of the trail as quickly as it had appeared.

But that didn't help Tom. B.J. recalls: "I can still picture it in my mind. When Tom's horse sucked back and swapped ends, it almost threw Tom over the front of the saddle. He was eyeball to eyeball with that grizzly bear and the only thing that saved Tom was that he had a death grip on that saddle horn and managed to pull himself back in the saddle. It was like something out of a Bugs Bunny/Road Runner cartoon."

When B.J. related the incident to me, along with the description of the bear, we were certain it was the same black grizzly we had both previously come across. About a month after their trip into the Moosehorn, the large grizzly with the unusual blackish coat and the typical vast home range of an adult male bear was fattening up in preparation for hibernation. He was in the foothills just east of Jasper National Park, one mountain range over from the Moosehorn Valley. But he never made it into his den before the winter storms blew into the backcountry. We received notice from the Alberta Fish and Wildlife in Hinton that the magnificent bear, after spending its entire life avoiding confrontation with humans, had been hit and killed by a train on the Grande Cache rail line near Big Berland Provincial Recreation Area.

◆ ◆ ◆

Park Wardens Bob Barker and Al Stendie were well into their careers when I started mine. Mac Elder was at the tail end of his career. The three of them were among the last to manage backcountry districts year round. After they retired from the Warden Service I asked them to sum up their experiences with the great bear.

Bob began his 35-year career with Parks Canada in 1967, remaining in Jasper the entire time. Bob was the last to have his family with him in a backcountry district year round. His wife, Barb, and infant daughter, Cheryl, joined him in the Brazeau District from 1970 to 1972. Cheryl was just six weeks old when she experienced her first trip on horseback, her parents taking turns holding her in the saddle in front of them on the 30-kilometre journey into Brazeau warden cabin. Another family member was along for the ride: their Siamese kitten, carried in the jacket pocket of whichever parent was not preoccupied with Cheryl.

In countless grizzly encounters, both on foot and on horseback, only once did a grizzly behave aggressively towards Bob. He was travelling with Patrolman Alfie Creighton to Isaac Creek warden cabin on the South Boundary. Alfie was in the lead with his horse when a young three to four-year-old grizzly startled them at close range as it approached on the trail. The bear spooked Alfie's horse. The horse spun around 180° and ran into the pack horses and Bob's horse. The horses bunched together in a medley, nervously crashing into each other and spinning circles while Bob and Alfie tried to calm them. The bear moved a few metres off the trail and shook its head as if in defiance at the horse party's intrusion into its territory. It paced back and forth growling, snarling, and popping its jaws. "The grizzly," as Bob put it, "was just a young teenager, likely venturing out and establishing a territory of its own...unafraid, assertive, and very reluctant to back down. The horses sensed that this grizzly was behaving differently." Eventually, the bear, taking its time and not wanting to lose face, slowly backed off into the brush. Bob said, "It was the only time I ever felt even mildly threatened by a grizzly."

Al also spent his entire career in Jasper. He never had a close call with a grizzly in the backcountry. He recalls one particular bear in the 1970s, however, that kept him company from a distance for a few years in the Blue Creek District. Al often saw the grizzly in the upper Blue Creek Valley between Topaz warden cabin and Hardscrabble Pass that leads into the Willmore. Al said, "The grizzly showed up every spring at Topaz. He'd take a chunk of wood off the corner of the cabin when he went by. He would then spend most of his time up on the slopes towards the pass. Come autumn, he'd come back down the valley and take another chunk out of the corner of the cabin—sometimes there'd be bite marks, sometimes claw marks. I painted the cabin one year. Well, he didn't seem to like my paint job and he came back the next spring and took another chunk out of the cabin." It may have been Al's cabin but the bear was making it clear it was in his territory, possibly testing the cabin as well to see if it could be broken into. Al commented,

"The grizzly never bothered me, the horses, or Kelly (his dog). He ignored us and went about each summer foraging and digging out a ground squirrel or two."

Mac had many exciting grizzly encounters. His closest call occurred in the early 1960s when walking from Willow Creek to Seldom Inn on the North Boundary. Mac, accompanied by his Alaskan Malamute, recalls wandering off the main trail to inspect something, "when suddenly a boar grizzly came right at me out of nowhere." Although the general rule is to hit the dirt and play dead, Mac said, "I had the time to climb a small pine tree. The bear was ferocious...mad as hell. He reached up and came within a foot of my boots. And then he seemed confused; it was as if he was thinking, 'I don't know what I got but I don't want it.' The bear then sauntered off into the woods. And my dog during the whole encounter went off and hid, tucking his nose under some willows."

The latest generation of park wardens are experiencing much the same encounters with grizzlies as the generations that came before them, albeit less frequently. They're not patrolling the backcountry as often or as extensively as their predecessors. The great bear is still out there, though, claiming the wilderness as its domain.

CHAPTER TWENTY-SEVEN

Wolf Pack

It was almost noon on September 10, 1986 when I reached the summit of Folding Mountain to patrol the boundary for poaching activity. It took most of the morning to climb the 2300 metres up its northeast ridge from the Terris Sawmill Road. Folding Mountain is situated eight kilometres east of Jasper's East Park Gate, where the western fringes of the foothills meet the massive uplifted folds of the Rocky Mountains along the eastern boundary of Jasper National Park.

My destination was Mystery Lake, another 11 kilometres to the south. I planned to camp at the lake and walk to Fiddle warden cabin the next day. Roughly two-thirds of my trek would take me along a series of three alpine ridges east of the Jasper National Park boundary and then another two alpine ridges that follow the park boundary. The ridges fan out along the southern shoulder of Folding Mountain, each one losing an average of 350 metres in elevation, then gaining approximately the same elevation before the summit of the next—a high-elevation roller coaster. These ridges and numerous alpine basins comprise the area between Folding Mountain and Mystery Lake, where Rod Wallace and I wanted to increase our autumn hunting season boundary patrol. The latter third section of the trek would lead off the summit of the last ridge and back into the province. I would then have to bushwhack down steep terrain to Folding Mountain Creek, which drains into the eastern end of Mystery Lake.

When Rod dropped me off near the old Terris Sawmill site that morning, the temperature was hovering around the freezing mark. It was drizzling rain with high cloud and light winds. The weather forecast for the rest of the day was for the same. Three hours later, at the summit, I took off my heavy pack and turned to look towards the town of Hinton, 30 kilometres to the northeast. I was alarmed at what I saw. The forecast was wrong.

A massive dark blue-black wall of cloud stretched across the eastern horizon above the foothills between Hinton and me. The easterly wind was picking up, pulling this giant and frightening cloud towards me. It was going to pack a hell of a punch.

Anticipating that this horrific weather would hit me within a half hour, I took shelter behind a boulder to reduce the impact of the approaching wind. I scanned the ridges ahead and compared the terrain I was about to set out on to the contour lines and features on my topographic map. This left me with a good mental picture of the terrain in case visibility would be obscured. I hunkered down and ate lunch. Halfway through an energy bar and sandwich, the storm arrived with gale force winds and heavy snow. The clouds closed in, darkening my world.

Within minutes I found myself in a whiteout, unable to see more than 15 metres in any direction. I had to reassess my plans. I could turn around, descend Folding Mountain, and abandon my journey. I wasn't about to do that, although I was apprehensive at what lay ahead if the nasty weather continued for long. Or I could sit out the storm, hoping it would be a short-term squall. I sensed that it wasn't.

I decided to continue south along the ridges towards Mystery Lake. Maintaining my direction in the whiteout meant following along the crest of each ridge. If I veered off too far to my right on the relatively flatter portions of the ridge and lost elevation, I knew I would have to backtrack to regain the ridge crest. The same applied if I veered too far to the left. Finding my direction in the mountains was second nature to me. When the weather was clear I used the sun. During periods of overcast, I used features of the surrounding terrain as a guide, and I usually had my topographic maps along for reassurance. I had never carried a compass in my life (the Global Positioning System was still a few years away); I prided myself on having a good sense of direction.

A few hours later I reached the third summit south of the main peak of Folding Mountain at the park boundary. My pace had been slow, as the whiteout forced me to continually assess my direction. Fortunately the snow had tapered off and was beginning to melt. The remaining snow on the ground, combined with the dense cloud I was walking through, had turned the world to white and shades of grey. I had difficulty making out any landscape features beyond a few metres. Other than trusting that staying along the ridge crests would keep me on route, I was losing my sense of direction. Equally distressing, despite wearing good quality rain gear, I was soaked to the skin and cold.

Although quite certain I was indeed on the third summit, I was unable to find the Jasper National Park boundary marker on its broad rounded crest. From the third summit, the ridge veers off into two separate ridges, one of which heads southwest towards the steep eastern face of Fiddle Peak that drops into a canyon along the Fiddle River. There are no trails in this part of the canyon; its rock walls drop almost vertically into torrential river currents. It was not the route I wanted to take.

I set out to what I thought was the southeast ridge, but soon afterwards I began to doubt myself. When I had turned around in the extreme whiteout conditions looking for the park boundary marker, I had lost my sense of direction. Nevertheless, I followed my gut feeling and continued on. I gained approximately 300 metres in elevation and reached what I thought was the fourth summit. I continued on to the fifth. My map indicated that I should reach this last summit within a half hour. After a half hour, I had gained and regained elevation and was standing on top of what I hoped was the last of the five summits. But I hadn't gained as much elevation as I should have. I seriously questioned whether I was on the summit of the fifth ridge or on the ridge below the steep east face of Fiddle Peak—the ridge that takes a long descent into the canyon on the Fiddle River. I was lost.

Not knowing where I was remains to this day one of the most disturbing, angst-filled hours of my life. Only those who have been lost in the wilderness, fearing for their survival, know that feeling. It's dreadful. I was also tired and hypothermic. And, I had my sense of pride: I had never expected that I would get lost in the mountain wilderness that was my birthplace and home, even taking into account it was over 11,000 square kilometres in size. I had made a serious mistake. For the first time in my life, I wished I had taken a compass.

I had to make a decision. Should I go back—and where was back? Not an option. Should I stop and camp for the night on the ridge and wait out the weather? Not an option either. I was exposed to the wind, cold, and snow and had no idea how long the storm would last. I decided to descend off the summit and into the nearest basin the terrain would force me into. Still in dense cloud and with snow falling again, I began my descent. I traversed back and forth across a scree slope until I reached a gully. As I descended further into the basin and into thickets of trees and shrubs alongside a creek, the snow changed to pouring rain. My clothes were sopping wet. With my backpack weighing heavily on my shoulders and the hopelessness of being lost weighing heavily on my mind, I kept moving to avoid serious hypothermia.

I carried on, trudging downhill for another hour through a dense forest of trees and shrubs until the creek I was following joined a larger creek. Was this Folding Mountain Creek or was it any one of the other numerous creeks in an approximate 40 square-kilometre area? That depended on which ridge I had dropped off of and in which direction I was headed—I had no idea.

At last the rain let up and turned into a light drizzle and the clouds lifted. The slope began to level off. A half hour later the forest cover began to thin and the trees gave way to a large open meadow. Emerging from the dark forest, I walked up to the top of a small grassy knoll to behold a panorama that is etched forever in my mind as one of the most emotionally stirring I have ever experienced.

The tranquil waters of Mystery Lake lay before me. The rain had tapered to a light shower and mist from the lake was rising up the slopes of the surrounding forest. The effect was surreal, almost ghostly. I was elated! I had found my way. I was *not* lost. I never *was* lost. Incredibly, with all the twists and turns and ups and downs over the past eight hours in cold, wet, and whiteout conditions, I was exactly where I wanted to be! I had arrived at the east end of the lake.

I experienced an overwhelming sense of relief. As I stood on the knoll surrounded by the wild landscape, time stood still. I was in one of those "feeling of oneness" euphoric states: spiritual bliss. It was the same meditative state I had experienced a few years before while jingling my horses in the early morning in the Moosehorn Valley under a brilliant luminescent sky of northern lights.

Seemingly in slow motion, my senses, specifically my sight, brought me out of my dreamlike state. I became aware once again of my surroundings. Looking away from the lake and forested slopes, I focused on the meadow immediately below the knoll. I was not alone. Not more than 15 metres away, standing stiff-legged from stopping dead in its tracks due to my sudden appearance on the knoll, was a magnificent black wolf.

Frozen in stance, we stared at one another for several seconds. The wolf's intense amber eyes seemed to pierce right through me. Then, just off to my right, I noticed some dark forms emerge from the mist-shrouded, shadowy edge of the forest. It took a few moments for the forms to take shape: six more wolves, moving as a group, were loping towards their big black companion and me. Startled, they scattered into a wide arc behind what I assumed to be their leader, the great black wolf standing before me, the alpha male. They paced back and forth nervously, their eyes on me. I remained motionless, thrilled at this incredible encounter with the wolves while still overjoyed to know that I wasn't lost.

The alpha male retreated towards the pack. All seven wolves were alarmed and nervous, yet curious, a typical reaction when meeting humans in the wild. I expected them to flee at any second. Instead, the group slowly spread out. One or two wolves backed off towards the lake on my right while another two retreated to my left. The remaining wolves didn't know what direction to go in. There was some tail wagging and other body language. A few wolves barked uneasily. Finally, they grouped together and ran off to my right, along the northern shore of the kilometre-long lake.

Not wishing to trouble them, I headed for the hiking/horse trail along the lake's south shoreline. Minutes later, the wolves, now on the opposite shore, stopped running. After taking a quick look at me across the lake, they postured, and with tails wagging, each held at different hierarchical positions, rubbed up against one another. A few wolves, in a submissive gesture, licked the faces of the more dominant members of the pack, with the alpha male receiving the most attention. Comfortable that they had distanced themselves from me and had re-established pack harmony, they settled down, held their heads to the sky, and howled. My encounter had been incredible, and now watching them and listening to their enchanting chorus left me enraptured.

After their musical interlude, the wolves trotted off towards the west. I followed along the south shore, reaching a campsite at the west end of the lake. The wolves were somewhere along the trail ahead of me. Wet and cold, without dry wood for a decent campfire, and with the rain, although light, still falling, I decided to forgo camping and push on to Fiddle warden cabin for the night. I hadn't seen any sign of recent hunting activity; who other than a crazy warden would set out on a trek like this in these weather conditions? A lone bighorn near the summit of Folding Mountain was the only large animal I had observed other than the wolves. It had been a long day, but it wasn't over yet. After a bit of food and some juice, I pulled on a dry undershirt, lifted my heavy pack onto my back, and set out for the cabin, 10 kilometres away.

A few minutes later, I intersected the wolves' tracks crossing the boundary back into the park and followed them for about two kilometres before they veered off the main trail. I continued my hike to Fiddle warden cabin, walking the last hour or so in the dark, the dull light from dying flashlight batteries barely illuminating the ground in front of me.

Chilled to the bone by the time I arrived at the cabin, I soon had a warm fire flickering in the old wood stove. I reached Jasper Dispatch on the SSB radio and asked the operator to call Rod at Pocahontas to inform him of my location. Rod responded a few minutes later from the warden station. He had been concerned about how my day had turned out after the storm. We chatted for a while before I prepared a late and welcome dinner. It was well into the night before the warmth provided by the hot food, the tea, and the fire brought my body core temperature back to normal inside that small log haven. Exhaustion settling in, I drifted off to sleep, reflecting on yet another of the many incredible encounters I had experienced with one of the most misunderstood animals on our planet.

◆ ◆ ◆

As with the great grizzly, our understanding of the wolf is heavily influenced by myth. Unlike the omnivorous grizzly, wolves are efficient killers. They are meat eaters. They *are* predators. A sense of loathing and hatred of predators permeates many cultures. We don't like the sight of a prey species being chased down, killed, and devoured. It's not pretty to watch. Of course, we are a predatory species as well, but the fishermen, farmers, and ranchers do our killing for us. Wolves, on the other hand, must survive in a harsh environment and make their own kills.

Wolves do not consider humans as prey. In the past century in Canada there is only one conclusive case of wolves attacking a human, and the attack did not involve wild wolves in a natural environment. In 1996, a young woman working as a caretaker at a forest and wildlife reserve near Haliburton, Ontario was killed by five captive wolves while feeding them in an enclosure.

Wolves may have been responsible for one other person's death. This case involved a geological engineering student killed at North Point Landing in northern Saskatchewan in 2005. He had multiple bite wounds and some flesh missing from his body. Black bear and wolf tracks were found nearby. No fewer than ten wildlife and forensic experts were called in to investigate, but they were unable reach a definitive conclusion as to which animal actually killed the man. It was known that black bears and wolves frequented a dumpsite close to the camp and were conditioned to human food.

In my many encounters, wolves have either fled or exhibited complete indifference. Most of the latter involved wolves habituated to people from frequent close contact. At other times, often in the backcountry, the wolves were very inquisitive. Wolves are intelligent and curious animals. They will often stand and stare, and sometimes cock their heads to one side, much like a dog trying to understand what its master is trying to communicate. They want to understand *us* better—what are our intentions, are we a threat? At some point, though, their natural fear of humans kicks in and they fade into the forest.

Thousands of outdoor enthusiasts in our national parks and other wild areas encounter wolves every year without incident. If humans were prey, I wouldn't be writing these words. Wolves encountering people with a dog, however, is an entirely different story. Wolves are very territorial and view other canine species as intruders. They sometimes attack and kill coyotes, foxes, or other wolves that are not members of their pack, occasionally consuming them. When they come in close contact with a person and a dog, they may act in a threatening manner—maybe even aggressively—towards the *dog*. And they might go in for the kill if the dog can be separated from its owner.

◆ ◆ ◆

At the end of October in 1984, Rick Ralf joined me at Willow Creek warden cabin for a few days. We decided to take our last ride together in the Willow Creek area before packing it in for the winter. Our destination was Kidney Lake, across the valley from the cabin. The morning brought a chilling -14°C. We saddled our horses after lunch when the temperature crept above zero. Gord Anderson's dog, Sara, had accompanied me over the last few weeks in the backcountry and was as keen as ever to explore. When we reached the Snake Indian River crossing a few kilometres before the lake, Rick hoisted Sara up into the saddle with me. My riding horse, Gander, was used to her joining me in the saddle for dangerous river crossings.

Shortly after crossing the river and riding through a meadow, we encountered, as Rick put it, "wolf tracks everywhere." Sara, back on terra firma, had her nose to the ground and the horses were alert: they knew wolves were about. Just seconds later, three wolves appeared on the trail ahead of us. I didn't have to say a word to Sara; she immediately sensed danger and positioned herself between the horses. The wolves took a good look at Sara and then receded into the forest. Five minutes later they began to howl.

We reached a ridge above the lake 20 minutes later, tied our horses to trees, and walked down to the shoreline. The wolves kept up their intermittent howling. Then all was silent. Sara seemed uncomfortable with the silence and glanced up to where the horses, 100 metres away and concealed from our view, were tied.

We returned to find the horses agitated. They had scuffed up the ground considerably with their metal shoes, as far away from the trees as their outstretched halter shanks had allowed. Fresh wolf tracks showed that the wolves had walked within 15 metres of the horses and had paced around the area. We calmed the horses down, tightened their cinches, and rode off, leaving a chorus of howls somewhere behind us. The wolves no doubt had their sights on Sara, but were likely curious as to our goings on as well. There are, incidentally, no recorded accounts in Jasper of a wolf, or grizzly or cougar for that matter, attacking a horse.

In the early 1970s, Al Stendie had a spooky incident with his dog Kelly while on horseback near Nellie Lake, four kilometres east of Blue Creek warden cabin. Riding along the trail on an otherwise quiet day, he described: "...sounds similar to the wind whistling through the trees, just very strange sounds. The sounds got louder and louder and then six wolves slowly appeared from out of the bushes beside us. Their voices changed to a very low moaning howl, very unusual. It was eerie; the hair stood up on the back of my neck. Kelly stuck like glue to the side of my riding horse. The horses were alert and kept their eyes on the wolves but weren't overly concerned. The wolves followed right alongside of us for half a kilometre before slowly moving off into the trees. Although spooked at first, I never felt threatened. Kelly, I think, felt otherwise."

Darro Stinson had an intriguing encounter with wolves while with his dog, Charlie, on the South Boundary in 1981. Darro had been camping along the Southesk River for a few days, keeping an eye on several hunting parties that were around for the spring grizzly hunt, legal on the province side of the park boundary, just across the river. Darro had been flown into the backcountry and was on foot, without his horses. He decided to break camp and move to Isaac Creek warden cabin.

Darro explained, "It was a beautiful warm spring day; the snow was melting. There were still patches of snow in the forest but the ground was bare in open areas. I stopped to have lunch on a sandy knoll under a tree. Charlie would always lie down beside me when we rested. After eating, I dozed off. I woke up to Charlie growling. He remained glued to my side. I sat up, looked, and was shocked to see three wolves lying on the trail 20 metres back in the direction we had travelled from. They sat up on their haunches when I did. They just sat there staring at us. Charlie was totally focused on the wolves. He then turned his head slightly, indicating something else off the side of the trail in the woods close to the three wolves. I stood up and couldn't believe what I was seeing—five more wolves. The wolves never moved; a few remained lying down, others were on their haunches. We watched each other for quite some time. Finally, I noticed it was getting dark and we still had six kilometres to go before reaching the cabin."

Darro was quite apprehensive when Charlie initially aroused him from his nap to discover that they were in the company of eight big wolves just a few steps away. But the longer they sat and watched each other, the more Darro relaxed. He was well aware that it is almost unheard of for wolves to act aggressively towards humans, as borne out by his previous close encounters with them. The wolves remained steadfast, however, engrossed by the man and his dog. Although spellbound by what he was experiencing and not fearing for himself, Darro was concerned for Charlie. Were the wolves waiting for them to make a move? Would they pounce on Charlie?

Darro lifted his backpack onto his shoulders. Charlie had remained silent since his warning growl that had awakened his master. He was just as fixated on the wolves as they were on him, and he did not budge from Darro's side. Charlie may have been a domesticated version of these impressive canines but he possessed their genes—he knew what their intensions were. He was nervous. Darro started walking down the trail with Charlie on his heels.

An hour later, with dusk fading to darkness, Darro emerged from the woods and out onto the gravel flats alongside Isaac Creek with Charlie still on his heels. So were the wolves. They had followed the pair for the entire six kilometres to the creek crossing that leads to Isaac Creek warden cabin. The pack never lost sight of Darro and Charlie, silently weaving through the dark foliage next to the trail like phantoms, keeping pace with man and dog. Finding it hard to believe that the wolves had followed them so far, Darro waded across the creek with Charlie by his side. Once across the creek Darro turned and looked back.

The pack was standing on the opposite bank looking at them. Moments later, their curiosity satisfied, the wolves vanished into the woods, perhaps disappointed that they hadn't had the chance to go after Charlie. At least they had escorted the pair out of their territory.

Charlie preferred to sleep out in the open on the porches of warden cabins at night. He liked to be aware of what transpired in the wilderness during the haunting hours of darkness. His eyes would be closed in slumber and dreams (maybe chasing rabbits or being chased by wolves), but his ears and nose always remained alert to signs of danger, serving as Darro's sentry. That night however, Darro brought him inside Isaac Creek warden cabin. Charlie didn't seem to mind.

Thousands of people have had the thrill of observing wolves in North America, mostly from the comfort of their vehicles. With the ever-increasing numbers of visitors descending on Jasper National Park in recent decades, wolf sightings have become more common. A select few visitors, mostly those hiking on backcountry trails, have experienced close encounters.

Encounters with wolves have increased dramatically in the Athabasca River Valley near Jasper townsite along with the increase in trail use by bikers, hikers, runners, and people walking their dogs. It is inevitable that conflicts occur when people and wildlife are brought together in large numbers. Frequent sightings of wolves on the Pyramid Bench trails above the townsite began during the winter of 2008. A pack of wolves moved into the area, claiming it as its territory. The wolves, as usual, did their best to avoid close contact with trail users. But that changed in November 2011.

On November 14, Wendy Niven, a long-time Jasper resident and avid 30-year trail user, took her male Entlebucher Mountain Dog, Helio, for a walk on the Pyramid Bench. Helio paused to smell something on a portion of the trail that parallels the Pyramid Lake Road and fell several metres behind.

In an account of the attack printed in the local Jasper paper, *The Fitzhugh*, Niven recalled, "I looked back to see Helio running toward me followed by a big Malamute-type dog. It wasn't until Helio ran past me full-tilt that I realized that the Malamute was a wolf. They tore off down the trail...I ran out onto the road hoping to divert the chase to a more open area, maybe away from the rest of the pack I was sure was around somewhere, where I thought Helio would stand more of a chance. When I heard high-pitched squealing in the woods...I ran as fast as I could back up the trail only to catch a glimpse of the wolf dragging Helio into the bush. I picked up the biggest stick I could find and started screaming at the wolf, hoping I could scare it into dropping Helio and running away. The wolf kept dragging Helio away and I kept following and screaming until I reached a place where the tumbled-down trees made seeing difficult."

Niven searched for Helio until nightfall, then reluctantly turned away and went home. The following day she returned with park wardens Steve Malcolm and Grant Peregoodoff to look for him. Upon finding the kill site, Niven said, "Nothing was left except a few bits of fur, some red snow, and Helio's torn collar. Am I mad? No. Wolves are wolves. They are a beautiful and an important part of our wilderness. Am I scared to go back? No. I have been reminded in a harsh way that even in our own Pyramid Bench backyard we are still in the wilderness. I for sure will be back."

Two months later, on January 9, 2012, Niven was back on the Pyramid Bench jogging along Cabin Lake Fire Road with her new dog, Tazz. She had returned to using the trails on numerous occasions along with hundreds of other trail users and scores of dogs. Incredibly, fate chose her for another encounter. The scenario began in much the same way as her first confrontation.

When Niven turned and yelled at the wolf, it kept approaching, intent on getting the dog at her heels. She threw a snowball at the wolf and it backed off momentarily but quickly returned. She continued to yell and throw more snowballs but the wolf refused to budge. The wolf eventually gave up pursuit of her dog when she headed back to town. The Warden Service subsequently closed part of the trail network on the Pyramid Bench for the remainder of the winter. Wolf sightings remained common on other areas of the Pyramid Bench and throughout the valley floor.

In June 2012, another Jasper resident, Kirsten Boisvert, was running on a trail with her Border Collie, Kona, near the Cottonwood Slough on the Pyramid Bench. Kona had ventured about 50 metres away from her when Kirsten heard a terrible shriek. She turned to see her dog sprinting back towards her, tail tucked tightly between his legs, with a wolf in pursuit. Kona ran straight to Boisvert, as did the wolf. She tried blasting capsicum spray at the wolf but was unable to get a direct hit. When the can was emptied she picked up a large stick, waving and thrusting it at the animal. She was able to keep the wolf at bay by constantly manoeuvring herself into a position facing the animal and blocking its advances at Kona who remained either at her side or behind her.

Boisvert eventually made it back to Pyramid Lake Road where she thought the wolf might give up its effort of making a meal of her dog. She was shocked, however, when it continued its pursuit for several hundred metres along the road. Finally, a vehicle appeared and the wolf retreated into the woods. The driver stopped and the pair jumped in.

There was a fourth confrontation on the Pyramid Bench. In October, 11 months after the first attack on Wendy Niven's dog, Karl Peetoom was running along Cabin Lake Fire Road when a lone wolf sprang out from behind tall grasses and shrubs and went for his Border Collie, Maggie. When Peetoom inadvertently dropped Maggie's leash, she ran away. The wolf gave chase and bit her several times before she managed to escape its grasp and run back to Peetoom. He grabbed her leash and collar and held her between his legs. The wolf followed and circled the pair, lunging at them in an attempt to separate Maggie so it could get at her. Karl emptied a can of capsicum spray at the wolf with little effect.

Peetoom and Maggie eventually made their way to Pyramid Lake Road, a short distance away. They stood in the middle of the road while the wolf continued to circle them. A truck came by a few minutes later. They scrambled inside and the driver called 911. Steve Malcolm arrived at the scene with fellow wardens Dave Smith and Landon Shepherd. The wolf had not strayed far. With its predatory fixation intensely focused on the dog, the wolf seemed oblivious to the people and vehicles. Steve walked towards the wolf. When the wolf turned tail and trotted into the woods, Steve ran after it to test its fear response. The wolf fled, but instead of leaving the area it made a wide circle around Steve and went right back to the vehicles in search of the dog. Although the wolf had not exhibited any threatening behaviour to the humans, its intense fixation on the dog and general lack of fear was troubling. This was the first of the four encounters on the Pyramid Bench in broad daylight; the other three occurred at dusk when there was less human activity. Considering the wolf was becoming bolder and this was the fourth attack on a dog in one year, Steve made the decision to put the wolf down.

The wolf, a healthy adult female, was one of a pack of nine that was in the area at the time. The description of the wolf and other details from each incident led Steve to conclude that it had been responsible for all four attacks. After the wolf was put down, there were no further wolf attacks.

CHAPTER TWENTY-EIGHT

Lashing Hooves

Stories involving wolf and bear encounters capture the public's attention; we seem to be far more interested in them than in other species. But our fascination with wolves and bears takes attention away from other animals, such as elk and moose, which also must be treated with caution and respect.

From the attention given to bear attacks, for example, one would think that they happen regularly. However, in Jasper National Park, in the 30-year period between 1983 and 2012, there were only two grizzly and two black bear attacks that resulted in injuries to five people. (These incidents are mentioned in an earlier chapter.) In the same 30-year period, *39* people in the park were injured—some fairly seriously—by elk.

Most of these injuries were the result of cows lashing out, kicking with their powerful legs and sharp hooves, to protect their young calves when they were approached too closely. Approximately 10 percent of the elk/human contact-encounters in Jasper are attributed to park visitors or town residents disturbing bulls at close range, particularly during the autumn rut. Although bulls have injured a few people, most of their contact-encounters have been directed at vehicles. Between 1983 and 2012, 29 vehicles sustained flat tires, punched in radiators, smashed windshields, and an assortment of dents and other damage.

Fortunately, the number of elk/human threat-encounters in the park has been markedly reduced in the last few years by various management actions, including ongoing hazing of elk away from areas of human habitation; relocating cows with newborn calves away from high visitor use areas; increased public education of the dangers in approaching elk; the fencing off of large grassed fields within the townsite to discourage elk grazing; and a realignment of fencing around the Jasper Park Lodge golf course to allow for natural wildlife movement corridors. The latter action has enabled wolves, cougars, and bears to access areas of the valley they hadn't used for 70 years, giving them the opportunity to do their part in controlling an unnaturally high elk population in the valley.

As dangerous as elk can be, I would advise even more caution when in close proximity to moose, and in particular, a cow with a young calf. If harassed, elk may kick out once or several times with their feet. Enraged moose, on the other hand, are more likely to knock their victims over and trample them repeatedly, sometimes to death. Fortunately, perilous encounters with moose in the Rocky Mountains are rare, largely because they are fewer in number than elk but also because they don't frequent habitat close to human activities to the extent that elk do.

One of the most frightening encounters I experienced with an animal was with a cow moose that had been attacked by a cougar. I was headed out to the Fiddle River trailhead after spending nine days in the backcountry accompanied by my horses, Anita and Jock, and their favourite canine friend, Sara. About an hour's ride downstream from Fiddle warden cabin, the river is squeezed between a steep mountain slope on one side that drops directly into the rushing waters and an impermeable thicket of small dense trees on the other side. The trail follows along the river floodplain about 10 metres away from the water's edge and next to a thicket of trees. As we were coming around a bend in the trail, the horses and Sara, as they often did, sensed some form of threat before I did. The horses became nervous, and Sara, in the lead at the time and detecting danger, dropped back and crowded in close beside them.

Thirty seconds later we were challenged by an old cow moose standing in the middle of the river. Several long bloody claw marks along her neck and back were telling: she had been attacked by a cougar and had taken to the water for protection. The cougar, likely alarmed by our approach, was nowhere to be seen. The moose turned to face us with ears back, raised hackles, and a defiant stare. My initial thought, that she would remain in the river as we passed by, quickly vanished. The horses' nervousness and resistance to moving forward confirmed my fear that she was poised for an aggressive attack.

Before I could react, Jock's muscles tensed under my saddle a split second before the moose leapt out of the water and charged. Jock, in his attempt to flee, reared up, spun around, and crashed into the side of Anita who had only managed a quarter turn. Almost thrown from the saddle, I reined back on Jock and turned him into a tight circle to prevent him from breaking into a full gallop/half-buck retreat that would have sent me flying. I managed to hang on to Anita's halter shank, winning a tug-of-war battle with her as she tried to escape this terrifying scene and saving myself a second time from being tossed from the saddle. I had lost sight of the moose and was expecting her to ram us or else go after Sara.

Once I had the horses controlled to a nervous on-the-spot prance, I looked around and saw that the cow moose had stopped her charge at the riverbank. She appeared ready to attack again. I managed to get further control of the horses and directed them back up the trail.

Satisfied that we had retreated, the cow moose headed back into the water. Her charge had been a defensive move. Distraught from being attacked by the cougar, likely somewhere nearby on our side of the river, she had also perceived us as being a threat.

I sized up our situation. We had no way around her. We could either return to Fiddle warden cabin or go forward and face another charge, possibly a much more aggressive one. Intent on our destination, I ruled out returning to the cabin. I also dismissed my initial thought to retreat several hundred metres back and wait out whatever scenario would play out between predator and prey; that could go on all day.

I assessed the state of Sara and the horses. Sara was both bewildered and terrified. She stood trembling, tail tucked low between her legs, looking up at me. During the moose's charge she had barely avoided getting trampled by the spooked horses. Within the same seconds, she had to keep an eye on the moose, fearing that she might be the prime target of its abrupt attack, while also wondering in which direction to flee. Sara had been on several long trips with me and was an experienced backcountry traveller. She was always cautious around bears, and her canine instinct kept her close to the horses and me in the presence of wolves. But she had never had reason to fear an ungulate species; a deranged moose intent on harm was a new and alarming experience for her.

This was a new experience for the horses as well, and they were clearly distressed, still nervously jostling about as I attempted to calm them down. They flared their nostrils, shook their heads, and snorted several times to shake off the remaining adrenalin in their system. Drawing large breaths of air, they inhaled moose, cougar, rage, and fear. As for me, my hands were shaking. I waited several more minutes to give the four of us—and the moose—time to settle down.

Deciding I was much safer out of the saddle than in it, I dismounted and took the halter shanks of both horses. Stepping in front, I tried to coax them forward. The moose stood her ground at the edge of the river. The horses initially refused to budge, but with a little more prodding they gingerly took a few steps. With further prodding, they took several more steps until we were close to a right angle from the moose.

And then, with a flurry of bodies, the whole scenario played out again.

I was grateful for not being in the saddle this time around. I did, however, receive a few muscle strains from a tug-of-war with the horses while clutching the ends of outstretched halter shanks when they turned tail. We retreated.

After regaining our composure once again, I turned the horses to face the moose. I was intent on giving it one more harrowing try and to get it over with as quickly as possible. I remained on foot in front of the horses, holding their halter shanks. Sara kept close to my side away from the moose. After much coaxing, I succeeded in getting the horses to move ahead. I kept them moving, breaking into a slow run as we got near the cow.

She put her head down, raised her hackles and stamped the ground. Anticipating another charge, I picked up the pace as we passed by her. Incredibly, she didn't make a move. About 50 metres past the cow, we halted. The horses, Sara, and I turned our heads in unison and glanced back. The moose was standing in the same spot, glaring at us. Relieved that none of us was harmed, I pulled myself up onto Jock's saddle and we continued on. I wished I could have witnessed the outcome of the cow's standoff with the cougar. Nonetheless, I was elated by yet another wildlife experience in Jasper's backcountry.

CHAPTER TWENTY-NINE

Expanding Horizons

In the spring of 1989, I began to contemplate a move. Until this time, I had never considered leaving Jasper National Park. I had travelled a fair amount in Canada and abroad but I had never worked anywhere else. It seemed time for a new chapter in my life. I had recently separated from my wife, Julia, and we had no children so I had few constraints.

Jack Willman, Chief Park Warden of Elk Island National Park, told me that a warden position would be available in his park later in the spring. Jack needed a warden whose main interest and experience was with resource management, specifically wildlife management. Thinking that I could always request a transfer back to the mountains at some point in time, I decided it was time to expand my horizons. I took Jack up on his offer.

Elk Island National Park is situated within aspen parkland habitat about an hour's drive east of Edmonton. The 194-square-kilometre park comprises primarily aspen-spruce forest interspersed with dry grasslands, shallow lakes, and numerous wetlands.

More than 90 percent of aspen parkland habitat in Alberta, Saskatchewan, and Manitoba has been converted to agricultural cropland or otherwise seriously altered. Elk Island is one of the few protected areas representing the last remaining 10 percent of Canada's aspen parkland ecosystem. This habitat supports over 250 bird species—a bird watcher's paradise. The park is most noted for its abundance of elk, plains bison, wood bison, moose, and deer. The management of the former three species is what captured my attention when I transferred to Elk Island.

One peculiarity sets Elk Island apart from other national parks: it is enclosed by a two and a half-metre fence. Because agricultural land and suburban acreages surround much of the park, the fence is required to keep Elk Island's large population of elk, bison, and moose off private land and the Yellowhead Highway, which bisects the park. Wood bison and plains bison are kept separate to keep their purebred genes intact, as they would otherwise interbreed. Plains bison are on the north side of the park, wood bison on the south.

Because the park has been totally fenced off from the surrounding agricultural land for over a century, bison and elk have been unable to disperse as population numbers increase. Predation, another population control mechanism, was removed from the ecosystem by government predator control programs in the first half of the 20th century; wolves, bears, and cougars, all native to the area, were virtually wiped out. Solitary or small groups of these predators from other wild land areas that have somehow weaved their way through a myriad of human obstacles in heavily populated urban and suburban areas have had difficulty re-colonizing the park. Most of those that are able to get anywhere near Elk Island end up meeting the sights of a gun barrel along the way. Suggestions to reintroduce these predators back into the park have been considered but not implemented to date.

With dispersal and predation no longer keeping bison and elk populations in check, it is left to Parks Canada staff to do so. Allowing populations of these ungulate species to outgrow their food supply in the park is not an option. The park's vegetation resources would become severely stressed, unpalatable weeds would gain a foothold, and mass starvation would occur. For the most part, moose and deer are able to self-regulate their numbers without interference. Parasites control moose populations, and deer readily move in and out of the park through small gaps under the fence dug by coyotes.

◆ ◆ ◆

During the first half of the 20th century, elk and bison were controlled with culling programs, and the meat was sold or given to charitable organizations. Towards the latter half of the century, the park began large-scale relocation programs. These either augmented dwindling populations of elk and bison in North America or reintroduced them into areas where they had been extirpated for up to 150 years.

During the last three decades in particular, these relocation programs have made a lasting contribution to wildlife conservation throughout North America and as far away as Russia. We relocated elk to the Yukon, British Columbia, other parts of Alberta, Saskatchewan, Ontario, Kentucky, Tennessee, and North Carolina. We relocated plains bison to Alberta, Saskatchewan, Manitoba, and Montana. Wood bison found new homes (or rediscovered old ones) in Alberta, British Columbia, Manitoba, the Yukon, the Northwest Territories, Alaska, and the Republic of Sakha in Russia. As of 2014, Elk Island has successfully provided a total of 885 wood bison, 1088 plains bison, and 4690 elk to conservation initiatives. The reintroduction of these species into thousands of square kilometres of wild areas has restored and enriched entire ecosystems.

◆ ◆ ◆

When I transferred to Elk Island, my intentions were to work there for a few years, gain experience working with the ungulate relocation programs, and then return to Jasper. I ended up staying for all but one year of the remainder of my career. I coordinated the elk management program for 16 years. During the winter months, when I wasn't organizing the trapping, handling, and relocation of elk, I was busy with handling plains and wood bison. I never tired of working with these animals or on the many conservation projects to relocate them. Park wardens, other park staff, and volunteers dedicated their winter months to these programs. Additional staff from numerous cooperating agencies, notably veterinarians from the Canadian Food Inspection Agency and biologists from the Canadian Wildlife Service, were essential to program operations. We were privileged to work alongside, and develop many lasting friendships with, personnel from the dozens of agencies we worked with in relocating elk and bison to areas under their jurisdiction.

Besides my regular park warden duties during the summer months, I coordinated a trumpeter swan reintroduction program with CWS biologists Len Shandruk and Gerry Byersbergen. Trumpeters have a wingspan of 2.3 metres and an average weight of 12 kilograms. They are the largest waterfowl in North America, not to be confused with tundra swans that breed in northern Canada or the non-native European mute swan that is found in city parks across the country. The trumpeter swan, once numbering in the hundreds of thousands, came close to extinction by the early 1900s due to subsistence hunting for its meat and demand for its down and feathers. Like most waterfowl in North America, swans lost most of their habitat to increasing human settlement. When Canada and the U.S. made an agreement under the Migratory Birds Treaty to stop the hunting of trumpeters in 1917, there were only about 130 left in Canada and the Lower 48 states.

The reintroduction program involved relocating family groups of trumpeters from the Grande Prairie area in Alberta to Elk Island National Park. The park and the remaining aspen parkland habitat in the surrounding area, known as the Beaver Hills, is now home to a growing population of trumpeters. Because of this program and many other trumpeter restoration projects across North America, their numbers have now surpassed 50,000. In 1978, the Committee on the Status of Endangered Wildlife in Canada (COSEWIC) designated the trumpeter as a species of special concern; then in 1996, COSEWIC declared that this majestic swan could be removed from the list—a conservation success story. (Trumpeter swans, however, are still considered as "threatened" under Alberta's Wildlife Act).

One of my most gratifying responsibilities in Elk Island was being a training officer for new members entering the Warden Service. Mentoring new recruits was both a challenge and immensely rewarding. Their eagerness to learn the ropes and their constant energy transferred back to me. There wasn't a day when I didn't feel privileged to be a mentor in their long and hard grind to obtain the skills required of a park warden.

The new recruits attended various training courses in the mountain parks as part of their training program. I arranged backcountry hiking and horseback trips in Jasper for the recruits I mentored. Of course, they needed someone with experience to train them, and that became my way of getting back into the backcountry at least once every summer.

I remained in touch with my peers in Jasper throughout my time in Elk Island. Apart from a year spent in Australia, I never missed an opportunity to arrange my own trips into Jasper's backcountry, often with horses, sometimes with a friend or another park warden, and always to one or more of our warden cabins.

◆ ◆ ◆

In 2002, I jumped at the chance to take part in a one-year work exchange between Parks Canada and Parks Victoria in the state of Victoria, Australia. Park Ranger Kane Weeks, then working in Lake Eildon National Park in Victoria, had requested a work exchange with a park warden in Canada. Kane and I made contact and expressed our shared interest in an exchange.

There were two hurdles for me to overcome before an exchange could be arranged. First, I had to pass the idea by my wife Chrystyne whom I had met shortly after moving to Elk Island from Jasper. Chrystyne is an adventurous explorer and will agree to almost any travel arrangement at the drop of a hat. She saw the exchange as a golden opportunity for both of us. Working as a substitute teacher allowed her the freedom to take an extended vacation. She planned to leave the cold Canadian winter for several months to travel the South Seas, including a one-month stop to visit me.

The second hurdle was more problematic: Parks Victoria, the agency that administers all national parks in the state of Victoria, had an international exchange program while Parks Canada did not. After two months of persistent and often frustrating work dealing with the required bureaucratic hurdles, I arranged for the exchange. In the process, I developed an exchange program between Parks Canada and Parks Victoria with assistance from Kane and from Parks Victoria senior management in Melbourne.

In September of 2002, after spending two weeks with Kane helping him settle into Elk Island, I stepped out of a Qantas 747 in Melbourne and into the eucalyptus-scented air of southeastern Australia. My supervisor, Andy Miller, Ranger in Charge of Lake Eildon National Park, met me at the airport. Andy drove to a small cottage that Kane had arranged for me to rent in the town of Alexandra, 90 minutes north of Melbourne and 20 minutes from Lake Eildon.

It was midday in Australia and Andy suggested I take it easy, get some sleep, and start work the next day. I had not slept for 34 hours (I can't sleep on planes) but was too charged up to think about rest. I took a moment for a quick reality check. *I was in Australia on my first day of a one-year work exchange!* I was standing on the soil of the great and ancient continent down under, the land of koalas, kangaroos, kookaburras, king parrots, and yes, many of the most venomous snakes in the world. There was no time to rest—not on this day.

I asked Andy to take me to the park, show me around, and introduce me to my new workmates. And so started what was certainly one of the most fascinating and invigorating years of my career.

Lake Eildon became my home park in Australia. I also worked in six other national parks, two state parks, and two marine parks. While on a one-month vacation, I volunteered in two national parks and one state park along the Queensland coast in eastern Australia and one national park in the Northern Territory. Although different in terms of culture, geography, resources, and landscapes, I found it was fairly easy to adapt my environmental knowledge and field skills to the job at hand in Australia. My duties included varying aspects of the same work I did back in Canada: resource management, public safety, law enforcement, and public relations.

◆ ◆ ◆

Before leaving Australia, I attended the 2003 International Rangers Federation Conference at Wilsons Promontory National Park located on the southernmost tip of the mainland, just north of Tasmania. Parks Canada wardens Don Waters and Shaun McKenzie also attended the conference that brought together 220 delegates from 40 countries. It was a great privilege for the three of us to have had the opportunity to attend the conference and to represent our agency and country.

As my time in Australia wound down, I vowed that the value of my experiences would not end when I returned home. Before I went to Australia, I had prepared a PowerPoint presentation that focused on the responsibilities of a Canadian national park warden and other Parks Canada staff. I gave the presentation to all interested staff in the Australian parks I had worked in or visited and at the annual Parks Victoria Awards Day Conference in Melbourne.

Apart from giving Parks Victoria staff a taste of the working lives of their Parks Canada counterparts, I promoted interest in the development of a formal exchange program between the two countries. Meanwhile, my exchange partner, Kane Weeks, was doing the same thing, networking with Parks Canada employees and management in Canada.

A few weeks before I left, I met with Chief Executive Officer Mark Stone, Human Resources Project Officer Di Barrett, and other senior Parks Victoria managers in Melbourne. We discussed my exchange with Kane and how their staff had spoken enthusiastically about the possibility of developing a formal long-term exchange program between the respective national park agencies. They all expressed interest in opening a dialogue with Parks Canada.

In the autumn of 2004, a year after I had returned from Australia, Di Barrett informed me that Parks Victoria senior officers had contacted Parks Canada managers in Ottawa to establish an exchange process. Shortly afterwards, I was contacted by Parks Canada's national office in Ottawa requesting my help in creating an exchange program using the proposal I had developed earlier as a template.

In May of 2005, six Parks Victoria staff arrived in Canada to work as stewards of the environment. Five months later six Parks Canada employees, representing various sections within their respective parks, left for Australia to do the same. In the following years, approximately 30 park staff participated in the exchange program.

The experience gained from the exchange program had enormous benefits for the individuals involved, the hundreds of park staff they came in contact with, and the professional reputation of both agencies. We exchanged ideas, perspectives and values, and built relationships that supported the transfer of skills, expertise, and knowledge. We learned that there is more than one way of doing business and that there are different solutions to similar issues. We developed fresh insights and new approaches in managing ways to conserve and protect our invaluable natural environment.

Just as important, the accumulated knowledge and experiences gained through the exchange program allowed us to better foster public awareness and understanding of the need to protect our wild spaces.

There are many stories yet to tell of my time in Elk Island and my one-year work exchange in Australia; perhaps one day I will write about them.

CHAPTER THIRTY

Changes... and Parks for Profit

When I returned to Elk Island from Australia in the autumn of 2003, I was immersed in an issue that would evolve into the most significant change that park wardens had faced in a century—the acquisition of sidearms (handguns) and the dissolution of the Warden Service.

To understand how this major transformation came about, we have to go back to 1909, when national park fire and game guardians—the predecessors of today's park wardens—began a typical day by preparing their horses for travel in Canada's first national park, Rocky Mountains Park (known today as Banff National Park). Once the diamond hitch was tied off on top of the tarp covering each pack horse's load and the riding horse was readied for travel, the fire and game guardian slipped his last item into a leather scabbard on one side of the saddle—a rifle.

In those heady, pioneering days of national park establishment, rugged and ragged outdoorsmen (hunters, trappers, outfitters, and other bushmen of various backgrounds) signed on as fire and game guardians. Their chief mode of travel, and often only friend, was the horse. The fire and game guardian's weapon of choice, the rifle, was used mainly for killing "vermin" during the days of predator control, to shoot animals suffering from injury or sickness, or to kill an animal that was deemed a threat to public safety. Occasionally, when faced with dwindling food supplies, they were allowed to bag the odd animal to fill their larder. Although never officially sanctioned for use on people, the rifle was always close at hand to defend against armed poachers or other men of disrepute roaming the wilderness.

Fast-forward to the mid-1950s. The title of fire and game guardian had long since been changed to "park warden." Park visitation had increased dramatically since the end of World War II, and travel by train or motor vehicle replaced the horse as the primary mode of transportation in the busy lower valleys of the Rocky Mountains. Horses remained the leading form of travel in the backcountry. To keep abreast of the demands created by the growing numbers of park visitors, wardens spent as much time along the high visitor use areas of their mountainous territory as on the backcountry trails. This scenario was playing out in most other national parks across Canada.

Over the next few decades, we steadily acquired a wider range of duties. Public safety and law enforcement responsibilities filled more of our time. Into the 1970s and '80s, criminal activity increased. Lawbreakers were better armed and more dangerous than in the past. We responded by increasing our patrols and enforcing not only national park offences but also criminal code offences, once the domain of the RCMP. As we became more involved in law enforcement, we found ourselves at greater risk from hostile or combative law-breakers. Consequently, we attended upgraded law enforcement training programs, learned self-defence techniques, and acquired batons, handcuffs, body armour, and pepper spray.

Many wardens, especially those immersed in law enforcement, began to voice concerns over safety issues. They demanded sidearms comparable to those carried by provincial enforcement agencies and other federal enforcement officers. Our rifles, kept in scabbards secured to riding saddles or stored in patrol trucks, had been used for resource management purposes and never intended for law enforcement.

By the end of the 20th century, the Warden Service was divided into two camps: those arguing for handguns, and those opposed to the arming of all wardens. Many believed it was time to formally split the Warden Service into three independent functions: law enforcement, public safety, and resource conservation. This way, only those who were in the Law Enforcement Function would have the authority to carry handguns. It was never clear in which direction our employer, Parks Canada, wanted to take the issue.

Of the hundreds of wardens I worked with throughout my career, only a handful wanted to give up the multi-function aspects of the job we thrived on. We wanted it all. We realized, however, that training for and performing the job of all three functions in a safe and effective manner was becoming more challenging. Most of us leaned towards specializing in one or perhaps two functions. The way I saw it, there was no right or wrong view of how each of us approached our career or how we envisioned an inevitable restructuring. Somehow we had to arrive at the best option: we had to compromise.

In June 2000, the issue came to a head: a park warden filed a complaint with a federal occupational health and safety officer on the grounds that he was not provided with the necessary protective equipment (specifically a sidearm) to carry out his law enforcement duties. In due course, a Canada Labour Code ruling directed Parks Canada to take the necessary measures to either correct the hazards inherent in a park warden's law enforcement duties or to protect wardens from these hazards.

Over the next eight years, that decision was repeatedly challenged, appealed, overturned, and upheld in numerous courtrooms and by a number of quasi-judicial bodies. Finally, in May 2008, then Environment Minister John Baird announced Parks Canada would designate armed enforcement officer positions in the national parks. Because not all wardens would be armed, a formal split of the Warden Service was unavoidable. Only those who choose to engage in law enforcement retained the title "park warden."

The remaining former wardens became "resource management specialists," "public safety specialists," or both. I retired in 2010 as a resource management/public safety specialist. Resource management has since been divided into a number of fields: wildlife, fire and vegetation, aquatic, environmental management, and cultural.

Change was inevitable; I could see it developing in the '70s when I joined the Warden Service. Losing the title "park warden," along with 100 years of tradition, was hard to take for many who chose not to carry sidearms. We were proud of our title and the job that came with it. The change brought disappointment, stress, tension among opposing camps, and distrust in management's ability to resolve the issues. Although several processes weren't handled as smoothly as they could have been, we had no choice but to take up the challenge and adapt. We had to move forward.

◆ ◆ ◆

A year and a half after my retirement, I dropped by the Resource Conservation Office (the former Park Warden Office) in Jasper to chat with some of my former colleagues and collect documents while researching material for this book. It was May 1, 2012. I couldn't have picked a worse day.

The federal government had been planning for several months to cut 3,800 jobs in 10 federal departments and agencies across the country. On the last day of April, the axe dropped. Parks Canada took a huge hit; 638 jobs were eliminated and 1,038 seasonal employees were cut back to shorter terms. All sections within the national parks were affected: visitor services, communications and interpretation, trades and maintenance, administration, park wardens, and those in the newly created resource management and public safety positions. Also affected were biologists, historians, social scientists, and archaeologists working out of Parks Canada regional offices.

In the four years since the restructuring of the Warden Service, resource conservation staff and park wardens had adjusted quite well to their new positions. Many had adapted to their new titles within the structure of their old roles. But they now faced a new disruption: as with other Parks Canada staff, they were stunned by the cuts in their ranks.

Ongoing, massive layoffs of long-term staff reduced the number of employees who had devoted their lives to working for Parks Canada. Hiring freezes prevented any meaningful recruitment. Staff morale suffered. Employees, frustrated with having to squeeze funds out of shoestring budgets, mourned the loss of their peers. They were left looking over their shoulders, wondering who would be next.

Despite everything, the remaining park staff soldier on with the endless passion they have always had for their work. Setbacks in programs, cuts in services, and job elimination are old hat to national park employees. Mac Elder, a park warden faced with low wages, harsh working conditions, and ongoing threats of lay-off early in his career in the late 1950s, talked about having a good sense of humour when handling adversity. When we were discussing the 2012 cuts, he said to me, "Lester B. Pearson (prime minister of Canada in the mid-1960s) once told us that funding would always be limited and that the government couldn't supply us with both pencils and pay checks."

Sadly, even the park staff *not* affected by the latest cuts cannot assume career stability. Many staff have either moved on to other jobs or are in the process of doing so. Consequently, Parks Canada has lost thousands of years of corporate knowledge and experience.

Due to ongoing budget shortages, long-term projects and programs developed over decades to protect and preserve the ecological integrity of our parks have fallen short of their objectives. Years of dedicated work in species-at-risk programs, wildlife and vegetation restoration, wildlife/human conflict management, aquatic restoration programs, control of non-native species, environmental assessment monitoring, and prescribed burning programs have been affected. Scientific research and monitoring initiatives that track everything from single species threats to the health of entire ecosystems and the impact humans have had on the parks have also suffered setbacks. Parks Canada's ability to provide adequate public safety, critical to the well-being of visitors, has been reduced.

Layoffs affecting employees in visitor services, interpretation and communications, and trades and maintenance, have seriously affected these programs in their respective parks. Having to pay for park entrance fees, only to face deteriorating park infrastructure and a lack of education and information programs, does not give the public a positive park experience.

Other challenges threaten our national parks. Successive governments—of which the Harper government was by far the worst offender—have largely ignored the value of the natural environment, placing national parks in peril. In a society structured around economic growth with minimal consideration towards environmental responsibility, our governments continue to value commercial interests over the long-term ecological, social, and economical benefits of protecting wilderness.

Much of the montane habitat, which contains the greatest diversity of plants and animals in the Rocky Mountains, has been destroyed, altered, or fragmented. Wildlife has had to compete for the montane: a century of incremental expansion of hotels, bungalow camps, campgrounds, ski hills, golf courses, and large scale tour operations has left once pristine wilderness fragmented with a patchwork of infrastructure to support townsites and the tourist industry. Lower river valleys are choked by railways, highways, secondary roads, pipeline corridors, hydro and power stations, landfills, trade waste pits, gravel pits, and sewage plants. Wildlife corridors, critical to many animals for daily movement and migration routes, have been lost, food resources have been compromised, and disturbances from human activity have adversely affected numerous species. Consequently, many plant and animal species have declined considerably in number. Some species (such as grizzly bears in Banff National Park and moose in both Jasper and Banff national parks) are at critically low populations. Woodland caribou (a species dependent on higher elevation habitats) have recently disappeared from Banff National Park and face imminent extirpation from Jasper National Park.

In the 1990s, Parks Canada recognized that commercial operations had reached their limit in many national parks. To counter the enormous impact that humans have on the environment, Parks Canada changed its policy regarding these operations. In Jasper, for example, the 2010 Jasper National Park Management Plan restricted further development and halted the expansion of existing accommodation. Restrictions were imposed on large-scale tour operations incompatible with park recreational policies. These policies promote public appreciation of the natural environment through activities that to do not adversely affect the park and its wildlife.

Unfortunately, numerous development proposals continue to be approved. In many cases, Parks Canada has circumvented environmental assessment procedures by caving in to the demands and pressures of developers. Environmental concerns have been disregarded. Parks Canada has ignored strong opposition to increased commercialism as expressed at public consultations by environmental groups, Aboriginal communities, former Parks Canada employees, and the general public.

Shockingly, park management plans have been rewritten, amended, or otherwise altered to grant new leases and expand development on existing leases. Parks Canada desperately needs to re-evaluate its support of commercial and private interests that contradicts its own policies. Too often, commercial ventures have taken precedence over the protection of ecological integrity. Tourism is important to the national parks but a balance must be struck between visitor use and preservation.

Despite the challenges ahead, I remain cautiously optimistic for the future of our parks and remaining wilderness areas. Since the beginning of the environmental movement in the late 1960s, Canadians have become increasingly aware of ecological principles and of human impact on the environment. Most understand the urgency to preserve and protect the planet. This entails using its resources sustainably and reducing our ecological footprint on what little natural habitat remains. Many are standing up to governments and industry to challenge misguided economic and political policies that favour short-term economic gain and profits for a few, over the protection of Canada's wilderness.

CHAPTER THIRTY-ONE

My Last Jingle – a Final Ride

Backcountry operations in Jasper National Park have not been spared budget restraints and cuts. Daily operating tasks, patrols, and ongoing projects and programs that require backcountry work have suffered. Only three part-time resource management specialists now cover Jasper's 10,860 square kilometres of area zoned as "wilderness" under the 2010 Management Plan. This comprises 97 percent of the park's total area. The park's horse herd has been cut from 65 to less than 30, with plans for further downsizing.

Trail maintenance has also suffered. Backcountry trails coordinator Jim Suttill supervised a crew that fluctuated between one dozen and two dozen employees each year over a three-decade period. He oversaw the work of contractors that employed another half dozen staff for trail projects. When Jim retired in 2011, he was left with a skeleton crew of three. Jim summarized each incremental budget slash by the federal government as "a slow death by a thousand cuts."

Most backcountry trails in the park are no longer maintained and within a decade will be impassable due to fallen timber, new growth, and unsafe or collapsed bridges that span treacherous river crossings. Warden cabins are seldom used now; without routine maintenance, many are aging beyond repair. The downsizing of the park horse herd and the move away from the traditional backcountry warden's role spells an uncertain future for Jasper's large tracts of wilderness.

◆ ◆ ◆

Shortly before my retirement, I took one final horse trip on the North Boundary of Jasper with Park Warden Brad Romaniuk. I had supervised Brad when he started with the Warden Service in Elk Island National Park and had taken him on his first back-country horse trip into the Fiddle River Valley a few years previously. Carrying on a century-old tradition, I instructed him on the finer points of packing a horse and throwing the proverbial diamond hitch, an important initiation rite for new recruits in the backcountry. Brad had since transferred to Jasper and had mastered the skills of working and living in the wilderness. Throughout our 10-day trip, it became clear to me that I had nothing further to pass on to him. I had, in effect, handed him the torch.

On the evening of our last day of the trip, we stepped off the porch of Willow Creek warden cabin and out into the meadows to check on our four horses. Fifteen minutes later, we found them in a scattered grouping of trees that border the eastern fringes of the pasture. They were contentedly grazing on tender grasses in the crisp autumn air, just as much in their element as we were in our mountain paradise. I walked up to Wrangler, the nearest horse to me, and stroked the back of his shoulders. As was my habit, at the end of each day in the backcountry I gave silent thought and sometimes an appreciative word or two to the ponies for their service and companionship. They may not have understood my words but they understood my tone of voice—friendship, thanks, and respect.

The horse has defined the life of backcountry wardens as much as the wilderness in which they travelled. The horses have carried us, borne our possessions and tools on their backs, courageously taken us across raging rivers, led us safely home to the comfort of our cabins in the darkness of night, alerted us to danger, and skidded wood needed for cooking meals and providing warmth in the cold stillness of autumn nights. We found joy in their companionship, laughter at their antics, and sadness when death took them away.

With those thoughts on my mind, Brad and I bid goodnight to our trusted friends and turned back towards the cabin.

I was left with the realization that the next morning might be my last experience with the ponies—my last jingle and final ride.

Upon reaching the cabin, Brad and I watched the sun as it set over the ancient mountain range along the upper reaches of the Snake Indian Valley. The brilliant globe of light and warmth shot golden rays across the remote landscape as it sank between a few layers of cloud. Behind the rays, the silhouetted peaks stood in grandeur, backlit by bright bands of gold, orange, and red. Slowly, the colours faded as if not wanting to leave—or did I not want them to leave? Just as the sun was about to disappear behind the mountains, it dropped beneath a cloud and with one last blaze of glory flashed its brilliance over the valley. Then the light gave way to a darkening azure sky and finally to the first of an infinite number of stars sparkling like gems against a blanket of black.

As our world darkened around us, a pack of wolves began their ritual evening howl from a nearby rendezvous site. Surrounded by my wilderness home, I pondered my purpose and existence within the vast cosmos.

More than any other location, it was the Snake Indian Valley that captured my imagination when, as a youth, I listened to the wardens spinning their tales of wolves, bears, and bighorns. It was in this valley that I "threw my first diamond" across the back and over the packs of a spirited horse. It was where I began my journey following in the footsteps of the old guardians of the wilderness I had admired since childhood. And it was to this valley that I returned, to honour those who had come before me and to wish happy trails to those who will come after, and to bring closure to my career.

Brad and I were up early the following morning to jingle the horses and bring them in for their oats before we saddled and packed them—for me, one final time.

It had snowed 15 centimetres overnight; an early autumn warning that turned the world white and reminded us winter was on its way. After walking the horses in from the meadow, we prepared our own sustenance for the day, a traditional cowboy breakfast of bacon, eggs, and pancakes, cooked on the old cast iron wood stove in the log cabin.

We relayed our departure plans to the Park Warden Office during the 08:00 a.m. radio call, cleaned up, boarded the windows, locked the door, and prepared the horses for travel. With the diamond hitches tied and tightened on the pack horses and the cinches snug on our riding horses, we swung up and into our saddles and turned away from the Snake Indian Valley. The soft crunching of the horses' hooves in wet snow broke an eerie silence in the calm mountain air as we rode out the pasture gate.

Glossary

105mm recoilless rifle A high-powered recoilless weapon first developed in the early 1950s and fielded in the Korean War. A later prototype was used to control avalanches in North America.

alpine High mountain elevations above the tree line comprised of tundra-like plant communities including wildflowers, low-growing plants, mosses, and lichens.

avalauncher gun A gun that uses bottled, pressurized nitrogen to propel a projectile carrying one kilogram of explosives to avalanche starting zones up to a few hundred metres away.

backcountry Undeveloped wilderness habitat; in the Canadian Rockies often considered as one or more day's travel (by foot or horseback) from developed areas.

bergschrund A crevasse near or at the top of a glacier formed by the downward flow of ice separated from a stagnant portion of the same ice sheet above.

biodiversity The variety of life found in an ecosystem, including the natural processes and connections between species.

bivouac A temporary camping spot under little or no shelter above the treeline.

blaze A small portion of bark cut from a tree with a knife or an axe to mark an undefined trail or route.

bushwack To make one's way through dense vegetation where no path exists.

cirque A crescent-shaped steep-sided basin at the head of a valley or on a mountainside formed by glacial erosion.

cold shoe The shaping and fitting of a horse's metal shoe without the use of a forge to heat the metal.

confluence A merging together of two or more creeks or rivers.

coniferous Cone-bearing seed plants, the great majority of which are trees. Most conifers are evergreens, with thin needle-like leaves.

corduroy Logs placed side by side across wet areas of a trail.

cornice An overhanging mass of hardened snow or ice formed by wind action at the edge of a mountain precipice.

crevasse A deep crack or chasm on a glacier.

deciduous A tree or shrub that sheds its leaves annually.

depth hoar Large-grained, weakly bonded crystals near the base of the snowpack that are formed as a result of large fluctuations in temperature.

extirpated A species that has become extinct in a given geographic area.

frontcountry High visitor use areas in the national parks that are easily accessible by vehicle, including day-use trails (as compared to backcountry areas that generally take one or more days to reach by foot and require overnight camping).

guide *(horse)* Responsible for leading a group of clients on a horse excursion and insures the welfare and safety of each client.

halter shank A rope attached to a horse's halter. The leading end can be tied to an object (e.g., hitching rail) or used to lead a horse.

headwaters The source of a creek or river.

hobbles Leather straps buckled to the lower part of a horse's leg above its hoof. A short length of chain is attached to each leather strap. Hobbles discourage the horse from straying too far too fast.

home range The area in which an animal lives and travels. It is generally much larger than its territory, which it actively defends.

jingle Finding and bringing back horses from their grazing areas. The sound of a jingling bell attached around the neck of one or more horses indicates their whereabouts (e.g., in dense forests or under limited lighting conditions).

krummholz A group of stunted trees at the upper reaches of subalpine forests.

mineral lick A natural mineral deposit where animals can obtain essential mineral nutrients which may not be otherwise available in nutrient-poor soils.

monoculture An ecosystem consisting of only one flora species; sometimes used to describe a habitat of very limited biodiversity.

montane In the Rocky Mountains, habitats found along the lower elevation valleys and slopes, generally comprised of mixed wood forests interspersed with grasslands and wetlands. They are rich in biodiversity.

mountaineer One who climbs mountains for sport.

outfitter *(horse)* The owner of a horse outfitting business who takes clients on backcountry horse excursions; may also act as a guide and wrangler with small groups.

parabolic microphone A microphone that uses a parabolic reflector (dish) to collect and focus sound waves into a receiver.

pass A low point between two mountains or a mountain range affording the lowest possible navigable route of travel.

permanent snow patches Pockets of snow that do not melt entirely during the summer.

rabies A contagious and often fatal viral disease that attacks the central nervous system. It is transmitted by the bite of an infected animal.

scree A collection of loose, broken rocks on a mountain slope. Walking on it is often difficult as it can shift when stepped on.

single side band A shortwave frequency (more properly called a "mode") used to transmit and receive radio messages over long distances.

snow pack The successive layers of snow formed during the winter with each new snowfall.

snow pit A deep pit dug vertically into the snow pack that reveals the successive layers of snow formed during the winter.

snow profile An assessment of snowpack conditions based on observing and recording snow layers and performing snow stability tests. Used in conjunction with other measurements (e.g., current weather conditions) to assess avalanche hazard.

surface hoar *(frost)* Feathery crystals that form on the snow surface during clear and calm conditions. Forms a persistent weak layer when buried in mountain snow packs.

sweeper A fallen or leaning tree that extends out over the surface of a river.

technical climb A climb on a mountain or rock face that generally requires rope and some form of protective aid.

territory *(animal)* An area occupied by a single animal, mating pair, or group that is vigorously defended against intruders, especially of the same species.

the province A term used by park wardens to describe provincial lands adjacent to national parks.

wrangler *(horse)* Responsible for the care and use of horses owned by an outfitting business.

whumpf The sound made when a weak layer in a snow pack collapses. This shifting of the snow pack usually results in an avalanche.

Bibliography

Books

Burns, R.J., and Mike Schintz. *Guardians of the Wild: A History of the Warden Service of Canada's National Parks*. Calgary: University of Calgary Press, 2000.

Calvert, Cathy, and Dale Portman. *Guardians of the Peaks: Mountain Rescues in the Canadian Rockies and Columbia Mountains*. Calgary: Rocky Mountain Books, 2006.

Camp, Frank. *Roots in the Rockies*. Ucluelet, BC: Frank Camp Ventures, 1993.

Dettling, Peter. *The Will of the Land*. Calgary: Rocky Mountain Books, 2010.

Dixon, Ann. *Silent Partners: Wives of National Park Wardens*. Pincher Creek, AB: Dixon and Dixon Publishers, 1985.

Feldhamer, George. A., Bruce C. Thompson, and Joseph A. Chapman. *Wild Mammals of North America: Biology, Management and Conservation*. 2d ed. Baltimore: The John Hopkins University Press, 2003.

Foster, John. E., Dick Harrison, and I.S. MacLaren, eds. *Buffalo*. Edmonton: The University of Alberta Press, 1992.

Herrero, Stephen. *Bear Attacks: Their Causes and Avoidance*. New York: Lyons & Burford, 1985.

Jasper Community History Committee. *Jasper Reflections*. Jasper, AB: Jasper Community History, 1996.

Jeck, Leonard. *Female Grizzly Rights: Grizzly Attack – A Seventeen-hour Ordeal*. Jasper, AB: Leonard C. Jeck, 1982.

Kane, Paul. *Wanderings of an Artist Among the Indians of North America: From Canada to Vancouver Island and Oregon through the Hudson's Bay Company Territory and Back Again*. London: Longman, Brown, Green, Longmans, and Roberts, 1859.

MacGregor, James G. *Pack Saddles to Tête Jaune Cache*. Edmonton: Hurtig Publishers, 1973.

MacLaren, I.S., Eric Hoggs, and Gabrielle Zezulka Mailoux. *Mapper of Mountains: M.P. Bridgeland in the Canadian Rockies, 1902-1930*. Edmonton: The University of Alberta Press, 2005.

McClung, David, and Peter Schaerer. *The Avalanche Handbook: 3rd Edition*. Seattle, Washington: The Mountaineers Books, 2006.

Moberly, Henry John. *When Fur Was King*. London, ON: J.M. Dent & Sons, 1929.

Murphey, Peter J., Robert W. Udell, Robert E. Stevenson, and Thomas W. Peterson. *A Hard Road to Travel: Land, Forests and People in the Upper Athabasca Region*. Hinton, AB: Foothills Model Forest, 2007.

Patton, Brian, and Bart Robinson. *The Canadian Rockies Trail Guide: A Hikers Guide to Banff, Jasper, Yoho, Kootenay, Waterton Lakes, Mount Assiniboine & Mount Robson*. Banff, AB: Summerthought Ltd., 1986.

Potter, Mike. *Fire Lookout Hikes in the Canadian Rockies*. 2d ed. Calgary: Luminous Compositions, 2008.

Power, Megan. *The History of Jasper*. Banff, AB: Summerthought, 2012.

Schintz, Mike. *Close Calls on High Walls*. Calgary: Rocky Mountain Books, 2005.

Journals, Articles, and Reports

Ballantyne, E.E. 1956. "Rabies Control in Alberta: Files of the Alberta Veterinary Medical Association." *Canadian Journal of Comparative Medicine* 20.1: 21-30.

Bertch, Barbara and Mike Gibeau. 2011. "Grizzly Bear Monitoring in and around the Mountain National Parks: Mortalities and Bear/Human Encounters. 1980-2010. Fourth Annual Report. August, 2011". *Parks Canada.*

Bertwistle, Jim. 2002. "A Description and Analysis of Wildlife Mortality on Transportation Corridors in Jasper National Park, Canada." *University of Alberta.*

Bradford, Wes, and Ivan Phillips. 1986. "Ungulate Mortalities (Highway and Railway 1980-1986) Jasper National Park." *Resource Conservation, Jasper National Park.*

Bradford, W., Kaye R., Phillips I., and Wallace R. 1986. "Wildlife Monitoring Program, Jasper National Park." *Resource Conservation, Jasper National Park.*

Bradley, Mark, and Lalenia Neufeld. 2012. "Climate and Management Interact to Explain the Decline of Woodland Caribou (Rangifer tarandus caribou) in Jasper National Park." *Rangifer* Special Issue 20:183-191.

Campbell, Carolyn. April 2012. "Caribou Habitat Protection: It's Urgent to Reduce Industry's Bootprint." *Wild Lands Advocate* 20.2: 6-9.

Carbyn, L.N. April 1974. "Wolf Population Fluctuations in Jasper National Park, Alberta, Canada." *Biological Conservation* 6.2: 94-101.

Carbyn, L.N. 1975. "Wolf Predation and Behavioural Interactions with Elk and other Ungulates in an Area of High Prey Diversity." *Canadian Wildlife Service.* Edmonton.

Cichowski, Deborah. 2010. "Status of the Woodland Caribou (Rangifer tarandus caribou) in Alberta: Alberta Wildlife Status Report No. 30 (Update 2010)". *Government of Alberta and Alberta Conservation Association*. Edmonton.

Davidson, Tom, and Dave Norcross. "Bison Reintroduction, Jasper National Park: Interim Report." *Warden Service, Jasper National Park*. (1978).

De Caen, Susan Alexandra Jane. 1997. "The Human History of the Yellowhead Corridor: Recommendations for a Cultural Interpretive Program for Jasper National Park: MEDes." *The University of Calgary*.

Eckert-Lyngstad, Nicole. 2013. "The Backcountry as Home: Park Wardens, Families, and Jasper National Park's District Cabin System: 1952-1972." Edmonton: *University of Alberta*, 2013.

Government of Canada. 2000. "Canada National Parks Act" (S.C. 2000, c. 32). Ottawa: *Department of Justice*.

Holland, W.D., and G.M. Coen., eds. "Ecological (Biophysical) Land Classification of Banff and Jasper National Parks, Volume I: Summary." *Alberta Institute of Pedology Publication* M-83-2. Edmonton. (1983).

Jenness, D. F.R.S.C. 1939. "The 'Snare' Indians." *Proceedings and Transactions of the Royal Society of Canada* ser. 3. 33(2): 103-105. Ottawa.

Karasiuk, D.J., R.G. Kaye, and L.M. Cole. 1978. "The Wildlife Inventory of Jasper National Park: Interim Report." *Canadian Wildlife Service*. Edmonton.

Kaye, Rob G. 1981. "Bear Mortalities and Bear/Garbage Management Practices – Jasper National Park: 1916 – 1980." *Parks Canada*.

Kaye, Rob G. 1983. "Interactions Between Bears and Humans. A Background Paper for the Four Mountain Parks Planning Program". *Parks Canada.*

Kaye, Rob G., and J. Roulet. 1983. "The Distribution and Status of the Wolf. A Background Paper for the Four Mountain Park Planning Program". *Parks Canada.*

Kaye, Rob G., and J. Roulet. 1983. "The Distribution and Status of Woodland Caribou. A Background Paper for the Four Mountain Park Planning Program". *Parks Canada.*

McDonald, Al., and Rob Kaye. 1983. "Caribou Report, Wildlife Monitoring Program – Jasper National Park." *Parks Canada.*

Ralf, Rick. 1995. "Bear Relocations and Mortalities for Jasper National Park, 1975-1995." *Parks Canada.*

Ralf, Rick. 1995. "History of Bear/Human Conflict Management in Jasper National Park: 1907 to 1995." *Parks Canada.*

Rogers, Jason. 2011. "Checklist of the Birds of Jasper National Park." Banff, AB: *Bow Valley Naturalists.*

Roush, William Morgan. 2004. "A Substantial Upward Shift of the Alpine Treeline Ecotone in the Southern Canadian Rocky Mountains", Victoria, BC: *University of Victoria.*

Wallace, Rod, Rob Kaye, and Tom Davidson. 1982. "Interim Backcountry Management Guidelines." *Resource Conservation, Jasper National Park. Parks Canada.*

Wallace, Rod, Rob Kaye, and Ivan Phillips. 1983. "Interim Wildlife Monitoring Plan, Jasper National Park." *Resource Conservation, Jasper National Park. Parks Canada.*

White, Clifford A., Charles E. Olmsted, and Charles E. Kay. 1998. "Aspen, Elk, and Fire in the Rocky Mountain National Parks of North America." *Wildlife Society Bulletin* 26.3: 449-462.

Winkler, Terry and Wes Bradford. 2007. "Bear/Human Conflict Management: Year End Report: 2006." *Resource Conservation, Jasper National Park.*

Woody, N.G. 1980. "Evaluation of Bear Management in Jasper National Park." *Warden Service, Jasper National Park.*

Woody, N. "Bear Management: 1981." *Warden Service, Jasper National Park.*

Woody, N. "Bear Management: 1982." *Warden Service, Jasper National Park.*

Logbooks

Jasper National Park Wardens. "Park Warden Cabin Logbooks." *Jasper National Park Cultural Resource Files.*

Blue Creek Cabin Logbook: 1959-1974.

Blue Creek Cabin Logbook: 1979-2003.

Brazeau Cabin Logbook: 1953-1977.

Brazeau Cabin Logbook: 1979-1992.

Fiddle Cabin Logbook: 1979-1999.

Isaac Creek Cabin Logbook: 1983-1992.

Seldom Inn Cabin Logbook: 1979-1995.

Vega Cabin Logbook: 1979-2005.

Whitehorse Cabin Logbook: 1979-2008.

Willow Creek Cabin Logbook: 1979-1991.

Wolf Pass Cabin Logbook: 1980-2002.

Acknowledgements

I must first pay homage to the many friends who persuaded me to write this book so that they could live vicariously through my exciting (if somewhat dangerous and reckless) childhood, when I learned the ways of wildlife and the wilderness, and my career as a national park warden.

I had the amazing good fortune to grow up under the shadow of the Stetsons worn by the generation of park wardens that came before me in my hometown of Jasper. It was they who gave me the inspiration to become a guardian of the wild—*just like them.* I was honoured to have many of these wardens as mentors when I began my career, and I was overwhelmed by their support and encouragement when it came to documenting some of their history. With great respect, thanks go in particular to Gord Anderson, Bob Barker, Alfie Burstrom, Mac Elder, Bob Haney, and Al Stendie. I want to honour the memory of Park Wardens Toni Klettl, Mickey McGuire, and Norm Woody for their leadership and mentoring skills. Their legacy lives on through those of us who had the privilege to work with them.

A special thanks to retired Senior Park Horseman Denny Welsh for hitching his horse to a tree in our yard when I was a boy while he courted his wife-to-be, Theresa, who lived in the upstairs suite of our house. I wanted a horse—*just like his.*

It was through the generation before me that I was able to provide a historical perspective of events and adventures in this book. And for those who have left us to ride wild horses in the hereafter—their voices can be heard in many of the book's tales.

This book could not have been started (let alone completed) without the support and enthusiasm of many of my former Parks Canada colleagues. They and the following individuals contributed to the writing of this book: Gord and Sharon Anderson, Lawrence Baraniuk, Bob Barker, Julie Bauer, Bette Beswick, Bradley Bischoff, Al (B.J.) Bjorn, Wes Bradford, Alfie and June Burstrom, Kathy Calvert, Ludwig (Lu) Carbyn, Jim Chesser, Terry Damm, Kelly Deagle, Dr. John Di Toppa, Mike Dillon, Ann and Peggy Dixon, Nicole Eckert-Lyngstad, Cathy and Mac Elder, Deke Hammel, Bob Haney, Pam Jeck, Gary Kaye, Loni Klettl, John Kofin, Steve Malcolm, Michael Mitchell, John Niddrie, Dave Norcross, Steve Otway, Karl Peetoom, Ivan Phillips, Ross Pigeon, Dale Portman, Rick Ralf, Brad Romaniuk, Greg Slatter, Duane Sept, Al Stendie, Darro Stinson, Jim Suttill, Patti Walker, Rod Wallace, Denny and Theresa Welsh, and Ric West.

Thanks to Cultural Resource Specialist Mike Dillon and Human/Wildlife Conflict Specialist Steve Malcolm (both former park wardens) for granting unrestricted access to all the Jasper Warden Office files I required when researching material for the book.

I am most grateful to John Ketcham and John Kofin, who reviewed the text at various stages of progression to offer feedback and edits. My sincere thanks to Sharon Perrin for bringing clarity, consistency, and focus to the manuscript. My appreciation goes to the many park employees (working and retired) who provided critical analysis of various portions of the manuscript. I also thank Cathy Reed for the final editing and proofreading of the manuscript and Iryna Spica for her masterful touch in the design and formatting of the book.

I am totally indebted to my wife Chrystyne and sister in-law Larissa Blavatska for their literary expertise. They devoted countless hours reviewing and meticulously editing my manuscript. They demonstrated to me that writing a book is not a solitary experience.

Finally, I must thank Chrystyne for her unwavering support in seeing me through the exhaustive experience of documenting a large part of my life.

In thanking all of you, including those who provided reviews and edits of my original manuscript, I take full responsibility for any errors or omissions that may appear within the pages of this book. And lastly, my apologies to anyone whom I may not have acknowledged; please know that I am grateful to all who helped me bring this book to life.

About the Author

Rob Kaye was born and raised in the town of Jasper, Alberta, in Jasper National Park. Fascinated with nature and entranced by the Rocky Mountains from an early age, he learned the ways of wildlife and the wilderness. Rob's early outdoor adventures led to a lifelong passion to protect the natural environment. Rob worked with the Canadian Wildlife Service for three years before realizing his dream of becoming a park warden with Parks Canada. His 33-year career included one year as a park ranger in Australia. Rob specialized in backcountry management and resource conservation. He retired in 2010 and currently lives on Vancouver Island.